THE WILL TO STAY WITH IT

Role Models of Determination

Emerson Klees

Cameo Press, Rochester, New York

Cameo Press
P. O. Box 18131
Rochester, New York 14618

Library of Congress Control Number 2002190409

ISBN 1-891046-01-2

Printed in the United States of America
9 8 7 6 5 4 3 2 1

THE ROLE MODELS OF HUMAN VALUES SERIES

"Example teaches better than precept. It is the best modeler of the character of men and women. To set a lofty example is the richest bequest a man [or woman] can leave behind."

Samuel Smiles

The Role Models of Human Values Series provides examples of role models and of lives worthy of emulation. The human values depicted in this series include teamwork, entrepreneurial ability, perseverance, motivation, and determination. Role models are presented in biographical sketches that describe the environment within which these individuals lived and worked and that delineate their personal characteristics.

These profiles illustrate how specific human values helped achievers reach their goals. Readers can glean helpful insight from these examples to use in strengthening the human values that are so important to our success and happiness. Each book in the series includes a prologue / introduction that highlights factors that contributed to these achievers' success.

The Role Models of Human Values Series
One Plus One Equals Three—Pairing Man / Woman
Strengths: Role Models of Teamwork (1998)
Entrepreneurs in History—Success vs. Failure:
Entrepreneurial Role Models (1999)

Miniseries
Staying With It: Role Models of Perseverance (1999)
The Drive to Succeed: Role Models of Motivation (2002)
The Will to Stay With It: Role Models of Determination
(2002)

LIST OF PHOTOGRAPHS

Page no.

Cover design by Dunn and Rice Design, Inc., Rochester, NY
Photographs by C. S. Kenyon, Rochester, NY

PREFACE

"Every great example takes hold of us with the authority of a miracle and says to us, 'If ye had but faith, ye, also, could do the same things.'"

Abraham Jacobi

The Will to Stay With It: Role Models of Determination is the third of a three-book miniseries within the Role Models of Human Values Series. The other two books are *Staying With It: Role Models of Perseverance* and the overarching book, *The Drive to Succeed: Role Models of Motivation*. The miniseries contains ninety-five biographical sketches.

This book provides role models of determination worthy of emulation through profiles of thirty-five strong-willed men and women. The biographical sketches represent seven categories of determination:

- **R**eformers / Pioneers—women who were activists and trailblazers
- **E**cclesiastics / Religious Leaders—men who were church leaders and martyrs
- **S**cientists / Inventors—individuals who were innovators and developers
- **O**rganizers / Planners—people who were creators and managers
- **L**uminaries / Notables—men and women who were writers, painters, and humanitarians
- **V**ictors / Leaders—military men / visionaries
- **E**ntrepreneurs / Achievers—people of accomplishment

These determined people inspire us by example.

Profiles of Lucretia Mott, Lucy Stone, Elizabeth Blackwell, and Antoinette Brown are reprinted from *The Women's Rights Movement and the Finger Lakes Region,* those of Orville and Wilbur Wright and Steve Jobs from *Entrepreneurs in History—Success vs. Failure: Entrepreneurial Role Models,* and of Elizabeth Barrett Browning and Lillian Gilbreth from *One Plus One Equals Three—Pairing Man / Woman Strengths: Role Models of Teamwork.* Biographical sketches of Frederick Douglass, Harriet Tubman, Thomas Garrett, and Levi Coffin are from *Underground Railroad Tales with Routes through the Finger Lakes Region,* of Andrew White and Brigham Young are from *People of the Finger Lakes Region,* and that of DeWitt Clinton is from *The Erie Canal in the Finger Lakes Region.*

TABLE OF CONTENTS

Page No.

Page No.

PROLOGUE

"The Will To Do is the greatest power in the world that is concerned with human accomplishment, and no one can in advance determine its limits.... It is a power we can direct and to just the extent we direct it do we determine our future. Every time you accomplish any definite act, consciously or unconsciously, you use the principle of the Will. Every person possesses some 'Will To Do.' It is the inner energy which controls all conscious acts. What you do directs your life forces.... Your will has a connection with all avenues of knowledge, all activities, all accomplishments."[1]

Theron Q. Dumont, *The Power of Concentration*

Determination is the quality of being resolute or firm in purpose in the pursuit of a goal. It is also thought of as will or as the will to achieve. In *The Psychology of Self-Determination*, Edward L. Deci cites William James:

> The first psychologist to discuss will in detail was William James, who in the second volume of *The Principles of Psychology (1890)* outlined a theory of will. It is a state of mind with which everyone is so familiar that a formal definition could hardly elucidate it. For him, to will is to desire an outcome that the person believes is attainable. It is a state of mind or an image that precedes voluntary behavior. The behavior follows the image, and if the person's beliefs about being able to achieve the outcome were accurate, the outcome would be achieved.[2]

In the words of William James:

> Desire, wish, will are states of mind which everyone knows and no definition can make plainer. We desire to feel, to have, to do, all sorts of things which are at the moment not felt, had, or done. If with the desire there goes a sense that attainment is not possible, we simply wish; but if we believe that the end is in our power, we will the desired feeling, having, or doing shall be real; and real it presently becomes, either immediately upon willing or after certain preliminaries have been fulfilled.[3]

Obviously, to have the determination or the will to achieve a particular goal, a goal must exist. Understanding the importance of goals and goal setting is a prerequisite to the comprehension of the quality of determination, as well as of motivation and perseverance, in moving toward a goal.

The establishment of attainable goals is critical to the success of any endeavor; however, its importance is not universally understood, perhaps because we have an inherent fear of failure to reach our goals or because we do not know how to establish reasonable goals. Some people think that the more that they want something, the greater the disappointment if they do not get it. They are afraid to risk failure and the accompanying anguish.

Another fear in setting goals is fear of success. Lack of self-confidence and self-esteem are usually factors in this case. Individuals may feel, subconsciously, that they do not deserve the success for which their conscious self is striving. These individuals tend to magnify the difficulty of attaining a particular goal and may become discouraged from setting a goal.

Also, some people subscribe to the philosophy of "whatever will be, will be." These individuals think that everything is preordained. The viewpoint that fate dictates the outcome of everything that they do is a demotivating influence in setting goals. Their fatalistic outlook prevents them from extending themselves in establishing goals and from expending effort in reaching those goals. Setting an attainable goal is the first step in achieving success. The goal may be a "reach" goal or a "stretch" goal, but it must be attainable.

INTRODUCTION

"The miracle, the power, that elevates the few is to be found in their industry, application, and perseverance under the promptings of a determined spirit."

Mark Twain

Examples of determination are all around us. The accomplishments of relatives, friends, acquaintances, and neighbors serve as role models for us. The slightly built grandmother who lifts a car that has fallen off its jack onto her grandson is one example. Another is provided by Theron Q. Dumont in *The Power of Concentration:* "The house of a farmer's wife caught on fire. No one was around to help her move anything. She was a frail woman and ordinarily was considered weak. On this occasion she removed things from the house that it later took three men to handle. It was the 'Will To Do' that she used to accomplish her task."[4]

The national news also provides us with role models of determination; Lance Armstrong is an outstanding example. In October 1996, just after the world-class bicyclist turned twenty-five, he was diagnosed with testicular cancer that had spread to his stomach and lungs. After he began chemotherapy, doctors discovered that he had two marble-sized brain tumors. He was told that his probability of survival was about fifty percent.

Having cancer changed Armstrong. His agent and friend, Bill Stapleton, noted, "He became an adult. He became more focused in his priorities. He also became a more caring, more giving person. In addition, when he returned to bicycling competition, he was fifteen pounds lighter and better able to cycle in the mountains."[5]

Armstrong met his wife, Kristin Richards Armstrong, when she was doing public relations work for the Lance Armstrong Foundation, which he had founded in 1997 to aid other cancer patients. They were married in May 1998, and, in October 1999, their son, Luke David Armstrong, was born. Armstrong admits to being passionate about his family. In his opinion, "passion separates the ordinary from the extraordinary."

Armstrong began to display his desire to compete when he was ten years old and developed an interest in running. He knows where he gets his intensity. "My mother is very passionate and very strongwilled. She's a scrapper. She's a fighter." She challenged her son to set a goal for himself. "If you don't have a goal, you don't have anything to beat. He always had this insatiable desire to win. All I helped him do was channel those desires."[6]

In between chemotherapy cycles, Armstrong rode his bike; not far, but he rode. He missed the 1997 racing season while recuperating. In early 1998, he began to train seriously. He dropped out of a race in February and considered retiring. Two months later, he and his trainer cycled 100 miles a day in the North Carolina mountains where Armstrong rediscovered his enthusiasm for riding. He performed well in races late in the 1998 racing season and decided to train for the Tour de France. He had only completed the Tour de France once, in 1995, when he finished 36th.

In 1999, Armstrong completed the 2,288 miles of the Tour de France in 91 hours, 32 minutes, and 16 seconds: a record of 24.95 miles per hour. He dominated the race by beating his nearest competitor by seven minutes and twenty-seven seconds. His doctor observed, "[Armstrong's victory] is astonishing. Probably it is less ... a physical feat than a mental and emotional feat. Physically, it is more conceivable for me than his emotional and mental recovery."[7]

Armstrong set another goal for himself—to win another Tour de France. He won that race in 2000 and again in 2001. In winning these three races, he displayed the determination for which he is known.

The thirty-five individuals described in biographical sketches in this book are notable role models; we can learn from them.

WILL

There is no chance, no destiny, no fate,

    Can circumvent or hinder or control

    The firm resolve of a determined soul.

Gifts count for nothing; will alone is great;

All things give way before it, soon or late.

    What obstacle can stay the mighty force

    Of the sea-seeking river in its course,

Or cause the ascending orb of day to wait?

Each wellborn soul must win what it deserves.

Let the fool prate of luck. The fortunate

    Is he whose earnest purpose never swerves,

    Whose slightest action or inaction serves

The one great aim. Why, even Death stands still,

And waits an hour sometimes for such a will.

Ella Wheeler Wilcox

CHAPTER 1

REFORMERS / PIONEERS

"Every human mind is a great slumbering power until awakened by keen desire and by definite resolution...."

Edgar Roberts

Chapter 1 provides biographical sketches of women pioneers who were determined to make changes in the role of women in society. They dedicated their lives to making reforms.

Lucretia Mott was one of the most experienced early leaders of the Women's Rights Movement, having gained that experience organizing and speaking in public to support the antislavery and temperance movements. She believed in doing and not just talking about making reforms. Lucretia Mott and Elizabeth Cady Stanton were the movers behind the first Women's Rights Convention in Seneca Falls, New York in 1848.

Lucy Stone, "the morning star of the Women's Rights Movement," was one of the first women to speak in public on the subject. She led the Women's Rights Movement in New England. In 1869, when the New Englanders split off from the women's rights effort directed by Elizabeth Cady Stanton and Susan B. Anthony and formed the American Woman Suffrage Association, Stone was one of its leaders. When the factions rejoined in 1890 as the National American Woman Suffrage Association, she was elected head of the executive committee.

Florence Nightingale knew at a young age that she wanted to become a nurse, but she had to overcome the objections of her parents. She proved her worth in caring for England's casualties in the Crimean War where she encountered poor organization and inadequate medical supplies. She addressed the shortcomings and initiated policies that were used in England's future conflicts. Nightingale was a dynamic woman who initiated reforms on the strength of her will. Upon her return to England, she implemented hospital improvements as a contributor to the Royal Sanitary Commission.

Elizabeth Blackwell knew that she wanted to be a medical doctor, but first she had to earn money to pay her tuition. Because she was a woman, she was rejected by twenty-eight medical schools before being accepted by Geneva Medical College. She encountered ostracism when she began her medical studies and lack of acceptance when she finished them. She was rejected for further study by hospitals in the United States, England, and France, but she persevered and added to her medical education where she could. She eventually founded a dispensary in lower Manhattan and the first medical school for women in the United States.

Antoinette Brown earned a Master of Arts degree in theology at Oberlin College in 1850, but her name did not appear on the roll of the Oberlin Theological School until 1908. Realizing the College's reluctance to ordain her a minister, she chose to find a position with a church and to be ordained in that church. She became an accomplished author and public speaker, and she was active in the Women's Rights Movement and the Association for the Advancement of Women. Also, she was a mentor and role model for young women who joined the ministry in increasing numbers after she had pioneered that career for women.

These women blazed trails that made it easier for women who came after them. They inspire us.

LUCRETIA MOTT Women's Rights Movement Leader

"[Lucretia Mott's] achievements, combined with her undeniably beautiful character and innate spirituality, do much to fulfill the ... title, 'The Greatest American Woman.' Of her contemporaries, Harriet Beecher Stowe and Margaret Fuller were superior writers; Elizabeth Cady Stanton, Lucy Stone, and Susan B. Anthony devoted greater energy and longer service to the cause of suffrage, but no woman in American history ever combined so many outstanding talents or participated influentially is so many varied movements, and with such grace of charm, as Lucretia Mott. She was great in deeds, great in womanhood, and great in those attributes of femininity that women strive for, and men demand."[8]

Roberta Campbell Lawson

Lucretia Mott, senior stateswomen of the Women's Rights Movement and mentor of many of its younger leaders, was also a dynamic speaker for the antislavery and temperance movements. Lucretia Mott and Elizabeth Cady Stanton convened the first Women's Rights Convention in Seneca Falls, New York in 1848. Lucretia presided over that convention as well as the national Women's Rights Conventions in Syracuse in 1852 and in New York City in 1853.

Lucretia Coffin Mott was born to Thomas and Anna Folger Coffin on Nantucket Island on January 3, 1793. Three factors shaped her early life: being born into a Quaker family; growing up with the hardy, independent, and self-reliant people of Nantucket; and having a father who believed in educating his daughters. Quakers gave women virtual equality with men, permitted them to speak at Quaker meetings, and allowed them to become ministers. Even as a young woman,

Lucretia Mott was accustomed to speaking in public; she became a minister in her twenties and was an accomplished speaker by the time she became active in the antislavery movement.

When Thomas Coffin, a whaler, was away on his sailing vessel, Anna Coffin ran their shop, kept the accounts, and made buying trips to Boston. Lucretia was used to seeing women in positions of responsibility on the Island. In 1804, the Coffin family moved to Boston; eventually, they moved to Philadelphia, the hub of Quaker life.

After completing elementary school at the age of thirteen, Lucretia attended Nine Partners boarding school, an advanced Quaker academy near Poughkeepsie. The strong-willed Lucretia occasionally rebelled at the severity of the discipline. She could endure punishment for herself more easily than she could watch it inflicted on her classmates. The school build-ing was divided into a "boys'" side and a "girls'" side and boys and girls were not permitted to talk with one another. When a boy with whom she was friendly was confined to a closet on a diet of bread and water, Lucretia went to the boys' side of the school building to take additional food to him.

Lucretia received excellent grades at Nine Partners and, after graduating, taught at the school. She met and fell in love with James Mott, who also taught there. Lucretia Coffin and James Mott were married on April 4, 1811 in Philadelphia, where James had accepted a position in his father-in-law's mercantile business.

Lucretia and James had a strong, loving marriage. Lucretia thought that a marriage would be successful if "the independence of the husband and wife will be equal, their dependence mutual, and their obligations reciprocal."9 Later in life, Lucretia realized that the happiness of her wedded life was enhanced by the fact that she and James both had a "deep interest in the sacred cause of wronged humanity."

Lucretia became a hard-working nineteenth-century housewife and eventually mother of six children. She also was known as an excellent hostess who was accustomed to entertaining large numbers of guests. She read widely, particularly history, philosophy, political economy, and theology. She also read about women's rights; Mary Wollstonecraft's *A Vindication of the Rights of Women* was one of her favorite books. She developed a keen memory and an analytical, independent intellect.

As Lucretia's children grew older and needed less attention, she became more active in Quaker meetings. In 1821, she was appointed a minister at the age of twenty-eight. In 1828, when the liberal Hicksites split off from the orthodox Friends, Lucretia and James Mott faced a very difficult decision. Ultimately, after much deliberation, they joined the Hicksites.

Lucretia believed strongly in "inward spiritual grace" and the following of an "inner light." She thought that there was a place for individual interpretation, not just following fixed creeds or rigid rituals. Her view of religion was based on justice and reason that expressed itself in "practical godliness," that is, religion that was lived rather than merely believed.

Occasionally, James Mott's business suffered a temporary reversal. On one such occasion, Lucretia and a cousin established a school associated with the Quakers' Pine Street Meeting. The school was successful, and her earnings helped the family overcome their temporary financial difficulty. During this period of time, their son, Thomas, died of typhus, the same disease that had taken her father. Lucretia and James had difficulty recovering from the loss of their two-year-old son.

The decade of the 1830s was a time of reform, and the Quaker community in and around Philadelphia was an early, active participant in the antislavery movement. It offered opportunities for practical godliness for the Motts. Their home was a station on the underground railroad; the couple spent considerable time and effort helping escaped slaves.

Lucretia clearly stated her view of the antislavery movement: "I endeavor to put my soul in [the slaves'] stead—and to give all my power and aid in every right effort for their immediate emancipation. The duty was impressed upon me at the time I consecrated myself to the Gospel which anoints 'to preach deliverance to the captive, to set at liberty those that are bruised.'"[10]

The Motts not only provided food, clothing, and shelter to fugitive slaves, they risked physical injury. A slave who was running away from his master sought refuge at the Motts' house. He ran into their home, through the parlor, and hid in the rear of the house. James Mott barred the door to the enraged master and "calmly stood at the door with a lighted lamp barring the way. James barely escaped death when the angry master threw a stone ... past his head and it crashed into the side of the door."[11]

On another occasion, former slave Daniel Dangerfield, who had worked for years on a farm near Harrisburg, was brought to trial as a fugitive in Philadelphia. Lucretia rallied her friends in support of Dangerfield. In court, she sat directly behind the defendant. Edward Hopper, the Motts' son-in-law, who was the defense attorney for Dangerfield, called upon "witness after witness to testify about Dangerfield's long residence in Pennsylvania." Lucretia spoke with the judge, a fellow Quaker, during the recess: "I earnestly hope that thy conscience will not allow thee to send this poor man into bondage."[12]

After an all-night court session, Dangerfield was acquitted due to a technical error in the writ of accusation. Many people present at the trial credited Lucretia with having a major influence on the verdict. One of the men present said: "She looked like an angel of light. As I looked at her, I felt that Christ was here."[13]

Also, the Motts provided refuge for Jane Johnson and her two sons. Jane, a slave belonging to John H. Wheeler, U.S. Minister to Nicaragua, was attempting to take advantage of Pennsylvania's antislavery laws to gain freedom. William Still, a leader of the underground railroad, and Passmore Williamson, Secretary of the Pennsylvania Anti-Slavery Society, helped her to escape from her master. Wheeler took legal action to have his slaves returned.

An indictment was obtained against Williamson and his accomplices, who were accused of "conspired effort" to encourage Jane to run away. Lucretia accompanied Jane to the trial, attended all of the court sessions, and invited Jane to stay at the Mott home for several days. Lucretia convinced Jane to testify in her own behalf at the trial to show that she wanted to leave her master. Jane's testimony was a key factor in obtaining her release from bondage. Jane and her sons stayed several more days with the Motts and then were guided successfully via the underground railroad to Canada and freedom.

In December 1833, the American Anti-Slavery Society was formed in Philadelphia. Lucretia was one of four women invited to attend the first convention, but women were not permitted to join the new organization. They formed the Women's Anti-Slavery Association, and Lucretia was elected

President. When a Pennsylvania branch of the American Anti-Slavery Society was established, James Mott was a charter member. Again, Lucretia was not invited to join, but two years later the rules were changed to allow women members. She became an active, influential member.

Lucretia Mott was a firm supporter of Angelina and Sarah Grimké in their early efforts to speak in public to mixed audiences of men and women. Lucretia provided them with advice and encouragement when they were harassed for attempting to speak in public. Sex discrimination had existed from the beginning of the antislavery movement, but the prejudice against the Grimkés was more than Lucretia could bear. From this time onward, she was driven by the "woman question." It became "the most important question of my life."

When Lucretia accompanied her husband to London for the World Anti-Slavery Convention in 1840, she was prepared as a woman delegate to be rejected. When she was rejected, being prepared made it no less painful. Lucretia forced the issue of women's participation to the floor of the convention and out of the secrecy of the executive committee. However, she lost her proposal to allow women to be active members of the convention. Lucretia first met young Elizabeth Cady Stanton at the World Anti-Slavery Convention when they were relegated to the gallery with the other women merely to observe the activities of the convention.

Instead of sitting quietly in the gallery, Mott and Cady Stanton toured London while discussing "the propriety of holding a women's convention." Despite the twenty-two-year difference in their ages, they had much in common. Cady Stanton looked up to Mott, who was more widely read and had more experience participating in organizations and in public speaking. Mott became Cady Stanton's mentor. They agreed to call a meeting to address women's issues when they returned to the United States. The meeting did not take place for eight years.

Elizabeth and Henry Stanton stayed in England and on the Continent for a year; when they returned home to Boston Henry was busy studying law and Cady Stanton was occupied with raising their young children. Only after the Stantons moved to Seneca Falls did the meeting occur, facilitated by Lucretia Mott's attending a Quaker convention in the region and visiting friends and relatives in the area.

Mott and Cady Stanton met at the home of Jane and Richard Hunt in Waterloo. Also present were Mott's sister, Martha Wright of Auburn, and Mary Ann M'Clintock, a Quaker abolitionist from Waterloo. At this planning meeting for the convention, the women discussed their frustration with the limited rights of women and the discrimination they had experienced in the abolition and temperance movements. Cady Stanton was particularly vocal. All of the women had attended antislavery and temperance conventions, but Mott was the only one with experience as a delegate, orator, and organizer.

They prepared a notice about the first Women's Rights Convention to be held on July 19 and 20, 1848 in the Wesleyan Chapel in Seneca Falls. The women agreed to reconvene at the home of Mary Ann and Thomas M'Clintock in Waterloo on July 16 to plan an agenda for the convention. At the second meeting, Cady Stanton prepared the *Declaration of Sentiments* modeled on the *Declaration of Independence*. The only difference of opinion among the women was whether or not to include women's right to vote in the *Declaration of Sentiments*. Cady Stanton prevailed, and it was included.

On July 19, James Mott called the convention to order. Lucretia Mott then stated the goals of the convention and discussed the importance of educating women and of improving the standing of women in society. The *Declaration of Sentiments* was discussed and adopted with minor changes. The resolution about the right of women to vote was the only one not adopted unanimously. Some attendees were concerned that pushing the elective franchise might reduce the probability of achieving other goals. However, the resolution received enough support to be kept in the document.

Mott also spoke at the second Women's Rights Convention in Rochester two weeks later. This was a more intellectual audience, and several conservative clergymen quoted St. Paul on the duty of women to obey their husbands: "Man shall be the head of woman." Mott replied in her eloquent speech, "Many of the opposers of Women's Rights who bid us to obey the bachelor St. Paul, themselves reject his counsel—he advised them not to marry."[14] These clergymen learned to respect Mott's knowledge of the Scriptures.

In 1849, Mott prepared a speech entitled "Discourse on Woman," in which she rebutted many of the male speakers' objections to the Women's Rights Movement. She wrote: "The question is often asked, 'What does woman want more than she enjoys? What is she seeking to obtain? Of what rights is she deprived? What privileges are withheld from her?' I answer, she asks nothing as a favor, but as a right. She wants to be acknowledged a moral, responsible human being."[15]

In 1850, Mott convinced a Quaker businessman to raise funds to establish the Female College of Pennsylvania in Philadelphia. Also, Lucretia and James Mott were the principal sponsors of the Philadelphia School of Design for Women (now the Moore College of Art). In addition, the Motts helped Pennsylvania's first female attorney gain admission to the Commonwealth bar exams. Mott believed in doing things, accomplishing things, not just talking about them.

In the fall of 1850, Mott met women's rights leader Lucy Stone at the first national Women's Rights Convention in Worcester, Massachusetts. They became close friends and corresponded frequently. By the end of the following year, Stone had decided to devote herself to the Women's Rights Movement and not to divide her energies by working for the abolitionist movement.

Mott presided over the national Women's Rights Conventions in 1852 in Syracuse and in 1853 in New York City. The Syracuse Convention proved to be "a stormy and taxing" event at which Mott encountered many verbal attacks. Again, her critics at the meeting quoted liberally from the Bible. Mott and Antoinette Brown, an ordained minister, countered these critics. Most reviews in the newspapers referred to the convention leaders' "firm and efficient control of the meetings."

The New York City Convention was also rowdy. In fact, a mob broke up the convention on the first evening. The women retained their composure, and Lucretia congratulated them for their "self-reliance" at a meeting the following morning. Attendee Margaret Hope Bacon observed about Mott: "No one else had the poise and authority to keep order nor the leadership to carry the frightened women through such ordeals."[16]

More rowdies entered the convention hall during the day, interrupted the meetings, and became so unruly that the meeting was adjourned early. At the time of adjournment, "the hall exploded in confusion." Mott saw that some of the women were afraid to leave the hall, so she asked her escort to take them out to the street. Mott's escort asked how she would get out of the building. Mott reached for the arm of the nearest troublemaker and said: "This man will see me through." He was surprised, but he saw her safely through the exit door.

In May 1866, the American Equal Rights Association was formed in New York to work for the rights of all citizens, without regard for age, class, gender, or race. Mott was elected President. She said that she was willing to lend her name and influence to the cause if the young could be encouraged to continue the work.

James Mott died on January 26, 1868. Lucretia and James had been so close and compatible that she was "numbed" by his passing. She continued to be active and in 1870 was elected President of the Pennsylvania Peace Society.

On April 14, 1875, Mott was the honored guest at the centennial celebration of the Pennsylvania Abolition Society. Henry Wilson, Vice President of the United States, presented her to the gathering: "I ... present to you one of the most venerable and noble of American women, whose voice for forty years has been heard and tenderly touched many noble hearts. Age has dimmed her eye and weakened her voice, but her heart, like the heart of a wise man and wise woman, is yet young."[17]

In 1878, Mott attended the thirtieth anniversary celebration of the first Women's Rights Convention in Seneca Falls. She spoke at the celebration; her speech included a plea to give women the right to participate in making laws, so that there will be "harmony without severity, justice without oppression." Frederick Douglass and Belva Lockwood spoke to the convention on topics of equal pay for equal work, improved educational opportunities for women, and women's suffrage. Lockwood was the first woman lawyer admitted to practice before the U.S. Supreme Court and the first woman candidate for President of the U.S. to receive electoral votes.

On November 11, 1880, Lucretia Coffin Mott died in her sleep. Several thousand mourners attended her burial at Pairhill Cemetery. A member of the Peace Society made brief comments on her life and a silence fell over the mourners. Someone asked, "Will no one say anything?" Another replied, "Who can speak? The preacher is dead!"[18]

Lucretia Mott's portrait hangs in the National Gallery in Washington, D.C. Adelaide Johnson's sculpture of Lucretia Mott, Susan B. Anthony, and Elizabeth Cady Stanton stands in the U.S. Capitol. In *Century of Struggle*, Eleanor Flexner described the relationship of Lucretia Mott to the other principal leaders of the Women's Rights Movement: "Lucy Stone was its most gifted orator ... Mrs. Stanton was its outstanding philosopher ... Susan Anthony was its incomparable organizer ... Lucretia Mott typified the moral force of the movement."

LUCY STONE (1818-1893) Women's Rights Movement Leader in New England

"Woman will not always be a thing. I see it in the coming events whose shadows are cast before them, and in the steady growth of those great principles which lie at the foundations of all our relations. I hear it in the inward march of freedom's host and feel it deep in my inner being. Yes, a new and glorious era is about to dawn upon us, an era in which woman taking her place on the same platform with her equal brothers, conscious of her rights, her responsibilities, her duties, will arouse and apply her long slumbering energies for the redemption of this sin-ruined world. It will take a long time to effect that change; the evil is so deep-rooted and universal, but it will come."[19]

Lucy Stone

Lucy Stone was leader of the Women's Rights Movement in New England and organizer of the American Woman Suffrage Association founded in 1869. Stone, with the help of her husband and her daughter, published the *Woman's Journal*, "the voice of the Women's Rights Movement," for over forty-seven years. Elizabeth Cady Stanton referred to her as "the first person by whom the heart of the American people was stirred by the woman question."

Lucy Stone, third daughter of seven surviving children of Francis and Hannah Matthews Stone, was born on August 13, 1818 in West Brookfield, Massachusetts. Francis Stone was a well-to-do farmer and tanner; although he sent his sons to college and could afford to send his daughters as well, he refused to pay for the girls' education. When Lucy told him that she wanted to attend college, he asked, "Is the child crazy?" Lucy was alone among her peers in the early Woman's Rights

Movement in not having a supportive father. Susan B. Anthony, Lucretia Mott, and Elizabeth Cady Stanton all had fathers who believed in education for women.

At the age of sixteen, Stone taught district school and then studied at several area seminaries, including Mount Holyoke Female Seminary. In 1843, she enrolled at Oberlin College, the first coeducational college in the United States, specifically, to learn public speaking skills to use in advocating women's rights and the abolition of slavery.

Women students at Oberlin discovered early that the college had no intention of training them as public speakers. They learned how to write, but they were "excused" from participation in discussions and debates. Oberlin President Asa Mahan advocated that women should be taught how to speak as well as how to write, but he was outvoted by the faculty. The policy was apparently based on the words of St. Paul: "Let a woman learn in silence with all submissiveness."

Stone worked in the kitchen of the women's dormitory and taught in Oberlin's preparatory school to earn living expenses. She also taught remedial courses to adult African Americans. In her third year, her father agreed to lend her the money to stay in college for two more years, if she would sign a note to pay it back.

Stone's opinions about women's rights were formed early. She had observed her mother's lack of self-esteem due to overwork and to being controlled by an autocratic husband. The daughters' legacy in their father's will was $200 each; the sons divided the balance of the family money and property.

As a teacher, Stone was paid half the salary of comparable male teachers. She was not allowed to vote in the orthodox Congregational Church, even though she was a full member of the church. She built up an inner core of resistance to these inequities. Some women were beaten down by it; Stone added another layer to this inner core as each incident occurred.

Stone and Antoinette Brown, who would become the first woman minister in the United States, became close friends and confidants at Oberlin despite their differences of opinion. Stone was more radical than Brown on the subject of abolition. Oberlin was strongly antislavery—it was an active station on the underground railroad—but the college and community leaders belonged to the anti-Garrison branch of the movement.

Stone and Brown also had different views on religion. Lucy became a Unitarian; she left the Congregational Church because it approved of slavery and opposed women speaking in public. In particular, the Church condemned the Grimké sisters speaking to mixed audiences of men and women. Brown was disappointed that her friend, Stone, did not support her in her goal to become an ordained minister.

They secretly formed a female debating society to improve their speaking skills. One of Stone's reasons for wanting to become a public speaker was to fight for women's rights, particularly the right to work in any job that women's ability made them equal to men. One of her first public speeches was given at a gathering of Oberlin's African Americans to celebrate the ending of slavery in the West Indies.

In 1847, Stone graduated from Oberlin with honors. She was the first woman from Massachusetts to receive a college degree. She refused to write a commencement address because she was not permitted to present it. It was considered improper for women to participate in public exercises with men; however, thirty-six years later, she was an honored speaker at Oberlin's semi-centennial jubilee.

Abolitionist William Lloyd Garrison attended the commencement exercises in 1847 and described Stone to his wife: "She is a very superior young woman, and has a soul as free as the air, and is prepared to go forth as a lecturer, particularly in vindication of the rights of women. Her course here has been very firm and independent, and she has caused no small uneasiness to the spirit of secularism in the institution."[20]

Stone gave her second speech, the first outside of Oberlin, from the pulpit of the church of her brother, William Bowman Stone, a minister in Gardner, Massachusetts. She spoke about women's rights. William and another brother, Frank, were the only members of her family who supported her speaking in public. Her sister, Sarah, told her that public lecturing by a woman was against divine law.

In 1848, Stone was hired by the Massachusetts Anti-Slavery Society as a public speaker. The job required endurance, since she was sent on extensive speaking tours throughout the Northeast riding in rough carriages over rutty roads. Her advance posters were torn down, and she was heckled during her talks and jeered by both editors and ministers. One cold winter day, she was drenched when someone thrust a water hose through her carriage window.

Stone interwove the subject of women's rights into her antislavery speeches. The Anti-Slavery Society objected, but they did not want to lose one of their most effective speakers. She told them, "I was a woman before I was an abolitionist. I must speak for the women." They compromised; she could speak about women's rights during the week if she gave anti-slavery speeches on weekends.

Before the Women's Rights Convention in Seneca Falls and before she had heard that others were interested in the movement, Stone already considered the pursuit of women's rights to be her major work. She traveled widely lecturing on women's rights, making trips to the Midwest, the South, and Canada.

Later, Stone became one of the best speakers of the Women's Rights Movement. She had a beautiful voice, a sincere delivery, and an aura of authority and self-assurance. She usually spoke extemporaneously. However, she was somewhat dogmatic and intensely earnest; at times her lack of a sense of humor worked against her.

In the spring of 1850, Stone attended an antislavery convention in Boston at which attendees were asked if they had any interest in a women's rights convention. Nine women, including Abby Foster and Lucy Stone, met to plan the first national Women's Rights Convention that was held in Worcester, Massachusetts in October 1850.

Many distinguished people signed the call for this convention, which was organized by Paulina Wright Davis, including Ralph Waldo Emerson, William Lloyd Garrison, James and Lucretia Mott, Wendell Phillips, Gerrit Smith, and Elizabeth Cady Stanton. Paulina Davis, editor of one of the first women's rights publications, *The Una*, was nominated President of the convention.

Attendees included Antoinette Brown, Abby Foster, Angelina Grimké, Lucretia Mott, Ernestine Rose, and Sojourner Truth. Elizabeth Cady Stanton was unable to attend due to the recent birth of a child, but she prepared a speech that was read. The convention was Stone's introduction to the formal Women's Rights Movement and gave her the opportunity to meet many of its policymakers. After making a moving speech that helped to attract Susan B. Anthony to the movement, Stone left the convention as one of its leaders. She published the proceedings of the convention at her own expense.

Stone had resolved never to marry, so that she could focus her energies on her goals: the abolition of slavery and the attainment of women's rights. Her resolve lessened when she met Henry Blackwell, brother of pioneer doctor Elizabeth Blackwell, at an abolitionist meeting. Henry fell in love with Stone and courted her for two years. When she met Henry's older brother, Samuel, she suggested that he visit her friend, Antoinette Brown, on one of his many business trips. Stone and Brown eventually became sisters-in-law.

Henry persuaded Lucy to marry him only after he convinced her that she could be free within their marriage, and after he agreed to devote his life to the women's rights cause. They were married on May 1, 1855. Stone did not change her name to Blackwell; from this time onward, women who retained their maiden name after marrying were called "Lucy Stoners."

In 1857, Stone chaired the seventh national Women's Rights Convention in New York. Lucy's and Henry's daughter, Alice Stone Blackwell, was born that year. A son born prematurely died shortly after his birth in 1859. Stone was less active in the Women's Rights Movement during Alice's early years.

In 1858, Stone let her household goods be sold for taxes in protest against her lack of the vote. She used the incident, which was well-known among those familiar with the Women's Rights Movement, to write a protest against taxation without representation. In 1863, she supported the Women's Loyal National League. In 1866, she helped form and served on the executive committee of the American Equal Rights Association and the following year was elected

President of the New Jersey Woman Suffrage Association.

The break between the two factions of the Women's Rights Movement occurred in May 1869 at a meeting of the American Equal Rights Association. Susan B. Anthony, Elizabeth Cady Stanton, and the New York faction wanted to push for the elective franchise for women without waiting for African Americans to obtain their right to vote. The New Yorkers also wanted to address divorce laws and to work actively with trade unions. Generally, they were more liberal than their counterparts in New England.

The New Englanders, led by Lucy Stone, wanted to wait for African Americans to win the right to vote before working to obtain the vote for women. Also, the Boston branch was not interested in dealing with trade unions; their members preferred a more conservative approach.

In November 1869, Stone and the New Englanders formed the American Woman Suffrage Association "to unite those who cannot use the methods, and means, which Mrs. Stanton and Susan use." Lucretia Mott tried unsuccessfully to hold the two factions together. The new American Woman Suffrage Association admitted men and women on an equal basis and had many male abolitionists as members; the National Woman Suffrage Association remained principally a women's organization in which men could not hold office.

Stone founded and financed the American Association's weekly newspaper, *Woman's Journal*. Mary A. Livermore served as editor for two years, and then Lucy and Henry assumed editorial responsibility. With the help their daughter, Alice, *Woman's Journal* was "the voice of the women's movement" for over forty-seven years. Livermore expressed her optimistic thoughts on the future if women were given more responsibility in society:

> With her enfranchisement there will come a nobler era. Then, with the interests that are identical, with a humanity common to both, the masculine head married to the feminine heart, wisdom supplemented with love, man and woman shall together work out the great problems of life, and a nobler and better civilization shall come to the waiting future.[21]

In 1870, Lucy and Henry helped to establish the Massachusetts Woman Suffrage Association. Stone devoted much of her time to lecturing, drafting bills, and attending legislative sessions in support of improving women's status.

In 1890, Stone's daughter, Alice, and Cady Stanton's daughter, Harriet Stanton Blatch, were instrumental in bringing together the National and American Woman Suffrage Associations into the National American Woman Suffrage Association. Elizabeth Cady Stanton was elected President, Susan B. Anthony Vice President, and Lucy Stone head of the executive committee.

In 1893, at the World's Columbian Exposition in Chicago, Stone gave her last speech in support of the Women's Rights Movement. Shortly afterward, her health began to fail. She died in Boston on October 18, 1893, just after urging her daughter to "make the world better." Over 1,100 mourners attended her funeral.

The Kansas City *Star* noted that "one of the kindest, best-mannered and sweet-voiced of women was met with all sorts of ridicule.... Now all she did is considered right for women.... Lucy Stone will be widely honored and lamented." The Boston *Globe* observed that "it will take generations of coming women to realize the boon bestowed by such a life." The Cleveland *Leader* added that "when Lucy Stone died there passed from the earth one of the noblest women of the century."

FLORENCE NIGHTINGALE (1820-1910) Nursing and Medical Pioneer

"It was not by gentle sweetness and womanly self-abnegation that she had brought order out of chaos in the Scutari Hospitals, that, from her own resources, she had clothed the British Army, that she spread her dominion over the serried and reluctant powers of the official world; it was by strict method, by stern discipline, by rigid attention to detail, by ceaseless labor, by the fixed determination of an indomitable will."[22]

Lytton Strachey, *Eminent Victorians*

Florence Nightingale is known principally for her work at the military hospitals at Scutari, near Constantinople, during the Crimean War. However, her contributions were much larger than that. She was the driving force in the reform of British Army medical services during and after the Crimean War: in designing hospitals with the patient in mind, in the establishment of a school of nursing with higher standards than previous ones, and in the administration of medical services for the British Army in India.

This effort involved guiding those in positions of power in the British government, choosing chairmen for key committees, and generally steering medical and hospital reform, military and civilian, for over forty years. She provided direction for the careers of many Members of Parliament and advice to every Viceroy of India before he left England to assume his new duties.

Florence was born in 1820, the younger of two daughters of William and Fanny Nightingale, who owned two large country houses, Embley Park in Hampshire and Lea Hurst in Derbyshire. The family had rooms in Mayfair for the London social season and took frequent trips abroad. Florence grew into an attractive, lively young lady who was intelligent and a good conversationalist. She had many suitors and turned down two offers of marriage from men who waited years for her final answer.

Virtually all of Florence's friends were contented to become wives, mothers, and hostesses whose principal interests in life were social activities. Florence was bored with the social whirl and felt obliged to do something meaningful with her life. She viewed this as a call and entered this note in her diary: "On February 7, 1837, God spoke to me and called me to His service."

However, Florence did not know what form this service was going to take; she knew that it was going to have something to do with ministering to the sufferings of humanity. It did not become clear to her for seven years that her call was caring for the sick.

In the fall of 1842, while visiting the Baroness and Baron von Bunsen, the Prussian Ambassador to Great Britain, Nightingale asked them what a person could do to relieve the suffering of those who cannot help themselves. The Baron told her about the work of Pastor Fliedner and his wife at Kaiserswerth, Germany, where Protestant deaconesses were trained in the institution's hospital to nurse the poor who were sick. She had not considered nursing as a way of serving those in need, and she did not follow up on this suggestion.

By the spring of 1844, however, Nightingale was certain that her life's work was with the sick in hospitals. Thirteen years later she wrote, "Since I was twenty-four ... there never was any vagueness in my plans or ideas as to what God's work was for me."[23] In June 1844, Dr. Ward Howe, the American philanthropist, and his wife, Julia Ward Howe, later to become famous as the author of "Battle Hymn of the Republic," visited the Nightingales at Embley.

Nightingale asked Dr. Howe: "Do you think it would be unsuitable and unbecoming for a young Englishwoman to devote herself to works of charity in hospitals and elsewhere as Catholic sisters do?" Dr. Howe replied: "My dear Miss Florence, it would be unusual, and in England whatever is unusual is thought to be unsuitable; but I say to you 'go forward.' If you have a vocation for that way of life, act up to your inspiration and you will find there is never anything unbecoming or unladylike in doing your duty for the good of others. Choose, go on with it, wherever it may lead you and God be with you."[24]

Nightingale considered how to present to her parents her plan to spend three months in nursing training at nearby Salisbury Infirmary where the head physician was Dr. Fowler, a family friend. She broached the subject with her parents in December 1845, during a visit by Dr. Fowler and his wife to Embley.

The Nightingales were strongly opposed and could not understand why Florence wanted to "disgrace herself." She wrote to a friend that her mother was terrified, and the reason was "not the physically revolting parts of a hospital but things about the surgeons and nurses which you may guess." She wrote later that: "It was as if I had wanted to be a kitchen-maid."[25]

In June 1849, she received a second proposal of marriage—from Richard Monckton Milnes—"the man I adored." She rejected his proposal for a vocation that her parents would not let her pursue.

She reasoned:

I have an intellectual nature which requires
satisfaction and that would find it in him. I
have a passionate nature which requires satisfaction and that would find it in him. I have a
moral, active nature which requires satisfaction and that would not find it in his life.... I
could be satisfied to spend a life with him in
combining our different powers in some great
object. I could not satisfy this nature by spending a life with him in making society and
arranging domestic things.[26]

Nightingale was distressed because she knew what she
had to do, but she was prevented from doing it. Lytton
Strachey, in *Eminent Victorians,* writes: "A weaker spirit
would have been overwhelmed by the load of such distress-
es—would have yielded or snapped. But this extraordinary
young woman held firm and fought her way to victory. With
an amazing persistency, during the eight years that followed
her rebuff over Salisbury Hospital, she struggled and worked
and planned."[27]

While continuing to perform her social obligations,
Nightingale studied hospital reports and public health "Blue
Books." She built up a detailed knowledge of sanitary conditions that ultimately allowed her to become the foremost
expert in England and on the Continent in her subject.

Finally, Nightingale was given the opportunity to receive
nursing training at Kaiserswerth. Her mother and her sister,
Parthenope, went to Carlsbad to "take the waters" for three
months, and Nightingale was allowed to spend three months
in Kaiserswerth. Her spartan life started at five o'clock in the
morning and the work was hard; but, in her words, "I find the
deepest interest in everything here and am so well in body and

mind. This is life. Now I know what it is to live and to love life, and I really should be sorry to leave life.... I wish for no other earth, no other world than this."[28]

Nightingale met Dr. Elizabeth Blackwell, the first woman medical doctor in modern times, in the spring of 1851 in London, where Blackwell had come for further medical training. Nightingale invited Blackwell to visit her at Embley. While showing her around the grounds of the estate, Nightingale made an observation that indicated the strength of her commitment to hospital nursing. She admitted to Blackwell that every time she looked at Embley from the outside, "I think how I should turn it into a hospital and just where I should place the beds."

In the summer of 1852, Nightingale made arrangements, although she was a Protestant, to work at a Catholic hospital where the nurses were nuns, either with the Sisters of Mercy in Dublin or with the Sisters of Charity in Paris. Once again she had to cancel her plans when Fanny had hysterics and because her actions were adversely affecting her sister Parthe's health.

In April 1853, Nightingale heard of an opportunity that suited her parent's requirements. The Institution for the Care of Sick Gentlewomen in Distressed Circumstances had encountered problems and was to be reorganized and moved to another location. Nightingale received no pay for her position, and she had to pay the salary of a matron—"a superior elderly respectable person," which the institution's committee required her to have because of her youthful appearance. However, she was responsible not only for the management of the institution but also its finances. Fanny and Parthe were unhappy about her new position but were more tolerant than they had been of her earlier attempts to enter nursing.

Nightingale had one year of nursing experience in March 1854, when England and France declared war on Russia. In June, the British Army landed at Varna on the Black Sea. When they embarked from Varna for the Crimea there was a shortage of transport ships, so they had to leave hospital tents and regimental medicine chests behind. On September 30, the British and the French defeated the Russians in the Battle of the Alma with heavy casualties on both sides.

British casualties did not receive proper care, since there were no litters or hospital wagons to transport them to a site to receive medical attention. When the wounded were carried by their comrades to receive the care of a doctor, no bandages or splints were available, nor were there any anesthetics or painkillers.

William Russell's dispatches to the London *Times* brought the conditions of the casualties to the attention of the British public. Two weeks after the Battle of the Alma, he wrote, "It is with feelings of surprise and anger that the public will learn that no sufficient preparations have been made for the care of the wounded. Not only are there not sufficient surgeons ... not only are there no dressers and nurses ... there is not even linen to make bandages."[29]

Russell visited the French Army to see how their wounded were being treated. He found that their medical facilities and nursing care were excellent, and that fifty Sisters of Charity had accompanied their army. In another article to his newspaper, he asked, "Why have we no Sisters of Charity? There are numbers of able-bodied and tender-hearted English women who would joyfully and with alacrity go out to devote themselves to nursing the sick and wounded, if they could be associated for that purpose and placed under proper protection."[30]

The Secretary for War during the Crimean War was Sidney Herbert, a good friend of Nightingale and her family. Earlier, he had tried to help her when she had expressed an interest in going to Kaiserswerth for training. He wrote to ask if she would go to the Crimea:

> There is but one person in England that I know of who would be capable of organizing and superintending such a scheme; and I have been several times on the point of asking you hypothetically if, supposing the attempt were made, you would undertake to direct it.
>
> My question simply is, would you listen to the request to go and superintend the whole thing? You would of course have plenary authority over all the nurses, and I think I could secure the fullest assistance and co-operation from the medical staff, and you would also have an unlimited power of drawing on the Government for whatever you thought requisite for the success of the mission.[31]

Nightingale had already written to Sidney Herbert offering her services for such an expedition; their letters crossed in the mail. She immediately began interviewing candidates and ultimately selected fourteen nurses who, along with ten Catholic Sisters and fourteen Anglican sisters, accompanied her to Scutari. She was appointed Superintendent of the Female Nursing Establishment of the English General Hospitals in Turkey. This title caused her problems, since it was construed to restrict her authority to Turkey and to exclude her from the Crimea in Russia.

Nightingale arrived at the military hospital in Scutari on

November 4, 1854, ten days after the Battle of Balaclava, where the Light Brigade was decimated by pitting cavalry against artillery, and ten days before the Battle of Inkerman. She encountered a medical support system in total collapse, due to: insufficient planning, poor execution of the few plans that did exist, and generally inadequate administration hampered by bureaucratic constrictions.

The Commissariat was responsible for the procurement, finances, transporting, and warehousing of hospital supplies. The Purveyor was responsible for food for the sick—such as arrowroot, milk, rice, and starch—but did not procure them; the Commissariat did, and the organizations did not work well together.

Barrack Hospital, with four miles of beds, was not big enough. Nightingale had to plan, equip, and finance accommodations for 800 additional patients when the casualties from the Battles of Balaclava and Inkerman began to arrive. Open sewers, which ran under Barrack Hospital, were filled with lice, rats, and other vermin. Ventilation was poor and the stench was horrible. Some floors were in such bad condition that they could not be scrubbed. Nightingale noted that she had been in dwellings in the poorest parts of many cities in Europe, but she had not encountered conditions worse than that of Barrack Hospital at night.

Nightingale immediately became a purveyor of hospital supplies and a supplier of clothing to the patients. In her words, she became a general dealer in vegetables; clothing; dining utensils; personal hygiene items such as combs, soap, and towels; as well as hospital equipment, including bedpans, operating tables, and stump pillows.

Finances available to Nightingale were £7,000 sent to her from private sources in England and funds collected by the

London *Times* for aid to the sick and the wounded. An eye-witness wrote, "I cannot conceive, as I now look back on the first three weeks after the arrival of the wounded from Inkerman, how it would have been possible to have avoided a state of things too disastrous to contemplate had not Miss Nightingale been there, with the aid of the means placed at her disposal by Mr. MacDonald [of the *Times*]."[32]

British officialdom was totally out of touch with the needs of the hospital at Scutari. When asked by Mr. MacDonald what was the best way to employ the *Times* fund, Lord Stratford de Redcliffe, Ambassador to Turkey, replied that it should be used to build an English Protestant Church.

Although Nightingale complied with regulations, for example in requesting approval of a medical officer in obtaining supplies for the hospital, her active style offended Dr. John Hall, Chief of the Medical Staff of the British Expeditionary Army. He found ways to obstruct her efforts. In particular, he was initially able to prevent her from supporting the two large hospitals in the Crimea by a strict interpretation of her title, Superintendent of the Female Nursing Establishment in *Turkey*. He claimed that her responsibility did not extend to the Crimea.

Nightingale was furious to learn from a letter from Sidney Herbert's wife to Mrs. Bracebridge, her associate, that forty untrained nurses and Mary Stanley, their leader, were to arrive in Scutari the next day. Nightingale had been neither consulted nor advised of their arrival, and she wrote a blistering letter to Sidney Herbert expressing her feelings. Furthermore, they arrived with no funds on which to live. Nightingale lent Mary Stanley £400 for their immediate needs. Sidney apologized profusely, accepted the blame, confirmed Nightingale's position of authority, and offered personally to pay for the passage home of Mary Stanley's group.

Co-workers were in awe of Nightingale. Dr. Sutherland said, "She is the mainspring of the work. Nobody who has not worked with her daily could know her, could have an idea of her strength and clearness of mind, her extraordinary powers joined with her benevolence of spirit. She is one of the most gifted creatures God ever made."[33] She worked incredibly long hours and gave personal attention to the patients, even those with infectious diseases. The administrative load was overwhelming, and she had no secretary to share the paper-work burden. By the spring of 1855, she was physically exhausted.

Nightingale was becoming a legend in England. Queen Victoria wanted to recognize her for her services, but it was not clear what recognition was suitable. Dr. Hall was award-ed a K. C. B. and became Sir John Hall for his efforts. Florence wrote to Sidney Herbert that she supposed that the letters stood for "Knight of the Crimean Burial-grounds." No counterpart award existed for women at the time; later, the honor "Dame of the British Empire" came into use.

The Queen presented Nightingale with a brooch designed by the Prince Consort, a St. George's Cross of red enamel with the Royal cypher surmounted by a diamond crown. On the front was the word "Crimea" on a cross encircled by the words "Blessed are the merciful." On the back were inscribed the words, "To Miss Florence Nightingale, as a mark of esteem and gratitude for her devotion towards the Queen's brave soldiers, from Victoria R. 1855." It was accompanied by a letter from the Queen:

> You are, I know, well aware of the high sense
> I entertain of the Christian devotion which you

have displayed during this great and bloody war, and I need hardly repeat to you how warm my admiration is for your services, which are fully equal to those of my dear and brave soldiers, whose sufferings you have had the privilege of alleviating in so merciful a manner. I am, however, anxious of marking my feelings in a manner which I trust will be agreeable to you, and therefore send you with this letter a brooch, the form and emblems of which commemorate your great and blessed work, and which I hope you will wear as a mark of the high approbation of your Sovereign![34]

In August 1856, Nightingale returned home from Scutari. Within a few weeks of her return, she visited the Queen and the Prince Consort at Balmoral Castle and made an excellent impression. The Prince wrote in his diary, "She put before us all the defects of our present military hospital system and the reforms that are needed." The Queen observed, "Such a head! I wish we had her at the War Office."[35] Nightingale became an influential person, and she knew how to use that influence. She negotiated Sidney Herbert's appointment as chairman of a royal commission whose function was to report on the health of the army.

In an interview by the Royal Sanitary Commission in 1857, Nightingale was asked if she had studied the organization of civilian and military hospitals. She replied:

Yes, for thirteen years I have visited all the hospitals in London, Dublin, and Edinburgh, many country hospitals, some of the Naval and Military hospitals in England; all the hospitals in Paris and studied with the "Soeurs de

Charity"; the Institution of Protestant Deaconesses at Kaiserswerth on the Rhine, where I was twice in training as a nurse, the hospitals in Berlin and many others in Germany, at Lyons, Rome, Alexandria, Constantinople, and Brussels; also, the war hospitals of the French and the Sardinians.[36]

By her experiences, she had accumulated knowledge unequaled in Europe, perhaps in the world.

During six months of extremely hard work, Nightingale assembled and wrote in her own hand "Notes Affecting the Health, Efficiency, and Hospital Administration of the British Army." This comprehensive 800-page document contained far-sighted recommendations for reform in the areas of hospital architecture, military medical requirements, sanitation, and medical statistics.

Nightingale drove Sidney Herbert unmercifully to implement these recommendations as Chairman of the Royal Commission addressing this reform. She spurred him on even when his health began to fail. He devoted himself to implementing her reforms; when he died, he was viewed as a martyr to the cause. After his death, she referred to Sidney as her "master." However, when he was alive, no one wondered who was "master."

In December 1859, Nightingale published a nursing guide, *Notes on Nursing*. The following year, she opened the Nightingale Training School for Nurses at St. Thomas Hospital and became known as the founder of modern nursing. She did this concurrently with her ongoing efforts for medical and sanitary reform, which continued for over forty years. Administration was her strength; she established a cost accounting system for the Army Medical Services between

1860 and 1865 that was was still in use over eighty years later.

Nightingale's work with medical reform in India began with the Sanitary Commission of the Indian Army. She never traveled to India; she became an expert on medical and sanitary conditions there by analyzing, interpreting, and summarizing extensive surveys forwarded to her from hospitals on the subcontinent.

Although Nightingale was an invalid for many years, the amount of work she accomplished and the influence she wielded on her subject was substantial. For years, her residence was referred to as the "little war office." Her invalidism allowed her to avoid social events in which she had no interest and to concentrate her time and effort on tasks that she considered useful. She had many requests for visits from distinguished people, some of whom she declined to see. One of her visitors was the Aga Khan. Her comments on his visit were, "A most interesting man, but you could never teach him sanitation."

In November 1907, King Edward VII bestowed the Order of Merit on Nightingale, the first such award given to a woman. She died on August 13, 1910. Her family declined the offer of a national funeral and burial in Westminster Abbey, in deference to her wishes. She was buried next to her parents at Embley; her pallbearers were six sergeants of the British Army.

During the time when Nightingale was pleading unsuccessfully with her parents to allow her to undertake nursing training, her mother confided her concerns to her friends. As noted by Lytton Strachey in *Eminent Victorians,* "At times, indeed, among her intimates, Mrs. Nightingale almost wept. 'We are ducks,' she said with tears in her eyes, 'who have hatched a wild swan.' But the poor lady was wrong; it was not a swan that they had hatched; it was an eagle."[37]

Elizabeth Blackwell Statue, Hobart and William Smith Colleges, Geneva, NY

ELIZABETH BLACKWELL (1821-1910) First Woman Medical Doctor in the U.S.

"When you want a thing deeply, earnestly and intensely, this feeling of desire reinforces your will and arises in you the determination to work for the desired object. When you have a distinct purpose in view, your work becomes of absorbing interest. You bend your best powers to it; you give it concentrated attention; you think of little else than the realization of this purpose; your will is stimulated into unusual activity, and as a consequence you do your work with an increasing sense of power."

Grenville Kleister

Elizabeth Blackwell's desire to become a medical doctor did not develop slowly. It occurred as a significant emotional event in her early twenties while visiting a friend who was dying of cancer. Her friend said to her, "You are fond of study, Elizabeth. You have health, leisure, and a cultivated intelligence. Why don't you devote these qualities to the service of suffering women? Why don't you study medicine? Had I been treated by a lady doctor, my worst sufferings would have been spared me."[38]

Elizabeth considered the study of medicine. She knew that, although she was happy with her social life revolving around her parents, sisters, brothers, and friends in Cincinnati, it was not a fulfilling life for her. She did not feel challenged. She entered her personal reflections on pursuing the study of medicine in her diary, "The idea of winning a doctor's degree gradually assumed the aspect of a great moral struggle, and the moral fight possessed an immense attraction for me. This work has taken deep root in my soul and become an all-absorbing duty. I must accomplish my end. I consider it the noblest and most useful path that I can tread."[39]

Before undertaking medical studies, Elizabeth had to earn money to finance her education. Her father, Samuel Blackwell, had passed away at the age of forty-eight, leaving the family in debt. Her mother, Hannah Lane Blackwell, Elizabeth, and her brothers and sisters had worked since Samuel's death to pay off family debts.

Blackwell taught school in Asheville, North Carolina and then in Charleston, South Carolina to earn money for medical school expenses. She sent out applications to medical schools while teaching in Charleston. She wanted to attend medical school in Philadelphia, which she considered the medical center of the United States because of its four highly regarded medical schools.

Blackwell sent her first inquiry to Dr. Joseph Warrington in Philadelphia. His response was discouraging; he viewed men as doctors and women as nurses and recommended that she pursue a nursing career. However, he added that, "if the project be of divine origin and appointment, it will sooner or later surely be accomplished."[40] She applied to twenty-nine medical schools for admission and received twenty-eight rejections.

In late October 1847, Blackwell received an acceptance from the medical school of Geneva College, Geneva, New York. Dr. Benjamin Hale, President of Geneva College, was an open-minded individual who had recruited an extremely capable dean for the medical school, Dr. Charles Lee. The medical school later became part of Syracuse University and Geneva College was renamed Hobart College.

The circumstances surrounding Blackwell's acceptance were unusual. Dr. Warrington wrote a letter to Dr. Lee on her behalf. The Geneva faculty was unanimously against the admission of a woman to their medical school. However, they did not want to be responsible for rejecting the highly regarded Philadelphia doctor's request. The faculty turned the decision over to the medical students; they were confident that the students would vote against her admission.

Dr. Lee read Dr. Warrington's letter to the class and informed them that the faculty would let the students determine the issue. He told them that one negative vote would prevent Blackwell's admission. The students were enthusiastic about her admittance, and the single dissenting student was browbeaten into submission. She received a document composed by the students and signed by the chairman of the class:

> 1. Resolved—That one of the radical principles of a Republican Government is the universal education of both sexes; that to every branch of scientific education the door should be open equally to all; that the application of Elizabeth Blackwell to become a member of our class meets our entire approbation; and in extending our unanimous invitation we pledge ourselves that no conduct of ours shall cause her to regret her attendance at this institution.

> 2. Resolved—That a copy of these proceedings be signed by the chairman and transmitted to Elizabeth Blackwell.[41]

> T. J. Stratton, Chairman

Blackwell was overjoyed to receive the acceptance. She arrived in Geneva on November 6, having missed the first five weeks of the session. She was not sure what to expect from her fellow medical students; however, she had grown up with brothers and was not an overly sensitive young woman. She was well-mannered and dressed conservatively in Quaker style. The Geneva community was not ready for a female medical student, and, initially, she had difficulty finding a place to live. She moved into a drafty attic room in a boarding house and fed wood into a wood-burning stove to keep warm.

Eventually, Blackwell became aware that she was being subjected to a form of ostracism. The other boarders were unfriendly at mealtime, the women she passed on the street held their skirts to one side and did not speak, and one doctor's wife snubbed her openly. Her feelings were hurt by this treatment. She reacted by staying in her room and studying.

Blackwell's Professor of Anatomy was Dr. James Webster, who was friendly and sincerely glad to have her in his class. He predicted: "You'll go through the course and get your diploma—with great éclat too. We'll give you the opportunities. You'll make a stir, I can tell you."[42]

However, within a short time, he prevented Blackwell from attending a dissection. He wrote a note to her explaining that he was about to lecture on the reproductive organs and that he could not cover the material satisfactorily in the presence of a lady. He offered her the opportunity for dissection and study of this portion of the course in private. She knew that Dr. Webster had a reputation for being coarse in covering this material. He sprinkled his lecture with humorous anecdotes. The students liked this approach to the subject matter and responded by becoming somewhat rowdy.

Blackwell replied to Dr. Webster reminding him that she was a student with a serious purpose, and that she was aware of his awkward position, particularly "when viewed from the low standpoint of impure and unchaste sentiments." She asked why a student of science would have his mind diverted from such an absorbing subject by the presence of a student in feminine attire. She offered to remove her bonnet and sit in the back row of benches, but if the class wished she would not attend the class.

Dr. Webster acquiesced, and Blackwell attended the dissection, which was "just about as much as I could bear." She noted in her diary: "My delicacy was certainly shocked, and yet the exhibition was in some sense ludicrous. I had to pinch my hand until the blood nearly came, and call on Christ to help me from smiling, for that would have ruined everything; but I sat in grave indifference, though the effort made my heart palpitate most painfully."[43] Dr. Webster conducted the class without the usual anecdotes.

Blackwell was a self-disciplined student who maintained a friendly but impersonal relationship with her classmates. She considered how to spend her summer adding to her medical knowledge. One of the few places open to her was Blockley Almshouse in Philadelphia that cared for 2,000 unfortunates, most of whom were from the slums.

Again, Blackwell had to pay for being a pioneer. The resident doctors snubbed her and left a ward when she entered it. They neglected to enter the diagnosis and the notation of the medication used in treatment on the patients' charts. She had to make many of her own diagnoses. Her major accomplishment that summer was the preparation of a thesis on typhus for which she received compliments from senior staff physicians.

Blackwell worked hard during her second year of medical school. Although she had always received good grades, she approached her final exams with trepidation. When the results were compiled, Elizabeth had the best academic record in the class. However, the administration of Geneva College vacillated on establishing the precedent of awarding the first medical degree to a woman in the United States.

Dr. Webster defended her, saying, "She paid her tuition didn't she? She passed every course, each and every one with honors! And let me tell you, gentlemen, if you hold back, I'll take up a campaign in every medical journal."[44] Blackwell received her medical degree on January 23, 1849. Her brother, Henry, traveled to Geneva to share the experience with her. She was invited to participate in the academic procession, which she declined "because it wouldn't be ladylike."

Blackwell was the last student called to receive a diploma from Dr. Hale. In presenting her diploma, Dr. Hale used the word *Domina* in place of *Domine*. Elizabeth replied, "Sir, I thank you. By the help of the Most High, it shall be the effort of my life to shed honor on your diploma."[45]

Blackwell's brother, Henry, documented his recollections of the ceremony:

> He [Dr. Lee, who gave the valedictory address] pronounced her the leader of the class; stated that she had passed through a thorough course in every department, slighting none; that she had profited to the utmost by all the advantages of the institution, and by her ladylike and dignified deportment had proved that the strongest intellect and nerve, and the most untiring perseverance were compatible with the softest attributes of feminine delicacy and grace, to all which the students manifested, by decided attempts at applause, their entire concurrence.[46]

As Blackwell left the ceremony, the women of Geneva displayed their smiles and friendly faces to her. She was pleased to see this change in attitude; however, she recorded her true feelings in her diary: "For the next few hours, before I left by train, my room was thronged by visitors. I was glad of the sudden conversion thus shown, but my past experience had given me a useful and permanent lesson at the outset of life as to the very shallow nature of popularity."[47]

Blackwell returned to Philadelphia with the hope of being accepted by the medical community there. She attended lectures at the University of Pennsylvania, but it was obvious that she was not going to be given the opportunity to gain the practical medical experience she needed. She went to Paris for further medical training, arriving on May 21, 1849 after a brief stay in England. Blackwell had forwarded a letter of introduction from a doctor in Boston to Dr. Pierre Louis, a highly regarded physician practicing in Paris. Her interview with Dr. Louis was not successful. He advised her to apply to La Maternité, a center for obstetrics where 3,000 babies were born annually. She realized that Dr. Louis viewed her as a midwife.

Blackwell's letter of introduction to Dr. Roux was more successful. She attended some of his lectures, and he took her on a tour of the wards of Hôtel Dieu. However, Dr. Henri Davanne, Director-general of the Paris hospitals, withdrew her permission to accompany physicians on their rounds at these hospitals, which was allowed for scores of male medical students. Dr. Paul DuBois and Dr. Armand Trousseau denied her permission to attend lectures at L'Ecole de Médecine. Dr. Trousseau suggested that she disguise herself as a man. She had heard this recommendation before, and she was no more receptive of the idea now than she had been previously.

However, lectures at the College de France and the Jardin des Plantes were open to her.

In late June, Blackwell was accepted into La Maternité, due mainly to the efforts of the U.S. Ambassador to Turkey, who happened to be visiting in Paris. Even with this diplomatic assistance, she was accepted as an aide, not as a doctor. She lived in a dormitory with sixteen young, exuberant French girls from the provinces who were there to be trained as aides. She made the best of her circumstances and used every opportunity to add to her medical knowledge.

In October 1850, Blackwell returned to London and was pleased to hear that the medical council at St. Bartholomew's Hospital had approved her application for further study. Dr. James Paget, the distinguished surgeon, made a point of making her welcome. She had access to every department of the hospital except the department of female diseases, which was the decision of the Professor of Midwifery; he had nothing against her personally but felt that he could not approve of "a lady's studying medicine."

Upon completion of additional training abroad, Blackwell returned to New York and attempted to establish herself with the medical community. She was not accepted as she had been in London. Her application to work as an assistant physician in the department for women and children at a city dispensary was rejected. She requested permission to visit the women's ward of one of the city hospitals, and her request was ignored. She was advised to open her own dispensary.

Finally, Blackwell used half of her savings to furnish a set of rooms where she had to pay an inflated rent. The New York *Tribune* carried the announcement that Dr. Elizabeth Blackwell had opened an office and was accepting patients. Elizabeth's landlady contributed to her difficulty in establishing her practice. She indicated her disapproval of Elizabeth's profession by refusing to deliver messages to her.

Blackwell expressed her thoughts in a letter to her younger sister, Emily, who planned to follow in her sister's footsteps: "A blank wall of social and professional antagonism faces the woman physician that forms a situation of singular and painful loneliness, leaving her without support, respect, or professional counsel."[48]

Blackwell planned, wrote, and delivered a series of six lectures. In the lectures, she advocated more varied and extended education for women, increased physical activity for women including participation in sports, and health and hygiene courses for young women. She wrote a book incorporating many of the thoughts in her lectures. In late 1852, it was published as *The Laws of Life with Special Reference to the Physical Education of Girls.*

Although Blackwell's views about hygiene were gaining acceptance, she was jeered while walking around the city. She received not only scorn but also threatening letters. She was viewed as a person who lectured about subjects that should not be discussed in public. She was bothered most by women who would not consider having a woman doctor.

Blackwell wanted to do more than run a dispensary. She wanted to establish a hospital to care for the sick who were unable to pay for treatment, to educate women physicians, and to train nurses. She was forced to close her dispensary because the $5,000 she needed to continue was not available in 1855, a recession year. Finally, she bought a house in which to establish her hospital. Her sister, Emily, who had received her medical degree at Western Reserve University in Ohio, had received further medical training in Europe and was now a trained surgeon. Emily was eager to join the staff of the fledgling hospital.

Dr. Henry Ward Beecher, brother of Harriet Beecher Stowe, author of *Uncle Tom's Cabin*, spoke at the official opening of the New York Infirmary for Women and Children on May 12, 1857:

> Woman should be entirely a better physician than man. Her intuition, perception, and good mother wit should make her so. Indeed, she is particularly fitted for the study of medicine.... Besides, woman has a right to do whatever she can do well, and I welcome anything that tends to enlarge the sphere of her development. I am sure this Infirmary will grow and prosper. I expect to see it as one of the giant institutions of the land.[49]

Charles A. Dana, Cyrus W. Field, and Horace Greeley were trustees of the Infirmary.

In 1858, Blackwell traveled to England, where she became the first woman in the British Medical Register. She never wavered from her goal of establishing a medical college for women; nevertheless, she had to postpone her efforts due to the demands of the Civil War from 1861 to 1864. She assisted the war effort by selecting candidates for nursing training, whom she trained at one of the New York hospitals or her Infirmary, equipped them, and forwarded them to Dorothea Dix, Superintendent of Nurses, in Washington, D.C. In 1866, Blackwell established the first visiting nurse program in New York City.

In November 1868, Blackwell opened her medical college. For thirty-one years, the college filled a need in providing medical education for women. In 1899, it was incorporated into the Cornell Medical Center. A separate medical college for women was no longer required; qualified women could obtain admittance to other medical colleges. The infirmary continued to exist as a separate entity.

Blackwell returned to England in 1869, where she assisted with women's efforts in Britain to enter the medical profession. In 1870, she helped to found the British National Health Society. In 1876, she accepted a teaching position in gynecology at the London School for Women. Her book, *The Moral Education of the Young,* was published that year.

Blackwell's niece, Anna, said, "I stood in awe of her although she was sweet and serene. One felt she had conquered so much.... Like her father, she had a sense of fun, but she had a masterful persistence when she felt she was right."[50] Dr. Elizabeth Cushier, a peer of Elizabeth and Emily, observed:

> We may forget the early struggles of the doctors Elizabeth and Emily Blackwell, but what we should never forget is that the dignity, the culture, and the high moral standards which formed their character, finally prevailed in overcoming the existing prejudice, both within and outside the profession. By their standards, the status of women in medicine was determined.[51]

The infirmary founded by Elizabeth Blackwell is now New York Downtown Hospital. In 1899, Hobart and William Smith Colleges, successors to Geneva College, named its first residence hall for women Blackwell House. In 1926, the London School of Medicine paid tribute to Geneva College as having the "highest ideals of American justice and liberty in inaugurating a new era in the story of medical science by conferring on a woman the degree of M.D." Elizabeth Blackwell overcame all of the obstacles encountered by a pioneer. She was determined.

ANTOINETTE BROWN (1825-1921) First Woman Ordained Minister in the U.S.

"Let us not be content to wait and see what will happen, but give us the determination to make the right things happen."

Peter Marshall, U.S. Senate Chaplain

While in her teens, Antoinette Brown decided that she wanted to be a minister. No American woman had ever been ordained a minister; however, in the 1820s, a Methodist woman had attempted to preach in New York State but gave in to public opposition. Quakers, who considered all members ministers, permitted all women to speak at worship services, but women were not usually leaders of the church community.

Antoinette Louisa Brown, the seventh of ten children of Joseph and Abigail Morse Brown, was born in Henrietta, New York in May 1825. Antoinette indicated her interest in religion at an early age, when she gave a spontaneous prayer to conclude a family prayer meeting at the age of eight. In the following year, she joined the village Congregational Church, at a time when joining the church so young was rare.

The small Henrietta church was a member of the liberal branch of the Congregational Church, which emphasized God's mercy and forgiveness in addition to human goodness and initiative. The orthodox branch of the Church believed that humans were morally corrupt, sinful, and dependent upon an all-powerful God who would condemn them to hell if they did not obey His word.

Antoinette was active in her Henrietta church and spoke frequently at prayer meetings, at which any church member was permitted to speak. She decided to attend Oberlin College in Ohio, where her brother, William, studied theology. Oberlin was the first U.S. college to admit women to take courses with men. In the spring of 1846, she began her studies at Oberlin.

Oberlin had been founded in 1833 by ministers from New England and New York. By the time that Brown arrived, the College had developed its own ideology, which was a combination of liberal religion, practical training, and the politics of reform. The spiritual leader of the Oberlin community was Professor of Theology Charles Grandison Finney, who had impressed Brown's parents at a series of revival meetings in Rochester during the winter of 1831. He was a captivating speaker who advocated the individual's dual responsibility of commitment to God and working to create a better society. He suggested that this dual responsibility should be fulfilled by applying one's intellect and education to saving individual souls and to improving society. He became Brown's mentor.

In the winter of 1846-47, during Oberlin's lengthy vacation, Brown taught at a large private academy in Rochester, Michigan. The experience verified what she already knew: "God never made me for a schoolteacher." The headmaster encouraged Brown to give her first public speech. She spoke in the village church and was pleased that "it was fairly well received by the students and by the community."

Brown met Lucy Stone, who later became a leader of the Women's Rights Movement, at Oberlin. Brown and Stone became close friends and confidants despite their philosophical differences. Stone was more radical on the subject of abolition; she had left the Congregational Church because it approved of slavery and was against women speaking in public. Brown was disappointed that her closest friend did not agree with her goals:

> I told her of my intention to become a minis-
> ter. Her protest was most emphatic. She said,
> "You will never be allowed to do this. You will
> never be allowed to stand in a public pulpit nor
> to preach in a church, and certainly you can
> never be ordained." It was a long talk but we
> were no nearer to an agreement at the end than
> at the beginning. My final answer could only
> be, "I am going to do it."[52]

In the summer of 1847, Brown completed her undergraduate studies at Oberlin. She returned home to Henrietta and
practiced public speaking: "I go out into the barn and make
the walls echo with my voice occasionally, but the church
stands on the green in such a way that I have too many audi-
tors when I attempt to practice there. The barn is a good large
one however, and the sounds ring out merrily, or did before
father filled it full of hay."[53]

Brown returned to Oberlin in the fall to study theology.
She was called to this vocation, and she was motivated to use
her intellect, her ability as a public speaker, and her interest in
public reform. However, although Oberlin was committed to
providing women with a general education, the only profession that it prepared women for was teaching. In the Theology
Department, women were welcome to sit in on classes only
for self-improvement.

Brown was assigned to write essays on the passages in the
Bible stating that women should not preach: "Let your
women keep silence in the churches, for it is not permitted
unto them to speak.... Let the women learn in silence with all
subjection. I suffer not a woman to teach, nor to usurp author-

ity over the man, but to be in silence." She found confirmation of her choice of a profession in the words of the prophet Joel: "And it shall come to pass in the last days, saith God, I will pour out my spirit upon all flesh; and your sons and daughters shall prophesy."[54]

In her assigned essay, Brown observed that St. Paul's suggestion that women should learn in silence had been misinterpreted. She suggested that St. Paul only intended to caution against "excesses, irregularities, and unwarranted liberties" in public worship. Her essay was selected for publication in the *Oberlin Quarterly Review*.

In their last year, Oberlin theology students were allowed to preach in area churches but not to perform any sacraments. Brown said: "They were willing to have me preach, but not to themselves endorse this as a principle.... They decided, after much discussion, that I must preach if I chose to do so on my own responsibility." Although she was not given official recognition, Brown spoke in small churches nearby, usually on the popular subject of temperance.

Upon completion of her theology studies, Brown chose not to be ordained at Oberlin. Not only did she think that it would be "a delicate thing" because of Oberlin's stance on women ministers, but also she preferred the usual path of ordination by a local church that wanted her as a pastor. She cited "an instinctive desire to be ordained in my own church, and a belief that I could one day in the future be ordained by my own denomination, which was then orthodox Congregational."[55]

Brown did not participate in the graduation exercises. In later years, she observed: "We were not supposed to graduate, as at that time to have regularly graduated women from a theological school would have been an endorsement of their probable future careers."[56] Her name did not appear in the roll of the theological school class of 1850 until 1908.

In 1850, Brown attended the first national Women's Rights Convention in Worcester, Massachusetts, where she spoke to disprove the Biblical argument that women should not speak in public. She met Lucretia Mott and Elizabeth Cady Stanton, organizers of the Seneca Falls Convention two years earlier. Blackwell was introduced to many men and women who were active in social reform. She maintained her contacts with them, although she thought that her cause would probably not be best served by working with organized groups.

Liberal ministers such as William Henry Channing and Samuel J. May invited Brown to preach in their churches. Her oldest brother, William, who had initially opposed her choice of a vocation, invited her to speak in his church in Andover, Massachusetts. She pursued her calling in earnest, and she began actively to seek a church in need of a pastor.

During one of her speaking tours across New York State, Brown had visited South Butler. Members of the small Congregational church listened to her speak and then invited her to become their pastor. In the late spring of 1853, she moved to South Butler and gave two sermons every Sunday, one prepared and the other extemporaneous.

Brown's responsibilities included pastoral duties such as visiting the sick; she felt suited to her role as minister and noted, "My little parish was a miniature world in good and evil. To get humanity condensed into so small a compass that you can study each individual member opens a new chapter of experience. It makes one thoughtful and rolls upon the spirit a burden of deep responsibility."[57]

Brown's friend, Lucy Stone, met Henry Blackwell, broth-

er of the pioneer doctor, Elizabeth Blackwell, at an abolitionist meeting. Henry fell in love with Stone and immediately
began to court her. Stone suggested that Henry's older brother, Samuel, visit Brown while on his travels. The Blackwell
brothers were business partners in Cincinnati. Samuel called
on Brown while en route to Boston. Samuel "enjoyed the visit
exceedingly." She observed that "he stayed perhaps a half a
day and had a pleasant visit.... He was not handsome."[58] She
was preoccupied with church duties.

Brown's church appreciated her work, and the governing
body proceeded with planning her ordination. She already
administered the sacraments, but the ceremony would provide
public recognition of her ministry. Reverend Luther Lee, a
minister from nearby Syracuse, whom she knew from abolitionist meetings, agreed to preach the ordination sermon.

Reverend Lee based his sermon on the text, "There is neither male nor female; for ye are all one in Christ Jesus." He
said, "In the Church, of which Christ is the only head, males
and females possess equal rights and privileges; here there is
no difference.... I cannot see how the test can be explained so
as to exclude females from any right, office, work, privilege,
or immunity which males enjoy, hold or perform." He concluded by saying, "All we are here to do, and all we expect to
do, is, in due form, and by a solemn and impressive service,
to subscribe our testimony to the fact that in our belief, our
sister in Christ, Antoinette L. Brown, is one of the ministers
of the New Covenant, authorized, qualified, and called of
God to preach the Gospel of His Son Jesus Christ."[59]

During the winter of 1854, Brown's duties weighed heavily upon her. Her job was a difficult one, and her responsibilities caused her emotional strain. A minister's functions were
many and varied. He or she was expected to be tolerant and

understanding, but at times authoritative and judgmental. It was difficult for her to be a "father" figure. Her role would have been easier if she had the support of friends and associates. However, Susan B. Anthony, Elizabeth Cady Stanton, and Lucy Stone all disapproved of her church affiliation. They did not perceive Brown's ministerial duties as promoting change in women's status.

Brown felt isolated:

> It was practically ten years after my ordination before any other woman known to the public was ordained. It was therefore doubly hard for me—a young woman still in her twenties—to adapt myself to the rather curious relationship I must sustain either to home conditions or to those of a pastorate. Personally this was more of an emotional strain than the enduring of any opposition that ever came to me as a public speaker or teacher.[60]

This isolation affected Brown in a serious way. She questioned her faith, particularly the belief that the individual was condemned to eternal damnation unless saved by a stern God. She was motivated more by Charles Grandison Finney's teachings that stressed human goodness and striving to approach moral perfection. In July 1854, overcome by mental conflict and nervous exhaustion, she returned home to rest.

Samuel Blackwell helped Brown find herself during this difficult time. She observed: "In the midst of the blackness of darkness which was around me more or less that year in New York, Mr. Blackwell's optimism and the fact that he was passing through a very similar experience to my own ... enabled him to become to me a present help in time of trouble."[61]

Brown had stayed with the Blackwell family when she visited Cincinnati on the lecture circuit. Samuel's five sisters were all achievers: Elizabeth and Emily became doctors, Ellen and Marian were active in the Women's Rights Movement and other reform efforts, and Anna, who lived at the transcendentalist commune at Brook Farm for a while, was a newspaper reporter in Paris. Samuel was used to activist women.

At the end of 1854, Lucy Stone agreed to marry Henry Blackwell if he would agree to devote his efforts to women's rights. Perhaps motivated by his brother's action, Samuel proposed to Brown at about the same time. She hesitated, but then she considered some of the women whom she knew — Lucretia Mott was an example — who had children, husbands, and homes in addition to careers. After their marriage, she was known as Reverend Antoinette L. B. Blackwell.

After leaving the ministry, Brown earned her living as a public speaker as her friend, Lucy Stone, was doing. Before radio and television, the lecture circuit or lyceum was an important means of informing and entertaining people. Women speakers were usually paid less than men. Brown told the lyceum organizers that "my terms, from principle, are never less that the best prices received by the gentlemen of the particular association where I speak." She found the work to be satisfying, and she consistently received favorable reviews in the local newspapers of towns where she spoke.

In the late 1860s, Brown Blackwell devoted herself to writing. Her first large published work was *Studies in General Science*, a collection of essays. In 1875, her second work, *The Sexes Throughout Nature*, a compilation of essays first published in periodicals, was published. In 1876, she published *The Physical Basis of Immortality*, a synthesis of her philosophy. *The Philosophy of Individuality, or The One and the Many*, was published in 1893. Her last two books, *The Making of the Universe* and *The Social Side of Mind and Action* were published in 1914 and 1915.

Brown Blackwell was drawn to the Unitarian Church. Samuel Blackwell and three of his sisters had already joined the Unitarians. In the spring of 1878, she joined the Unitarian Fellowship and asked to be recognized as a minister. In the fall of 1878, the Committee on Fellowship of the American Unitarian Association acknowledged her as a minister.

Oberlin College finally recognized Brown Blackwell's status in 1879, awarding her an "honorary" Master of Arts degree, the degree that she had earned during three years of study in the Theological Department. One change from her studies thirty years previously was that she no longer was the only woman minister. In 1864, Olympia Brown, motivated by Brown Blackwell's talk to her class at Antioch College, was ordained a Universalist minister. By 1880, almost 200 women were recognized as ministers, and many held full-time pastoral jobs.

In addition to her participation in the Women's Rights Movement, Brown Blackwell was active in the Association for the Advancement of Women and the American Association for the Advancement of Science. Although she had not had the responsibility of a parish for decades, she considered herself a "minister emeritus" during her later years.

In June 1908, Brown Blackwell was invited to Oberlin College to receive an honorary Doctor of Divinity degree. In introducing her to Oberlin President Henry Churchill King at the commencement ceremony, Dr. Charles Wager spoke to the audience:

It is appropriate for the institution that was the first to provide for higher education of women to honor, at its seventy-fifth anniversary, a woman who has eminently justified that daring innovation, a woman who was one of the first two in America to complete a course in divinity, who as preacher, as pastor, as writer, as the champion of more than one good cause, has in the past conferred honor upon her Alma Mater, and who today confers upon it no less honor by an old age as lovely as it is venerable.[62]

In the spring of 1921, her health began to fail; she was at peace with herself. She was ready for death and looked upon it as a reunion with Samuel, who had preceded her in death, and all of her other loved ones. In late November 1921, at the age of ninety-seven, Reverend Antoinette L. B. Blackwell, the first woman minister, died in her sleep.

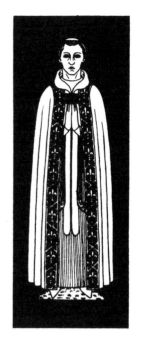

CHAPTER 2

ECCLESIASTICS / RELIGIOUS LEADERS

"For though with judgment we on things reflect, our will determines, not our intellect."

Edmund Waller, *Divine Love*

Chapter 2 provides profiles of men who displayed determination throughout their lifetimes. Three of them, St. Thomas Becket, St. Thomas More, and St. John Fisher, were sufficiently determined to die for their beliefs. Many similarities exist in the lives of **St. Thomas Becket** and **St. Thomas More**, even though they lived three centuries apart. Both served as Lord Chancellor of England for King Henry; Becket served King Henry II, and More served King Henry VIII.

More was raised in the clerical and legal life, whereas Becket grew up the business and political environment and was ordained so that he could serve both as Archbishop of Canterbury and Lord Chancellor. Becket participated in battles and in individual combat, activities that were not experienced by More. The outlook of the kings that they served were different. King Henry II wanted to control the Church, but he did not place himself above the Pope; King Henry VIII placed the Catholic Church in England under his jurisdiction.

Another difference between Becket and More is the manner in which they died. Becket was murdered in his cathedral after King Henry II uttered the words to his lieutenants, "[Who] will free me of this lowborn priest?" More was beheaded for refusing to acknowledge King Henry VIII as leader of the Church in England.

St. John Fisher was a well-educated cleric and author who served as Chancellor of Cambridge University and as Bishop of Rochester. He was a highly regarded intellectual in his time; it is surprising that he is not more widely known today. He died as Thomas More died, beheaded because he would not sign a document placing the jurisdiction of the Church in England under King Henry VIII. Fisher was executed before More and was the first English bishop to be sentenced to death in the courtroom.

Martin Luther was the first Protestant. He spoke out against misdeeds of the Catholic Church and suffered all of the tribulations of a reformer. For a time, he was sequestered in a castle until the controversy he had stirred up had subsided. Selling indulgences was one practice of the Catholic Church with which he disagreed. A Church member could commit a sin and then have that sin forgiven by paying money to the Church. The reforms that Luther sought were needed. He had sufficient determination and confidence in his beliefs to take on the established Church.

St. Ignatius Loyola began his life as a soldier, and members of the order that he founded, the Society of Jesus or Jesuits, are sometimes called "Soldiers of Christ." He was punished and imprisoned on several occasions early in his career for departing from the ways of the Catholic Church. He thought that he had been visited by Christ and that his path in founding the Jesuits had been preordained. The Jesuits have been known as authors and educators and have been a force within the Catholic Church.

These five men are outstanding examples of the importance of determination in being unwavering in our beliefs.

ST. THOMAS BECKET (1118-1170) English Religious Martyr

"The man who is just and resolute will not be moved from his settled purpose, either by the misdirected rage of his fellow citizens, or by the misdirected rage of an imperious tyrant."

Horace, *Carmina III*

Thomas Becket and King Henry II were friends as youths. Their thinking began to diverge when Henry made decisions that adversely affected the Church in England. Becket demurred when the young King asked him to be Archbishop of Canterbury because he knew that would be placed in the position of siding either with his conscience or his King. Becket's concerns were overridden, and he served as Archbishop of Canterbury; however, his fears became reality. Ultimately, King Henry viewed Becket as an obstacle to his desire for increased control over the Church. This view had fatal results for Becket; it cost him his life.

Becket was born in Cheapside, London on December 21, 1118 to Gilbert and Matilda Becket. Gilbert, who like his wife was born in Normandy, was a successful London merchant who acquired property, lived on rents, and served for a time as Sheriff. Matilda Becket, described as "pious and charitable," was a significant influence in shaping her son's character. John of Salisbury wrote of Thomas Becket: "From an early age he learned from his mother to fear the Lord and sweetly to invoke the Blessed Virgin, taking her as his guide in all his ways, as his patroness in life, and placing all his trust in her, after Christ."[63]

Young Thomas attended Merton Augustinian priory school for several years and continued his education in the schools of London. When he was sixteen, he enrolled in the arts course in Paris where Peter Abelard, Peter Lombard, and Robert of Melun taught. Becket admired and respected Abelard, who said, "By doubting, we come by inquiry; by inquiry, we come to truth."

At the age of twenty-one, Becket returned to England when his mother died and was instructed in the arts of falconry and hunting by Richer de Laigle, a Norman Baron who was a friend of his father. While hunting with Baron de Laigle, Becket had an accident that he associated with his call to destiny. Some biographers considered it a miracle; they viewed it as an indication that God saved his life that day so that he could "stand and fight for His tabernacles."

> The man and the boy had come to a rapid mill-stream crossed by a narrow footbridge. The knight dismounted and led his horse swiftly across the bridge. Thomas followed, all muffled in his hood—it must have been a cold day and the bridge, a mere plank, possibly had a thin coating of ice on it. Halfway across, Thomas's horse stumbled; Thomas held fast to the reins, and boy and horse plunged into the stream. The violent current swept Thomas along toward the roaring mill, with Richer and the rest of the hunting party following on the banks "with great and piteous cries."

> It seemed certain that Thomas would either be drowned or crushed by the mill wheel. At this moment the miller, knowing nothing of what was happening, suddenly shut off the water from his mill. In the ensuing silence he heard the shouts, came out of the mill, and "catching sight of Thomas in the water, quickly put in his

hand and pulled him out, barely breathing and half dead."[64]

Becket's carefree life changed when his father's fortunes suffered a reverse due to the loss of many of his rental buildings in a London fire. He went into service with an accountant friend of his father. Becket was a clerk and an auditor to the Sheriffs of London. He gained experience in the policies and methods of civic and mercantile finance in the City of London. His sphere of knowledge expanded to include diplomacy, finance, and politics as well as an acquaintance with the royal court.

In his mid-twenties, Becket reached a turning point in his career. He realized that one of the most stable environments in that time of trouble was the Church. Henry I's only legitimate heir was his daughter, Matilda. The future Henry II was an infant. English lords and Norman barons did not want Matilda to ascend to the throne because her husband, Geoffrey of Anjou, was unacceptable to them. They preferred Stephen of Blois, King Henry's nephew and grandson of William the Conqueror.

Becket's father knew the Archbishop of Canterbury well; they were both from the same region of Normandy. Members of Archbishop Theobald's household visited the Becket home frequently and were impressed by the potential of twenty-four-year-old Thomas, who was given a position on the Archbishop's staff. Becket was leaving the secular environment for the society of the Church; he was making more than just a job change. His duties involved being a secretary to a minister, which included such responsibilities as collecting the rents of the estates and overseeing the house property as well as helping the Archbishop with his correspondence. He observed how the Archbishop dealt with royal encroachment and political issues.

Archbishop Theobald groomed Becket for the position of Archdeacon, who was responsible for the administrative and legal functions of the diocese. He sent Becket to the University of Bologna to study canon and Roman civil law and then to the famous school of law at Auxerre for further study.

In *Thomas Becket,* David Knowles describes the Church in England in Becket's time:

> The intermingling of secular and church government in Anglo-Saxon history was unique in the Europe of its day. While it resembled other regions in several important aspects, such as the wide prevalence of the proprietary Church and the position of the King as overall controller of church affairs, as universal patron and governor-general, there were also significant differences.
>
> The papacy claimed nothing of the Church in England save the safeguarding of the faith and the bestowal of metropolitan dignity and the abiding loyalty of King and people manifested by the free gift of Peter's pence. There was not, in consequence, the faintest echo of tension between Pope and monarch.[65]

Upon Becket's return from Europe, he served as Provost of Beverly and as Canon at Lincoln and Canterbury cathedrals. In 1154, he was ordained a deacon, and Archbishop Theobald appointed him Archdeacon of Canterbury and gave him confidential assignments with the Church in England.

Becket made several visits to Rome and became known for his diplomacy.

When Henry of Anjou, great grandson of William the Conqueror, became King Henry II, he appointed Becket as Chancellor, the senior minister of the government. Chronicles of the time described the new Chancellor as "slim of growth, and pale of hue, with dark hair, a long nose, and a straightly featured face. Blithe of countenance was he, winning and lovable in conversation, frank of speech in his discourses but slightly stuttering in his talk, so keen of discernment that he could always make difficult questions plain after a wise manner."[66]

Becket was a hard-working, effective Chancellor and a close personal friend of young King Henry II. They had similar interests and spent much free time together. They thought alike, and Becket had a strong influence on the young King in his relationship with his subjects and in his decisions to make reforms, such as streamlining the judicial process.

As Chancellor, Becket lived well. When he went to France to arrange a royal marriage, he was accompanied by two hundred retainers and several hundred knights, squires, and servants with eight wagons. He gave magnificent entertainments and was very generous with gifts to the poor.

In 1159, King Henry went to war with France to reclaim the province of Toulouse that his wife, Eleanor of Aquitaine, had inherited. Becket, dressed in armor, led 700 knights into battle and fought French knights in single combat. Another cleric chided him for his military activities, telling him that he looked more like a falconer than a cleric.

When Becket returned to England, he participated in scheduled retreats at Merton and was subjected to the usual church discipline. At times, he appeared to give in to King

Henry in relinquishing some of the historical privileges of the Church, but at other times he argued with the King in defending the Church's rights.

When Archbishop Theobald died in 1161, King Henry asked Becket to be the next primate of the Church in England. Becket tried to convince the King to make another choice:

> Should God permit me to be the Archbishop of Canterbury, I would soon lose your Majesty's favor, and the affection with you honor me would be changed into hatred. For there are several things you do now in prejudice of the rights of the Church which make me fear you would require of me what I could not agree to; and envious persons would not fail to make it the occasion of endless strife between us.[67]

Becket resisted the appointment until Cardinal Henry of Pisa, representative of the Pope, overrode his concerns. Becket was elected primate of England in May 1162 and ordained a priest by Bishop Walter of Rochester. He was consecrated Archbishop of Canterbury by the Bishop of Winchester and received vestments from Pope Alexander III. Counter to the wishes of the King, Becket resigned his position as Chancellor of England.

Becket's world changed dramatically. He wore a hair shirt under his black cassock and linen surplice and lived an austere life of self-discipline. He gave alms to the poor, studied the Bible with Herbert of Bosham, visited the sick, and oversaw the work of the monks. Initially, his relationship with the King did not change; however, over time, the issue of church versus state caused differences of opinion between them. Unlike his much later successor, King Henry VIII, who considered the will of God to be his personal will, King Henry II realized that the will of God was of a higher order than his own personal desires.

The first conflict between Becket and the King occurred when Henry ruled that a tax on landowners (the Church was the largest landowner) should be paid to his treasury instead of to the King's officers, who in the past had protected landowners from overeager tax collectors. When Becket objected, he and the King argued; from this time onward, the King's demands were directed at the Church, not at landowners generally.

Another difference of opinion arose when Canon Philip de Bois was accused of killing a soldier. He was tried by an ecclesiastical court, according to long-established tradition, and was acquitted by the Bishop of Lincoln, the judge in the case. The King disagreed with the verdict and insisted that de Brois be tried again in a civil court. Becket insisted that de Brois could not be tried again for the same crime.

In October 1163, King Henry II called a council of bishops at Westminster, where he demanded that clergy accused of civil crimes be tried in civil courts. Contrary to Becket's advice to his bishops, the King bullied them into signing the Constitutions of Clarenden that reduced the authority of the Church in England, including the following changes:
- "No prelate should leave the kingdom without royal permission (preventing personal appeals to the Pope in Rome).
- No tenant-in-chief could be excommunicated against the King's will.
- The Royal Court was to decide in which court clerics accused of a civil offense should be tried.
- That custody of vacant Church benefices and their rev-

enues should go to the King."[68]

Becket's loyalty was questioned, and he was ordered by the King to give up some of his properties. The King attacked the Archbishop's reputation and accused him of financial misdealings dating back to his time as Chancellor. The Bishop of Winchester suggested that Becket be replaced as Archbishop, but no action was taken. Becket offered to use his own money to clear his reputation, but he was not permitted to do so.

In October 1164, the King called a council of bishops at Northampton. The Earl of Leicester confronted Becket with a message from the King: "The King commands that you render your accounts. Otherwise you must hear his judgment." Becket responded: "I was given the church of Canterbury free from temporal obligations. I am therefore not liable and will not plead with regard to them. Neither law nor reason allows children to judge and condemn their fathers. Wherefore I refuse the King's judgment and your and everyone's. Under God, I will be judged by the Pope alone."[69]

At the invitation of King Louis VII of France, Becket moved to the Continent. Henry forbade his subjects to give help of any kind to him. The Archbishop sent several Bishops to present his side of the argument to Pope Alexander III. Later he visited the Pope, who was temporarily residing at Sens, France, to discuss the Constitutions of Clarenden. Becket resigned as Archbishop of Canterbury, but the Pope reinstated him, telling him that to give up his office would be to "abandon the cause of God." Pope Alexander suggested that he stay at the Cistercian monastery at Pontigny.

Becket donned a monk's robe and abided by the rules of the monastery. In England, Henry seized the wealth and property of the Archbishop's relatives and friends and banished them from England. He sent them to Becket at Pontigny to cause him anxiety by their suffering. Henry told the Cisercians that he would confiscate all of their property in England if they continued to provide a refuge for Becket, who moved to the royal abbey at St. Columba as a guest of King Louis VII.

This strain continued for three years. The Pope appointed Becket as his official representative in England except for York, which was a separate See. The Archbishop excommunicated those enemies who had agitated against him; nevertheless, he attempted to placate the King. In 1169, in Montmiral, King Henry II met with King Louis VII, who favored Becket's position. They resolved the dispute between Becket and his King, at least temporarily. The Archbishop made plans to return to England. When he departed from France, he told the Bishop of Paris, "I am going to England to die."

On December 1, 1172, Becket arrived in England and led a procession to Canterbury along a route filled with cheering people. Despite the shouting crowds, the atmosphere was one of impending difficulty and strain. At the reconciliation with Becket in France, King Henry had agreed to punish Archbishop Roger of York and the Bishops of London and Salisbury, who had acted against the Pope's wishes.

Upon his return to England, Becket acted according to the Pope's desires; he suspended Archbishop Roger of York and excommunicated the two Bishops. They requested that their sentences be dropped. When Becket refused to back down, they joined King Henry who was touring western France, which was part of his dominions.

At Bur, near Bayeux, the three Bishops presented their disagreement with Becket to King Henry, who flew into a rage. Someone (probably Roger, who was usually the spokesman) said, "I assure you, my lord, while Thomas lives you will have no good days, nor quiet times, nor a tranquil kingdom." The King, known for his temper, yelled: "The man ate my bread and mocks my favors. He tramples on the whole royal family. What disloyal cowards do I have in my court, that not one will free me of this lowborn priest."[70]

Four Barons who heard the King's anguish, Reginald FitzUrse, William de Tracy, Hugh de Moreville, and Richard de Breton of Somerset, took the King at his word and departed for England without asking Henry's permission to leave. Becket was warned of potential trouble. The four Barons visited Becket at Archbishop's Hall at Canterbury to demand that he rescind his sentence for the three Bishops. The Archbishop refused, and the Barons left muttering threats.

Soon the knights returned and began to beat down the door. It was twilight, and vespers were being conducted. Becket and a small retinue walked down the cloister passageway toward the cathedral. His retinue included Robert de Merton, his confessor; William FitzStephen, a cleric; and Edward Grim, a monk.

FitzUrse called out: "Where is Thomas the traitor? Where is the archbishop?" "Here I am," Becket replied, "no traitor but an archbishop and a priest of God." Again, the knights asked him to countermand his orders for the three Bishops. He responded: "I cannot do other than I have done.... I am ready to die, but God's curse on you if you harm my people.... You owe me fealty and submission." FitzUrse replied, "I owe no fealty contrary to the King."[71]

Grim put his arms around the Archbishop and attempted to protect him. FitzUrse drew his sword and swung it at Becket, knocking off his fur cap, slicing off the top of his scalp, and cutting deep into his left shoulder. Grim extended his arm to protect the Archbishop from the blow and received a deep wound and broken bones in his arm. De Tracy swung his sword at Becket's head, causing him to fall to his knees. De Tracy struck again, and Becket collapsed onto the floor. De Briton administered the fatal blow to the head. De Moreville, who had been holding back the crowd entering the cathedral, did not strike the Archbishop.

When King Henry heard of the murder, he shut himself in his royal quarters and fasted for forty days, realizing that his outburst had triggered the Barons' action. Later, he repented in public and, in 1172, received absolution from the Pope. On February 21, 1173, Becket was canonized by declaration of the Pope.

Thomas Becket had the determination to give his life to protect the rights of the Church as he understood them. Many miracles were observed at his gravesite and at the invocation of his name, St. Thomas of Canterbury. Chaucer called him the "holy blessed martyr." He is revered with the feast of St. Thomas of Canterbury by the Roman Catholic Church, which considers him the defender of secular clergy.

ST. THOMAS MORE (1478-1535) English Statesman, Author, and Martyr

"In truth there is no such thing in man's nature as a settled and full resolve either for good or evil, except at the very moment of execution."

Nathaniel Hawthorne, *Twice-Told Tales*

Thomas More was imprisoned for treason and sentenced to death by a court of King Henry VIII for opposing Henry's control over the Catholic Church in England. In *Thomas More,* Richard Marius compares More and his King:

> Thomas More ... was, until his imprisonment at the last, a cruelly divided man, torn between the necessity of making his way in the secular world and the devout longing to simplify life and to prepare his soul for the eternal world to come. Henry VIII was also divided. He comes down to us as the worst tyrant ever to sit on an English throne. Yet he was all his life torn between the grandiose vision of a chivalric self and the inner reality, which was somewhat pathetic—the enduring, frightened child always longing for a firm hand that might lead his steps aright.[72]

Thomas More was born on February 7, 1478 in Cheapside, London to Sir John More, barrister and judge, and Agnes Grainger More, daughter of Thomas Grainger, the Sheriff of London. He attended St. Anthony's School, where he received an excellent classical education. At the age of twelve, he was received into the house of John Morton, Archbishop of Canterbury and Lord Chancellor of England. A custom of the time was to place boys with potential in the homes of people of high rank to learn their ways and manners. Archbishop Morton, soon to become Cardinal Morton, was taken with his young charge and observed: "This child here waiting at table will prove a marvelous man."

Cardinal Morton sent More at the age of fourteen to Canterbury College which later became Christ Church, Oxford University, where he studied with Linacre, the foremost Greek scholar in England. He also studied French, Latin, and mathematics and learned to play several musical instruments.

Two years later, More studied law at New Inn and, in February 1496, became a student at Lincoln's Inn. At the age of twenty-one, he traded witticisms at a dinner hosted by the Lord Mayor with Erasmus, the Dutch humanist, who had been teaching Greek at Cambridge and Oxford Universities. Without being introduced, Erasmus said, "You must be More or no one." More responded, "You must be Erasmus or the devil."

Years later, Erasmus described More:

> He seems born and made for friendship, and is a most faithful and enduring friend. He so delights in the company and conversation of those whom he likes and trusts, that in this finds the principal charm of life.... Though he is rather too negligent of his own interests, no one is more diligent in those of his friends.... He is so kind, so sweet-mannered, that he cheers the dullest spirit and lightens every misfortune. Since his boyhood, he has so delighted in merriment that he seems born to make jokes, yet he never carries it to the point of vulgarity, nor has he ever liked bitter pleasantries. If a retort is made against himself,

even if it is ill-grounded, he likes it, from the pleasure he finds in witty repartees.

He extracts enjoyment from everything, even from things that are most serious. If he converses with the learned and wise, he delights in their talent; if with the ignorant and foolish, he enjoys their stupidity! With wonderful dexterity, he accommodates himself to every disposition. His face is in harmony with his character, being always expressive of a pleasant and friendly cheerfulness and ready to break into smiles. To speak candidly, he is better adapted to merriment than to gravity of dignity, but he is never in the least degree tactless or coarse.[73]

In 1501, More was called to the bar and practiced law at Furnival's Inn. Three years later, he became a Member of Parliament, where he argued against the King's demands for money. He was described as being of medium height with a clear complexion and a penetrating voice, auburn hair, and blue-gray eyes. More's friends at this time included John Colet, dean of St. Paul's and founder of St. Paul's School, who became his spiritual advisor, and William Grocyn, Rector of St. Lawrence Jewry, where More taught a course on St. Augustine's *City of God*.

More struggled with his choice of vocation. He practiced the rules of the Church, assisted daily at Mass, and wore a hair shirt. He considered joining the Carthusian monks or the Friars of the Observance, but he felt no call either to life in the monastery or secular life; he was too much a man of the world.

More met John Colt of Essex and was introduced to his three daughters. He proposed to the eldest daughter, Jane, even though, as reported by his biographer and son-in-law, William Roper, in *The Life of Sir Thomas More:* "And albeit his mind most served him to the second daughter, for that he thought her the fairest and best favored, yet when he considered that it would be both great grief and some shame also to the eldest to see her younger sister preferred before her in marriage, he then of a certain pity, framed his fancy toward her and soon after married her."[74]

More and Jane were happy, and he educated her in literature and music. Jane was only sixteen and had been raised in the country, so More molded her to become the type of wife that a man in his position needed. They had three daughters and a son. The daughters received the same education as their son, John. More was a strong believer in education for women.

More sang in the local choir and asked his children to read from the Bible at mealtime. Biographer Thomas Stapleton comments on his charity:

> He used personally to go into dark courts and visit the families of the poor, helping them not with small gifts but with two, three, or four pieces of gold, as their need required.... Very often he invited his poorer neighbors to his table, receiving them graciously and familiarly. The rich were rarely invited, the nobility hardly ever. Moreover in his parish, Chelsea, he hired a house in which he placed many who were infirm, poor, or old, providing for them at his own expense.[75]

In 1509, King Henry VII died, and his eighteen-year-old son was crowned King Henry VIII. The young King was well-educated, a linguist, and an accomplished musician. He was known for his great physical strength, his quick thinking, and his personal courage. More's promotions were accelerated after young Henry became King. The year after the King's coronation, More became Undersheriff of London, a prestigious post in which he addressed the unemployment, injustice, and suffering of the poor.

In 1510, Jane More died, leaving her husband with four young children. Within a few months, he married Alice Middleton, a widow who was older than he. Alice was described as both a "practical and kindly woman" and as "harsh and worldly." More observed that she was "neither a pearl nor a girl."

In 1515, More traveled to Flanders to negotiate new trade agreements for England with the Hanseatic League, which consisted of cities in northern Germany. The following year he published *Utopia,* the work for which he is best known. In this socialist primer, the government of Utopia is guided by the principles of wisdom, fortitude, temperance, and justice, modeled on Plato's *Republic. Utopia* advocates communal life and freedom of thought but disapproves of enclosure of public land. Residents of Utopia have no possessions. All wear similar clothing and are forbidden to go to war except to add territory when population increase demands it.

In 1517, More became a judge in the Court of Requests, a member of the King's Council, and an agent of Lord Chancellor Cardinal Wolsey on diplomatic missions to Europe. In 1521, he was appointed Privy-counselor and Undertreasurer and was knighted for his services to the crown. Two years later, he was elected Speaker of the House of Commons.

In 1527, the King appointed More Lord Chancellor to

replace Cardinal Wolsey, who had irritated Henry by failing to obtain the nullification of his marriage to Catherine of Aragon. Considerable strain developed between the King and the Pope when Cardinal Campeggio's papal commission rejected Henry's request for annulment. The King, who did not want another cleric in the office of Chancellor, chose More.

King Henry VIII's justification for the nullification of his marriage to Catherine of Aragon was that she was the widow of his brother Arthur, a fact that he had obviously known when he married her. The real reasons were Catherine's inability to bear a son and Henry's infatuation with Anne Boleyn.

More, who considered Henry's marriage to Catherine valid, tried to avoid taking sides. When reporting on the case to Parliament in 1531, More declined their request to give his opinion. In the following year, the clergy was forced to submit their existing laws to a royal commission for review and to make no new laws without approval of the commission. Next, in Henry's "submission of the clergy," an Act of Parliament canceled payment to the Pope of the first year's income from Church appointments. More opposed these moves in public and resigned as Lord Chancellor after holding the post for less than three years.

More wrote to his friend Erasmus: "I saw that I must either lay down my office or fail in the performance of its duties. I could not carry out all the tasks imposed by my position without endangering my life, and if I were to die, I should have to give up my office as well as my life. So I determined to give up one rather than both."[76] This loss of employment reduced the More family to virtual poverty.

In 1534, Pope Clement VII declared the marriage of

Henry and Catherine valid and rejected annulment. Despite the Pope's ruling, Henry married Ann Boleyn. Henry forced Parliament to pass an Act of Succession, which required all King's subjects to take an oath that his marriage to Catherine was invalid, that his marriage to Ann Boleyn was valid, and that their children would be heirs to the throne despite the objections of "any foreign authority, prince, or potentate." The intent of the Act of Succession was to make the Church of England independent of the Catholic Church.

In April 1534, More and his friend, John Fisher, Bishop of Rochester, were requested to sign the Act of Succession by a royal commission at Lambeth. Although they both accepted the new line of succession, they declined to sign the Act because it defied the Pope's authority to make a decision about a sacrament of the Church.

More was placed in the custody of William Banson, Abbot of Westminster, and asked again to sign the Act. Thomas Cranmer, Archbishop of Canterbury, urged him to sign. When he refused a second time, he was imprisoned in the Tower of London, where he spent fifteen months. He had chest pains and was thought to suffer from a heart condition. In November 1534, More was charged with treason.

More's wife sold her clothing to pay expenses and twice unsuccessfully petitioned the King to release her husband for reasons of poverty and poor health. His family, particularly his daughter, Margaret, visited him frequently. On May 4, 1535, More and Margaret watched from his prison window the hanging of three Carthusian Priors and a Bridgittine Prior for not acknowledging Henry's supremacy over the Church.

Following these executions, Thomas Cromwell, the King's new Councilor, presided over further examination of More by the King's Council. When asked again whether he would sign the Act of Supremacy, More refused. Cromwell threatened torture.

On June 22, John Fisher, Bishop of Rochester, who was elderly and in poor health, was beheaded on Tower Hill for refusing to sign the Act of Supremacy. He was the first Bishop to be executed in England since Thomas Becket and the first to be sentenced to death in the courtroom.

On July 1, More was tried at the Court of King's Bench. He was permitted to sit during the trial because he was ill. He was charged with treason by "traitorously and maliciously attempting to deprive the King of his title of Supreme Head of the Church of England." Solicitor General Richard Rich declared that More had said that Parliament could not legislate King Henry Supreme Head of the Church. More told Rich, "I am sorrier for your perjury than for my own peril."

More was found guilty and was condemned to death by beheading. On July 7, More's friend, Sir Thomas Pope, told him that his execution was scheduled for nine o'clock. When More was led to the scaffold, he told the Lieutenant of the Tower, Sir Edmund Walsingham, "I pray you, see me safe up, and for my coming down, let me shift for myself."

More knelt on the scaffold and recited the psalm, *Miserere*, and then gave a final message to the people: "I call you to witness, brothers, that I die in and for the faith of the Catholic Church, the King's loyal servant, but God's first." He told the executioner, "Pluck up your spirits man, and be not afraid to do thy office; my neck is very short, take heed therefore you do not strike awry." He covered his own eyes and moved his long gray beard from the block so that it would not be cut by the executioner's axe "for at least it hath committed no treason."[77]

More's body was buried in St. Peter-ad-Vincula Church in

the Tower. In 1886, he was beatified by Pope Leo XIII; he was canonized in 1935 by Pope Pius XI.

ST. JOHN FISHER (1469-1535) Bishop of Rochester and Martyr

"Firmness, both in suffering and execution, is a character which I would wish to possess. I have always despised the whining yelp of complaint, and the cowardly feeble resolve."

Robert Burns

John Fisher was highly regarded by his peers. His contemporary, Cardinal Reginald Pole asked:

> What have you, or have you had for centuries, to compare with Rochester in holiness, in learning, in prudence, and in episcopal zeal? You may be, indeed, proud of him, for, were you to search through all the nations of Christendom in our days, you would not easily find one who was such a model of episcopal virtues.
>
> If you doubt this, consult your ambassadors; and let them tell you whether they have anywhere heard of any bishop who has such a love of his flock as never to leave the care of it, ever feeding it by word and example; against whose life not even a rash word could be spoken; one who was conspicuous not only for holiness and learning, but for love of country.[78]

John Fisher, one of four children, was born in 1469 to Robert Fisher, a prosperous textile merchant, and Agnes Fisher in Beverly, Yorkshire. Beverly was an important trading center that was not committed to either York or Lancaster during the War of the Roses. Robert Fisher died in 1477 when his son, John, was only eight years old. Agnes Fisher remarried a man named White and had four more children, including Richard, who was ordained a priest, and Elizabeth, who became a nun.

Young John attended the Beverly Minster grammar school, which had enjoyed a strong reputation since the tenth century; he received a solid education in Latin. In 1482, he enrolled at Cambridge University. Study at the time emphasized grammar, rhetoric, and logic, followed by astronomy, music, and geometry. His mentor was William de Melton, a highly regarded philosopher, teacher, and theologian, who later was Master of Michaelhouse College and Chancellor of York.

Fisher received a B.A. degree in 1488 and a M.A. degree in 1491, the year in which he was ordained a priest. He continued to study at Cambridge and in 1494 was elected Senior Proctor, an administrative position. He was not only a scholar but also a man of political affairs. As Senior Proctor, he was invited to the King's Court at Greenwich, where he met King VII's mother, Lady Margaret Beaufort, "mother, author, plotter, and counselor of union." Her patriotic maneuvering had resulted in the victory at Bosworth Field in 1485 that ended the War of the Roses. Lady Beaufort, Countess of Richmond and Derby, was considered the most learned and most noble lady in England.

In 1497, Fisher was elected Master of Michaelhouse College succeeding his mentor de Melton. He earned a Doctor of Divinity degree in 1501 and was elected Vice Chancellor of the University.

An early biographer describes Fisher at age thirty-two:

Tall and comely, he was six feet in height, very slender, lean and upright; well-formed, with black hair and dark eyes that were between black and gray. His forehead was smooth and large, his nose of a good and even proportion: he was "somewhat wide-mouthed and big-jawed, as one ordained to utter speech much, wherein was, notwithstanding, a certain comeliness; his skin somewhat tawny.... His face, hands, and all his body so bare of flesh as is almost incredible" through "the great abstinence and penance he used upon himself many years altogether, even from his youth. In speech he was very mild, temperate, and modest, saving in matters of God and of his charge."[79]

In 1502, Lady Margaret Beaufort chose Fisher as her personal chaplain and confessor. Lady Margaret, now a widow, dedicated the remainder of her life to God, and Fisher resigned as Master of Michaelhouse College to guide her on her spiritual path. He thought that, although he was her spiritual director, he learned more from her than she learned from him.

In 1503, Lady Margaret endowed a Chair of Divinity in Cambridge and became known as the "greatest benefactress Cambridge had ever known." In 1504, Fisher was elected Chancellor of Cambridge University and then Bishop of Rochester, a See that had been founded by St. Augustine.

Fisher was described at this time as:

A scholar and preacher who had the gift of government and the strength of will to impose discipline in studies and conduct. He had won

Ecclesiastics / Religious Leaders

the trust and confidence of those older than himself; they had valued his prudent judgment and his lack of self-interest. His outlook, however, was not limited to university life; he saw beyond that of the spiritual needs of ordinary folk; his desire was to educate priests and teachers who could administer to those needs as devoted pastors. He was not a radical reformer; his cast of mind was conservative. He built on well-proved foundations, retaining what was sound in the past but rejecting what had proved defective.... He recognized the good work of his predecessors and made it part of the fabric which was under his care.[80]

One of Fisher's main accomplishments was founding St. John's College, Cambridge University. The operation of St. John the Evangelist Hospital, its physical plant on the Cambridge campus, and its finances had declined dramatically. Fisher persuaded Lady Margaret to fund a second college at Cambridge for the study of theology with a master and fifty scholars on the hospital site. She had been considering endowing a new college at Oxford University, but the "dogged pertinacity" of Fisher convinced her to favor Cambridge.

Two events delayed the establishment of St. John's College: on April 21, 1509, King Henry VII died, and, on June 29, Lady Margaret passed away. The endowment for St. John's College was not mentioned in Lady Margaret's will. Her only reference to it was in an undated codicil. Her grandson, Henry VIII, could and did claim this legacy as part of his inheritance. Fisher fought to claim Lady Margaret's legacy to St. John's for seven years and finally was successful.

Fisher's determination to overcome many obstacles and to

carry out the last wishes of Lady Margaret was notable. A less strong-willed person would not have accomplished what he did in a virtually singlehanded struggle. Finally, in 1516, he obtained a papal Bull that, with one stroke, permitted the establishment of St. John's College.

Fisher's diocese, the diocese of Rochester, was the smallest and poorest in England. The Bishop was a humble man. He fasted so strictly that his health suffered, and he had to have "a little thin gruel" on fast days. He slept only four hours a night on a hard bed made of straw and mats. He was so devout that he teared up when he said Mass. He had an extensive library that he intended to donate to St. John's when he died. His friend Erasmus, who was also a friend of Thomas More, said of him: "There is not in that nation a more learned man nor a holier bishop."

In addition to being known as a fine preacher who avoided flowery sermons, Fisher was an author. In his first book, *De Unica Magdalena,* he attempted to prove that the three Marys in the Gospel had one identity. In several of his later books, he spoke out against Lutheranism and tried to disprove Luther's "heresy."

In the *Life and Death of Sir Thomas More,* E. W. Hitchcock and R. W. Chambers document a contemporary's opinion of Fisher:

> He was in holiness, learning and diligence in his cure and in fulfilling his office of bishop such that of many hundred years England had not had any bishop worthy to be compared unto him. And if all countries of Christendom were searched, there could not lightly among all other nations be found one that hath been in all things like unto him, so well used and ful-

filled the office of bishop as he did. He was of
such high perfection in holy life and straight
and austere living as few were, I suppose, in
all Christendom in his time, religious or
other.[81]

In May 1527, King Henry VIII attempted to have his marriage to Catherine of Aragon annulled on the grounds that
Catherine was the widow of his brother, Arthur. Henry wanted to marry Anne Boleyn and have the male heir that his wife
could not provide. Catherine had come to England in 1501 to
marry the fifteen-year-old Prince of Wales, Arthur. Six
months after their marriage, Arthur died. Leviticus said, "He
that marrieth his brother's wife doth an unlawful thing ... they
shall be without children." A papal dispensation had been
obtained permitting Henry's marriage to Catherine after he
ascended the throne.

Fisher was asked if he agreed that the marriage of Henry
and Catherine should be annulled. He ruled that, since the
Pope had permitted the marriage, it was valid. Fisher aroused
the ire of the King and of Anne Boleyn, niece of the Duke of
Norfolk, who was to become head of the King's Council.
When the Church in England gave in to Henry and allowed
his marriage to Anne Boleyn, Fisher became ill over the
extended disagreement with the King.

On February 20, 1531, an attempt was made to poison
Fisher. When that failed, he was shot at from across the river
at his home in Lambeth. In the fall of that year, he received a
message from Anne Boleyn advising him not to attend
Parliament "that he may not catch any sickness, as he did last
year." This message increased his determination to attend and
to speak out "should he die a thousand times."[82]

On March 1534, the new Act of Submission of the Clergy was passed, granting the King power over the Church in England. Fisher's friend, Sir Thomas More, resigned as Lord Chancellor. On Palm Sunday, Fisher was placed under house-arrest in the care of Bishop Gardiner of Winchester on trumped-up charges. The Imperial Ambassador observed that: "The real cause ... is his manly defense of the Queen's [Catherine's] cause."

On April 14, Fisher told the King's Commissioners that he could not sign the oath supporting the Act of Submission. He was imprisoned in the Tower of London, as was Sir Thomas More. Fisher was frail and ill during his fifteen months of imprisonment. His possessions were confiscated, including his library that had been intended for St. John's College, Cambridge. His See as Bishop of Rochester was declared vacant.

Fisher wrote to the King's Councilor, Thomas Cromwell, begging for clothing and for food that he could digest. Friends occasionally brought food items, and he and More shared gifts of edibles that they had received. Fisher wrote three spiritual books while in the Tower, two of them, *A Spiritual Consolation* and *The Ways to Perfect Religion,* for his sister, Elizabeth, who was a Dominican nun. In May, he watched from his window while a Bridgittine Prior and three Carthusian Priors were executed. Additional unsuccessful attempts were made to get him to sign the oath.

On May 20, 1535, Pope Paul III made Fisher a Cardinal "for his fame in virtue and learning" and negotiated for his release from prison. King Henry boasted, "He shall wear it (the hat) on his shoulders, for head he shall have none to sit it on."[83]

On June 1, 1535, a special commission was formed to try

individuals accused of acts of treason. On June 14, Fisher was interrogated by the commission in the Tower for saying: "The King our sovereign lord is not supreme head on earth of the Church of England." Fisher responded, "Sir, I will not deny that I so said to you, but for all my saying I committed no treason."[84]

On June 17, Fisher was tried by a special commission in Westminster Hall and found guilty of treason. Richard Rich, Solicitor General, testified that Fisher had told him during a prison visit "that he believed in his conscience, and by his learning assuredly knew, that the King neither was, nor by right could be, supreme head" of the Church in England. Fisher was astounded by Rich's testimony, not only by what he said but because Rich had told him that the content of their conversation was for the ears of the King alone. Fisher was sentenced to be beheaded.

On June 22, 1535, Fisher was told by the Lieutenant of the Tower that he would be executed at ten o'clock that day. He was taken to the scaffold, where he refused any help ascending the stairs. Everyone was amazed that he could climb the stairs without assistance in his emaciated condition. Fisher addressed the crowd: "Christian people, I am come hither to die for the faith of Christ's Catholic Church.... And I pray God save the King and the realm, and hold His holy hand over it, and send the King a good counsel."[85]

Fisher kneeled on the scaffold and recited the psalms *Te Deum* and *In te Domine Speravi*. The executioner blindfolded him and then raised his axe and severed his head from his body. His body was buried without ceremony at All Hallows Church, Barking and then reinterred in St. Peter ad Vincula Church in the Tower, where Thomas More's body was buried on July 6. In 1886, Fisher was beatified with Thomas More by

Pope Leo XIII; he was canonized in 1935 by Pope Pius XI.

MARTIN LUTHER (1483-1546) The First Protestant

"I have brought myself by long meditation to the conviction that a human being with a settled purpose must accomplish it, and that nothing can resist a will which will stake even existence upon its fulfillment."

Disraeli

A historian observed that "Luther's Germany was in many ways the most flourishing part of Europe." In his biography, *Martin Luther,* Leonhard W. Cowie provides a description of Germany in the 1500s:

> Politically, Germany was divided into many separate parts, and no single German state was as powerful as the kingdom of England, France, or Spain. Twelve million Germans lived in some 350 separate realms of varying sizes. Some were states ruled by princes or nobles, with titles such as archduke, duke, margrave, or count; others were bishoprics, where the bishop had both ecclesiastical and worldly authority. Some smaller territories were governed by the abbotts of monasteries.
>
> There were also free knights, who, in most cases, had no more than a castle and a domain of a few acres to govern and farm. Finally, there were the free cities. Some of these, like Augsburg and Nuremberg, owned large provinces.... All of the German lands except Prussia, in the east, were within the boundaries of the Holy Roman Empire, as were the Netherlands, Switzerland, and Bohemia. This empire claimed to be the successor of the old Roman Empire.[86]

On November 10, 1483, Martin Luther was born to Hans and Margaret Ziegler Luther in Eisleben, a small town in southwest Saxony. He was named for St. Martin of Tours, on whose day he was born. Hans Luther worked in the copper mines in nearby Mansfeld. The family was poor, but Hans had become a member of the middle class by leasing several mines and smelting furnaces. He was elected to the Mansfeld town council. Martin's parents were devout Catholics. Although they were strict disciplinarians, they were supportive of their children. Hans Luther hoped that his son, Martin, would become a successful lawyer and improve his status in society.

At the age of seven, Martin enrolled in school in Mansfeld where the emphasis was placed on learning to read and to write Latin, the language of the Church and of the field of law. Young Luther developed his interest in music while singing in the choir of St. Georges church across the square from the school. The boys' choir sang the *Te Deum, Benedictus,* and other Latin chants; his favorite was the *Magnificat,* which he translated into German in later years.

At the age of thirteen, Luther was sent to the boarding school of the Brothers of Common Life in Madgeburg, a city of 30,000 in the Elbe River valley thirty miles north of Mansfeld. He became familiar with monastic life from the Brothers, who encouraged personal religion among the people. The Dutch scholar, Erasmus, had been educated at a Brothers of Common Life school.

After only a year in Madgeburg, Luther's parents sent him to another boarding school, St. George's School in Eisenach, fifty miles from Mansfeld, near the Thuringian Forest. Eisenach was considerably smaller than Madgeburg but, nevertheless, was a religious center where he learned of the work of church orders, particularly the Franciscan friars.

In 1501, at the age of eighteen, Luther enrolled at the University of Erfurt, one of Germany's finest universities. Erfurt, capital of Thuringia, had a population of 30,000. Luther studied language, logic, and philosophy to earn his Bachelor of Arts degree in 1502. He then studied arithmetic, astronomy, geometry, and music to complete his studies for a Master of Arts degree, which he received in January 1505. He ranked second in a class of seventeen.

Luther's father was pleased that his son planned to study law at the University of Erfurt's College of St. Mary. In early July 1505, Luther walked home to Mansfeld to visit his family. During his travels on a hot summer afternoon, he encountered a violent thunderstorm. Lightning struck so close to him that he threw himself to the ground amid deafening claps of thunder. Luther was terrified and promised to undertake a career in the Church if his life were spared. He believed that this experience was a calling from God that he must heed.

Luther's father was extremely disappointed, and his fellow students at the University were surprised; however, Luther believed that taking this action was the only way to save his soul. St. Paul's conversion on the road to Damascus is somewhat analogous to Luther's decision to join a religious order because of this incident.

In August, Luther entered the Augustinian priory in Erfurt, which had seventy friars and was known for its theological learning. The Augustinian Vicar General for the province of Saxony was Johann von Staupitz, a deeply spiritual scholar who became Luther's friend and supporter.

Luther's six-foot by nine-foot cell was unheated during the winter. He dined in silence with the other novices and the friars in the refectory. After a one-year novitiate, he took vows of poverty, chastity, and obedience and continued his studies for the priesthood.

In February 1507, Luther was ordained and said his first Mass. He was a zealous friar who begged in the streets for food for the community, fasted, and flagellated himself. In 1533, he looked back on that time and thought, "I was a good friar and kept strictly to my order; I could say that if the monastic life could get a man into heaven, I should have entered."[87]

Luther gained considerable reputation as a scholar. In October 1508, his mentor, von Staupitz, was appointed Professor of Theology at the University of Wittenberg and invited Luther to join him as a lecturer. Wittenberg was a small university known for its collection of relics. The catalog of relics collected on a journey to Jerusalem by Frederick, Archduke of Saxony, listed 5,005 items, including a part of the burning bush seen by Moses, a piece of Jesus's cradle, and thirty-three wooden fragments of the Holy Cross.

Wittenberg University awarded Luther a Doctor of Theology degree in 1512 and appointed him Professor of Theology when von Staupitz retired. Luther's lectures included series on the Psalms and the Epistles of St. Paul. He studied Greek so that he could use Erasmus's Greek edition of the New Testament in his lectures. In 1517, an Augustinian friar from Cologne who attended Luther's lectures on the Epistle to the Galatians described him:

> He was a man of middling height, with a voice both sharp and gentle; it was soft in tone, sharp in the enunciation of syllables, words, and sentences. He spoke neither too rapidly nor too slowly, but evenly and without hesitation, very

clearly, and so logically that each part flowed naturally out of what went before. He did not get lost in a maze of language, but first explained the individual words, then the sentences, so that one could see how the content of the exposition arose and flowed out of the text itself. For it all hung together in order: word, matter, natural and moral philosophy.... There never was anything in his lectures that was not relevant and full of meaning.[88]

Although Luther worked hard and his reputation grew every year, he was troubled. He thought, "My life draws nearer and nearer to hell. Day by day I become worse and more wretched." He found no spiritual fulfillment in his religious observances even though he practiced them seriously. He commented, "Who knows whether these things please God? ... I was trying to cure the doubts and scruples of the conscious with human remedies, the traditions of men. The more I tried these remedies, the more troubled and uneasy my conscience grew."[89]

Luther was persevering and zealous in his religious observances, such as penances and lengthy services. He was admired and respected by the Wittenberg community, but he was concerned that he was getting no closer to God, no closer to salvation.

Luther observed: "It is God's eternity, holiness, and power which thus continuously threaten men throughout the whole of his life. God's everpresent judgment grasps hold of man in the loneliness of his conscience, and with every breath conveys him to the Almighty and Holy One to prosper or be destroyed."[90] He considered himself a sinner and worse, an unredeemed sinner. His peers did not understand his anxieties and attempted to assure him that his soul would be saved.

Luther's personal anxieties were accompanied by concerns about differences between the early Church and the Church of his time. Part of his dissatisfaction was the practice of saying Masses for the dead to ease their progress through purgatory toward heaven. He was critical of "those foolish and impious churchmen who swagger about with the gifts which they had received from the laity and think they are doing their job when they mutter a few prayers on behalf of their benefactors."[91]

Luther's first nagging doubts about his calling had occurred on trip to Rome in 1510. He traveled with another friar to the city that he considered the seat of the Vicar of Christ and the center of Christendom. He was concerned about stories of the scandals surrounding some of the Renaissance Popes and disturbed by the immorality, irreverence, and laziness of the clergy that he had observed on his visit.

In 1515, Luther experienced an epiphany while reading St. Paul's Epistle to the Romans:

> I greatly longed to understand Paul's Epistle to the Romans and nothing stood in the way but that one expression, "the justice of God," because I took it to mean that justice whereby God is just and deals justly in punishing the unjust. My situation was that, although an impeccable friar, I stood before God as a sinner troubled in conscience, and I had no confidence that my merit would appease Him. Therefore I did not love a just and angry God, but rather hated Him and murmured against Him. Yet, I clung to dear Paul, and had a great yearning to know what he meant.

Night and day I pondered until I saw the connection between the justice of God and the statement that "the just shall live by faith." Then I grasped that the justice of God is that righteousness by which, through grace and sheer mercy, God justifies us through faith. This immediately made me feel as if I had been born again and entered paradise through newly opened doors. The whole of the Scriptures took on a new meaning, and it became to me inexpressibly sweet in greater love, so that the passage of Paul became to me a gate of heaven.

If you have a true faith that Christ is your Savior, then at once you have a gracious God, for faith leads you in and opens up God's heart and will, that you should see pure grace and overflowing love. Thus it is to behold God in faith that you should look upon His fatherly, friendly heart, in which there is no anger nor ungraciousness. He who sees God as angry does not see Him rightly, but looks only on a curtain, as if a dark cloud has been drawn across his faith.[92]

St. Paul's words, "the just shall live by faith," became the cornerstone of Luther's beliefs. His thinking evolved to the realization that no one could ensure salvation by his or her own actions, such as fasting, praying, or doing penance. Salvation involved putting one's faith in God. Forgiveness by God is a key element of salvation. Luther's doctrine of "justification by faith" became the core concept of the Reformation.

In *Here I Stand: A Life of Martin Luther,* Roland H. Bainton describes Luther's epiphany: "In that single flash Luther saw the denouement of the drama of existence. There was God the all-terrible, Christ the inexorable, and all the leering fiends springing from their lurking places in pond and wood ... that they might seize his shock of curly hair and bolt him into hell."[93]

Attendance at Luther's lectures increased significantly. Philip Melanchthon, Professor at Wittenberg and loyal supporter of Luther, observed:

> He made these writings so clear that the light of new learning seemed to arise after a long and dark night. Here he distinguished between the Law and the Gospel, here he refuted the error which then reigned in the schools and assemblies, which teaches that men merit remission of their sins by their own works, and that men are justified with God by discipline as the Pharisees taught.... All devout people were much taken by the sweetness of his doctrine, and it was welcome to the learned, as though Christ appeared from darkness, prison, and filthiness.[94]

Luther did not claim that his doctrine was new. He acknowledged his debt to St. Paul, and he reminded his followers that St. Augustine had also espoused these concepts.

The principal point of departure of Luther's doctrine from existing Church doctrine was the belief that the personal relationship between God and each individual was the way in which grace was received by means of the individual's faith. The role of the clergy as mediator or representative for individual Christians was downplayed. He reduced the emphasis on attendance at Mass, receiving the sacraments, and performing other observances as requirements for salvation.

Luther's first acceptance was from the Professors of Theology at the University of Wittenberg and then from the rest of the University community. He disagreed with some of the practices of the Church; nevertheless, he continued to consider himself a loyal member. He did not consider himself primarily a reformer.

Renaissance Popes were under considerable financial pressure. Their expenditures as both princes and ecclesiastics were large. Patronage of talented architects and artists was expected by the public. In 1484, Pope Innocent VIII pawned his tiara to obtain money for operating expenses. Popes looked for additional sources of income, such as dispensations, fees, and obligatory legal payments from bishops and pastors. The sale of indulgences became a popular source of income for the church.

Payment of indulgences evolved over the years. Upon confessing his sins to a priest, a sinner was pardoned from eternal punishment for his mortal sins; nevertheless, the repentant sinner still had to suffer punishment for his sins, either during his lifetime or in purgatory. However, the Pope had the power to grant indulgences, allowing sinners to be absolved of doing penance for their sins in this life or by suffering less time in purgatory before entrance into heaven:

- In 1300, Pope Boniface VIII granted indulgences to everyone who participated in the Crusades.
- In 1476, Pope Sixtus IV granted the redemption of souls in purgatory to friends and relatives of the sinner on earth upon payment for indulgences.
- In 1510, Pope Julius II gave indulgences to everyone who contributed to building St. Peter's Basilica.

The sale of indulgences became a popular source of funds for the papacy. Abuses in the sale of indulgences motivated Luther to seriously question their use. In particular, he questioned Pope Leo X's granting permission to Archbishop Albert of Mainz to sell indulgences in Germany for the building of St. Peter's. Half of the proceeds went to the Pope, and the remainder were kept by Archbishop Albert, who was in debt to his banker. Many churchgoers from Wittenberg traveled to nearby cities to obtain indulgences from the Archbishop's agent, Friar Johann Tetzel. Luther was incensed when he saw people returning to Wittenberg with pieces of paper noting the indulgences purchased from Friar Tetzel.

Luther prepared a list of ninety-five arguments or theses including his disagreement with the selling of indulgences and nailed it to the door of Wittenberg's castle church. This act transformed a little-known Professor of Theology into an individual known throughout Germany and beyond.

Posting a notice on the door of the church was a means for a scholar to notify the community of his desire to debate the issues in the notice. Luther did not consider this action an act of defiance, and he certainly did not think of himself as a priest in revolt. No one came forward to debate with Luther. He made no attempt to disseminate his theses to a broader audience. However, those who agreed with his arguments translated his notice written in Latin into German, printed copies on many printing presses in Germany, and distributed them widely.

Luther opposed the abuse of indulgences both from money-raising and spiritual points of view:

> Indulgences are most pernicious because they
> introduce complacency and thereby imperil

salvation. Those persons are damned who think that letters of indulgence make them certain of salvation.... Peace comes in the work of Christ through faith. He who does not have this is lost even though he be absolved a million times by the Pope, and he who does have it may not wish to be released from purgatory, for true contrition seeks penalty.

Christians should be encouraged to bear the cross. He who is baptized into Christ must be as a sheep for the slaughter. The merits of Christ are vastly more powerful when they bring crosses than when they bring remissions.[95]

Luther had the backing of his fellow friars and professors at the University of Wittenberg as well as the support of Elector Frederick of Saxony. However, Archbishop Albert was upset by Luther's actions and was concerned when his agent, Friar Tetzel, encountered threats of bodily injury by the crowds. Archbishop Albert reported his concern to the Pope, who directed the Augustinian Order to exercise tighter discipline with their members. In April 1518, Augustinian authorities summoned Luther to Heidelberg. He defended his views ably and convinced many of his superiors to support him.

As Luther's support grew within Germany, Pope Leo summoned him to Rome. Instead of going to Rome, Luther appealed to Elector Frederick, who arranged a hearing for Luther in Augsburg with the noted Dominican theologian, Cardinal Cajetan. The Cardinal did not debate with Luther, he instructed him: "You have only a word of six letters to pronounce, and the whole business will be dropped: Revoco (I recant)."

Cardinal Cajetan tried to make Luther realize that his persistence would be perceived as opposing the authority of the Pope. Luther told him that pursuing the truth was more desirable than any alternative course of action. The Cardinal said, "I shall not talk to that creature again for he has deep eyes and marvelous speculative ideas in his head."[96]

Pope Leo X issued a papal Bull upholding the use of indulgences. He sent Carl von Miltitz, a papal chamberlain, as an envoy to Luther to ask him to retract his doctrine or to have Elector Frederick surrender Luther to papal authority. Von Miltitz accomplished neither goal but observed that public opinion in Germany was on Luther's side.

In January 1519, von Miltitz met Luther and was impressed by him. He said, "Martin, I imagined you were some aged theologian mumbling arguments to himself in a cozy corner behind the stove. I find you are young and strong and original."[97] Von Miltitz convinced Luther to write a letter to Pope Leo X telling him that he submitted to his authority; however, Luther retracted none of his theses.

Increasingly, Luther was viewed as attacking the Church. In his opinion: "The song was pitched in too high a key for my voice." He studied the role of the papacy in the history of the Church and could find no justification in the Bible for the Pope having authority over all Christians; furthermore, he could find no support for the argument that the early Church had accepted this claim. In Luther's opinion, the real authority in the Church was a council comprised of the bishops of all countries. He advocated the immediate formation of such a general assembly.

During the summer of 1519 in Pleissenburg, Luther debated his beliefs with Johann von Eck, a Professor from Ingolstadt and one of his most bitter detractors. During the ten-day debate, von Eck made Luther concede that even the Church council could err, and that the Bible was the true authority within the Church.

Luther's books were widely disseminated. He was a good writer but, since he felt so strongly about his beliefs, occasionally was overly aggressive. He admitted: "I am hot-blooded by temperament, and my pen gets irritated easily." His ardent supporter Melanchthon believed that: "the truth might fare better at a lower temperature." In 1520, Luther's *Three Treatises* were published:

1. *"To the Christian Nobility of the German Nation,* in which he requested the German princes to reform the Church because the clergy had done no reforming.

2. *On the Babylonian Captivity of the Church,* a declaration that Baptism and Communion were the only sacraments. Luther questioned the validity of Confirmation, Penance, Holy Orders, Marriage, and Extreme Unction as sacraments.

3. *Of the Liberty of a Christian Man,* in which Luther espoused that: 'A Christian is by his faith the free master of all things and subject to none' and 'A Christian is by his love a humble servant in all aspects and subject to all others.'"[98]

Luther concluded his *Three Treatises* with: "From faith flow love for God and delight in God, and, out of love, the free, unconstrained, happy life of service to our fellows.... A Christian lives, not in himself, but in Christ and his neighbors by love. By faith he rises above himself unto God; from God he stoops below himself by love; and yet he remains always in God and in divine love."[99]

In June 1520, Pope Leo X issued a papal Bull, *Exsurge Domine,* condemning Luther's books and ordering them to be burned. He gave Luther two months to recant or be considered a heretic by the Church. In January 1521, the Pope excommunicated Luther in another papal Bull, *Decet Pontificem Romanum,* which called for Luther to be arrested and conducted to an ecclesiastical court for trial.

Luther was still under the protection of the Elector Frederick. The court was to be overseen by Charles, who had been Holy Roman Emperor for just over a year. Charles convened the Imperial Diet in Worms to determine what was to be done about Luther. The Emperor gave him safe-conduct; however, the Swiss reformer Johannes Huss had been given safe-conduct to attend the Council of Constance in 1415, and he had been burned at the stake as a heretic.

Luther was greeted warmly as he approached Worms. Eminent residents of the city on the Rhine River rode out on horseback to welcome him, and 2,000 citizens saw him arrive in his cart. He told them, "God will be for me." Cardinal Aleandro of Venice, the papal delegate to the Diet, was awed by Luther's popularity with the German people. The Cardinal wrote, "Nine out of every ten cry, 'Luther,' and the tenth, 'Death to the Court of Rome.'"

At 4:00 p.m. the following afternoon, the Imperial Marchal conducted Luther to the Bishop's palace where Charles and the Diet were gathered. The Bishop's chamber was packed to capacity. One attendee described Luther: "A man of forty years of age, more or less, vigorous in expression and physique, eyes without distinction, mobile of countenance, and frivolously changing his expression. He wore the habit of St. Augustine, with leather girdle, his tonsure large and recently shaven, his hair closely clipped." The Emperor Charles was not moved by the man he saw. He said, "That man will never make me a heretic."

Cardinal Aleandro had collected Luther's books and placed them on a bench in the chamber. Luther described the proceedings: "This afternoon I faced the Emperor and the papal delegate, who asked me if I wished to repudiate my books; and I must say tomorrow whether I repudiate them. I merely requested a brief opportunity for consideration. If Christ grants me His blessing, I shall not recant a dot or a comma."[100]

At 6:00 p.m. the following day, Luther met again with the Diet. This time the meeting was held in the great hall of the Bishop's palace. Again, the meeting place was crowded with people. Luther had appeared nervous at the previous meeting and was unsure of himself that night; however, he had regained his self-assurance by the second meeting.

Luther admitted that he had been overly aggressive in stating his disagreement with the papacy; however, he said, "I do not set myself up to be a saint." He replied to the question of the previous day: "Unless I am convicted by Scripture and plain reason (for I do not accept the authority of Popes and councils, since they have often erred and contradicted each other), my conscience is neither right nor safe. God help me. Amen." He added: "Here I stand; I can do no other."[101]

Luther summarized the proceedings to a friend: "'Are these books yours' — 'Yes.' 'Do you recant?' — 'No.' 'Then get out.'" The Diet struggled with Luther for a week in an attempt to reach a compromise. Luther insisted: "The Pope is no judge of matters pertaining to God's word and faith; but a Christian man must examine and judge for himself."[102] Luther was asked to leave Worms and was given a safe-conduct for twenty-one days. Luther preached in monastery chapels along his route to Wittenberg and at the village church in Mohrs, his grandmother's village.

Luther and his companions were traveling through the Thuringian Forest after leaving Mohrs when they were intercepted by five armed horsemen. Luther's companions put on a show of resistance, so the driver could report that Luther had been overpowered. However, by prior arrangement, Elector Frederick of Saxony decided that Luther needed a cooling-off period and offered to hide him at Wartburg Castle. Frederick had left the arrangement to be made by others. When asked where Luther was, he could honestly say that he did not know.

At the castle, Luther was dressed as a knight and was addressed as "Sir George." He studied, wrote, and translated the Bible from Latin into German, so that it would be accessible to the people. He declared, "It [must] have its place in the hands, tongues, eyes, ears, and hearts of men." Within a year, using the version of Erasmus, he translated the New Testament. He did not complete the translation of the Old Testament until 1534. His German Bible and his emphasis on hymns were two key elements of the Lutheran Reformation.

While Luther was at Wartburg Castle, leadership of the Lutheran movement was provided by the moderate Philip Melanchthon and the more radical Andreas Karlstadt and Gabriel Zwilling. Melanchthon began to give both bread and wine at communion, a departure from the Catholic bread-only communion. The scholarly Melanchthon had difficulty containing Karlstadt and Zwilling, who wanted change at a faster rate. Upon his return to Wittenberg, Luther advocated the more moderate approach of Melanchthon; he was concerned about the possibility of losing many of the moderate members of the movement.

In 1524, the Peasants' Revolt occurred in southwestern Germany. Peasants, who were encouraged by Luther's attacks on the papacy, advocated rising up against the nobility and the clergy. Initially, Luther sympathized with the peasants until he realized that they were going too far when they became more violent. Luther wrote a pamphlet, "Against the Murdering, Thieving Hordes of the Peasants" in an attempt to restrain the peasants. He lost considerable support for the Lutheran movement by condemning the Peasants' Revolt.

Also that year, the first Lutheran hymnal, containing eight hymns including four written by Luther, was printed. Following these four hymns, Luther wrote twenty-four more. Later, he wrote an additional twelve hymns. One of his better known hymns, "A Mighty Fortress Is Our God," contains the lines:

> A mighty fortress is our God,
> A bulwark never failing,
> Our helper He amid the flood
> Of mortal ills prevailing.

In June 1525, Luther married Catherine von Bora, who had left the Cistercian convent of Nimptschen. Her parents, who either could not or did not want to provide a dowry for her, had sent her to the convent, where she rebelled. After leaving the convent, Catherine worked in the home of the burgomaster. She told a professor that she was interested in marrying Luther. Luther did not take her seriously until he realized that she meant it. Soon, he was very much in love with her. He observed to a friend, "My Katie is in all things so obliging and pleasing to me that I would not exchange my property for the riches of Croesus."[103] He called her Katie and occasionally "Kette," the German word for chain.

In 1526, Luther conducted his first Mass in German; however, it was more than just a translation of the Latin Mass into

German. Luther rejected the doctrine that the Mass re-enacted Christ's sacrifice on the Cross and the body and blood of Jesus was offered to intercede with God for the sins of man. Luther emphasized that a Mass was an event at which Christian worshippers met to praise God and to strengthen their relationships with Jesus Christ and with each other.

In 1529, Luther wrote his *Small Catechism,* a manual that described his Christian doctrine. The basis for his catechism was the Creed, the Lord's Prayer, and the Ten Commandments. Earlier, Zwilling had removed the statues on the side altars because they were viewed as idolatrous, but when some of the clergy wanted to remove the crucifix from the main altar, Luther objected. He said, "When I hear Christ speak, my heart forms the image of a man hanging on the cross. Far from it being a sin, it is well that I have the image in my heart. Why then should it be a sin to have such a picture before my eyes."

In 1530, King Charles returned to Germany with the goal of establishing religious unity in the country. He asked that Protestant princes state their position on religion. Melanchthon prepared the *Confession of Augsburg* to delineate their position. Melanchthon concluded his moderate summary of Lutheran doctrine by stating:

> This is almost the sum of our teaching. It can be said that nothing in it is discordant with the Scripture or the teaching of the Catholic Church or the Roman Church as it is known from ancient writers. We are judged unfairly if we are held to be heretics. Our disagreement is over some abuses which have crept into churches without due authority.[104]

Melanchthon's conciliatory words were not enough. Cardinal Campeggio, the papal delegate, insisted that the Lutheran movement must accept papal authority. Luther told Melanchthon, "Agreement on doctrine is plainly impossible, unless the Pope will abolish his Popedom." The Lutherans left Augsburg without resolution of the differences.

Between 1520 and 1560, Lutheranism expanded considerably by the dissemination of its doctrine with the help of the printing press. First, it spread to Scandinavia and then to France, the Netherlands, Switzerland, and the countries controlled by the Hapsburgs. Other denominations of Protestantism were developed by Calvin in Switzerland, Cranmer in England, and Knox in Scotland.

On February 18, 1546, Luther died of a heart attack in Eisleben; he was buried in Wittenberg. Two days prior to his death, he inscribed a friend's book with a passage from St. John's Gospel: "If anyone obeys my teaching, he shall never know what it is to die." Luther added a comment of his own, "How incredible is such a text, and yet it is the truth. If a man takes God's work in full earnest and believes in it and then falls asleep, he slips away without noticing death and is not sad on the other side."[105]

ST. IGNATIUS LOYOLA (1491-1556) Founder of the Jesuits

"The man who succeeds above his fellows is the one who, early in life, clearly discerns his object, and towards that habitually directs his powers. Even genius itself is but fine observation strengthened by fixity of purpose. Every man who observes vigilantly and resolves steadfastly grows unconsciously into genius."

Edward G. Bulwer-Lytton

Ignatius Loyola founded the Society of Jesus, a strong Catholic order. In *St. Ignatius and the Jesuits,* Theodore Maynard observes, "One cannot think of any religious group that has had so prodigious an effect upon the world. Each of the orders, working in its own way, has magnificent achievements to its credit; but the Jesuits may be considered the 'shock troops' of the Church, trained to strike anywhere with terrific impact."[106]

Ignatius Loyola was born on December 24, 1491 in Guipuzcoa in the Basque region of northwest Spain to Don Beltran, Lord of Loyola and Onaz, and Marina Loyola, daughter of a distinguished Basque family. Ignatius, christened Inigo, was the youngest of eleven children. The high-spirited youth, known for his physical courage, was sent by his father to live in Castile with Juan Velasquez de Cuellar, a provincial Governor of King Ferdinand of Spain. He was instilled with discipline and obedience, qualities of a successful soldier, and trained to be a skilled horseman and a polished courtier.

In 1516, Loyola joined the army of his relative, the Duke of Najara, and fought against the French in northern Castile and Navarre. Although trained as a soldier, he did not consider himself a professional. He was promoted to Captain and led a brave defense of the fortress of Pampeluna although vastly outnumbered. The Spanish surrendered the fortress after six hours of shelling when Loyola was struck in the right leg by a cannonball, shattering his shin. A French doctor attempted to set the broken leg and then had the wounded Captain conveyed by litter to his sister's residence at Anzuola.

Loyola's leg had to be broken again and reset, which left the sharp end of the bone protruding through the skin. Because the use of anesthesia was still in the future, he had to endure the pain of having the bone reset and the sharp end of the bone sawed off. He was neither tied down nor held during the procedure; clenched fists were the only indication of the pain he experienced. His right leg was now permanently shorter than his left, but wearing a higher heel on his right shoe compensated for this difference.

While he was recovering, Loyola's sister gave him *The Golden Legend, Lives of the Saints* and *The Life of Christ* in four volumes to read. His initial lack of interest was overcome; he read the books over and over. He was particularly captivated reading about the lives of St. Francis, St. Dominic, and the lesser-known St. Humphrey. He thought to himself, "It they could do this, I could do the same and more."

Loyola had to overcome his memories of serving as a courtier and of enjoying the finer things of life. He had been smitten by a lady of high station and could not forget her. He fantasized about what he "would achieve in the service of a certain lady, the journey he would make to the land where she lived, and the feats of arms he would perform for her."

Gradually, Loyola realized that his worldly thoughts disturbed him, but his thoughts about Christ and the saints left him with a feeling of peace and contentment. He considered doing penance for his past life. A significant emotional event occurred one night in August 1521:

> The point of no return, so to speak, occurred
> one night when, unable to sleep, he saw clear-
> ly before him the likeness of Our Lady and
> was filled with a sheer happiness that lasted
> many hours. He became conscious of a pres-
> ence that gave him a total revulsion from his
> old dissolute life. The experience completed
> his conversion. All the licentious images
> imprinted on his imagination were there no
> longer. He assigns no date to the vision but
> from that night to the day that he dictated this
> page of his autobiography, he was never again
> troubled by temptations of the flesh.[107]

Loyola read the New Testament and marked the passages
that moved him. He was filled with a strong desire to serve
the Lord and realized that he could help others by speaking
about God in his own words. He decided that going on a pilgrimage was the way to contemplate his new spiritual feelings
and to think about the course that his life should take. He
mounted a mule and traveled to the shrine of Our Lady of
Montserrat in the mountains above Barcelona. When he
arrived at the shrine, he removed his expensive clothing and
put on the sackcloth of a pilgrim.

Loyola confessed his sins and decided on a life serving
God and of penance for his past sins. He subsisted on alms
and for most of the year 1522 lived in a cave, where he went
to pray and meditate. He experienced doubts about his decision to leave the worldly life. He kept a journal of his inner-
most thoughts and insights that gradually evolved into his
widely read book, *Spiritual Exercises*. He revised and added

to these original journal entries over the next twenty years. For the remainder of his life, he looked back on his stay at Manresa in the scenic mountains above Barcelona as the most formative time of his life.

Loyola decided to make a pilgrimage to Jerusalem. Early in the fourteenth century, Pope Clement V had ruled that pilgrims must have the Pope's permission to visit Jerusalem. Loyola obtained the necessary permission from Pope Adrian VI in March 1523. He traveled to Venice to obtain passage, for which he was unable to pay, on a ship bound for the Holy Land. In September, Loyola reached Jerusalem, where he visited the Holy Sepulchre and traveled to the Mount of Olives. He had a vision of Christ on his way back to Jerusalem from the Mount of Olives.

Again, Loyola managed to obtain free passage—on a small ship bound for Venice. A year after setting out for the Holy Land, he returned to Barcelona and studied Latin for two years. He attended the University of Alcalá, near Madrid, where he studied logic, physics, and theology. He wore a plain gray habit, begged for food, and slept on the floor in a hospice for poor students. He was imprisoned for six weeks for teaching the Catechism to young children without having the proper authority.

Loyola enrolled at the University of Salamanca where, as in Madrid, he could not hold back his enthusiasm for reform. Again, he was imprisoned. He considered these imprisonments as trials designed to sanctify him. Nevertheless, they motivated him to leave Spain. In February 1528, he arrived in Paris where he studied Latin and philosophy at the College of Montaigu and the College of St. Barbara. However, he was not satisfied to be just a student; he wanted to expound on the value of the Catholic religion and to influence people's lives.

He convinced some of his fellow students to do good works for the benefit of others and to pray with him on Sundays and holy days.

The conservative Principal of the College thought that these activities distracted students from their studies. He decided to punish Loyola by a public flogging until Loyola explained to him what his small group was attempting to do. The Principal called an assembly of students and publically rescinded the punishment and announced that he now realized that the goal of Loyola's small group was to save souls. The Principal assigned another student, Peter Faber, to tutor Loyola in philosophy courses, preparing him to earn a Master of Arts degree in 1533. Loyola began studies in theology toward a doctorate, which ill health prevented him from completing.

Six theology students joined Loyola in his participation of "spiritual exercises." His small group consisted of Peter Faber; Francis Xavier, another Basque from a noble family; Nicholas Bobadilla, Diego Laynez, and Alfonzo Salmeron, Spaniards at the top of their class academically; and Simon Rodriguez, a Portuguese. In August 1534 on the feast of the Assumption in the chapel on Montmartre, they received communion from Peter Faber, who had recently been ordained a priest. They took vows of poverty and chastity and resolved either to preach in the Holy Land or to offer their services to the Pope.

Loyola returned to Spain to regain his health but stayed in contact with the other six members of the group. Two years later, they met in Venice but, because of the war between the Turks and the Venetians, were prevented from sailing to Palestine. They traveled to Rome and were received by Pope Paul III, who gave permission to those who were not yet ordained to receive Holy Orders.

Loyola took a year to prepare himself and did not say his first Mass until December 1538. Loyola was visited by God at a chapel in La Storta and was told, "I will be helpful to you in Rome." On their second visit to the Vatican, the Pope accepted their offer to serve the Lord. Initially, they referred to themselves as "the Company of Jesus." Faber and Laynez taught theology at the University of Rome. Loyola continued to teach among the people and to expand his "spiritual exercises."

The Company of Jesus decided to establish a religious order:

> After prayer and deliberation, they all agreed to this and resolved to add to the vows of poverty and chastity a third vow, that of perpetual soldierly obedience. At their head should be a General who should hold office for life, with absolute authority over every member, himself subject only to the Pope. A fourth vow required them to go wherever the Pope might send them for the salvation of souls. Professed Jesuits could own no real estate or revenues, either as individuals or in common; but their colleges might use incomes and rent for the maintenance of students. The teaching of the Catechism was to be one of their special duties.[108]

On September 27, 1540, Pope Paul signed the Bull authorizing the formation of the Society of Jesus, as the Jesuits were now called. On April 7, 1541, Loyola became the first "General" of the Society of Jesus. Jesuits used the title "General" for the individual in charge of their efforts to gain spiritual victories under the banner of Christ, not military victories, such as those won by the Templars during the crusades.

Loyola wrote the constitution for the Society of Jesus, which contained the following goals:

- "Sanctification of their own souls by a union of the active and contemplative life
- Instructing youth in piety and learning
- Acting as confessors of uneasy consciences
- Undertaking missions abroad
- Propagating the faith"[109]

Members dressed like the secular clergy. New members made a confession, followed the "spiritual exercises," and studied as a novitiate for two years followed by taking the vows of poverty, chastity, and obedience. After more years of study, they repeated in public their earlier vows that were now binding forever, and they were called "professed." The fourth vow was made at this time: to undertake any mission that the Pope commanded.

Loyola lived in Rome for the remainder of his life directing the worldwide efforts of the Society of Jesus. He founded a home for instruction of converted Jews, for fallen women who wished to reform, for poor orphans, and for poor young women to prevent their falling into danger. Missionary work began early. Loyola insisted that his missionaries speak the language of the country to which they were assigned. In 1540, Rodriguez and Xavier were sent to Portugal. In April 1541, Xavier sailed for India, where he introduced Christianity to a new part of the world. Xavier is considered by some biographers as the greatest missionary since St. Paul.

Peter Canisius, scholar and pious priest, founded Jesuit schools in Austria, Bohemia, and Germany. Luis Gonzales was sent to Morocco; other Jesuit missionaries went to the

Congo, Abyssinia, and South America. In 1542, Jesuits arrived in Ireland and England during a time when Protestantism was firmly established and Roman Catholics were persecuted. During this time, twenty-six Jesuits became martyrs in England and Wales.

Loyola and the Jesuits countered militant Protestantism. Nineteenth-century English Cardinal Manning later observed: "It was exactly what was wanted at the time to counteract the revolt of the sixteenth century. The revolt was disobedience and disorder in the most aggressive form. The Society was obedience and order in its most solid compactness."[110]

The Jesuits founded many colleges beginning with the Roman College of the Jesuits in 1551 and the German College in Rome the following year. Loyola recruited able teachers whom he provided with the latest equipment in establishing model institutions of higher learning.

In 1548, *Spiritual Exercises,* Loyola's principal written work that he had begun in 1522 in Manresa, was published in Rome. Performance of the exercises took four weeks:

- Week 1—Deliberation about sin and the consequences of sin.
- Week 2—Reflection on our Lord's life on earth
- Week 3—Contemplation of the Lord's Passion
- Week 4—Meditation about the Lord's Resurrection.

As described by Rev. Francis Xavier Talbot, S.J.:

> The *[Spiritual Exercises]* is a concise memorandum for the guidance of a director and an exercitant in the performance of a carefully planned series of reflection, meditations, affective aspirations, self-examinations, and resolutions. The aim of the *Spiritual Exercises* is: (1) the purification of the soul from disor-

dered affections and worldly standards; (2) the discovery of the Divine Will before making a choice of a state of life; (3) the consecration of the person's mind and will to the service of the Creator under the leadership of Jesus Christ.[111]

In his sixties, Loyola was worn out and ill; his offer to resign as General was rejected. His health failed while he wrote his autobiography. He died on July 31, 1556 after leading the Society of Jesus for fifteen years. When he died, 13,000 Jesuits toiled in thirty-two provinces. The able Father Laynez succeeded Loyola as General and with Father Francis Borgia led the Society of Jesus for many years. On June 27, 1606, Loyola was beatified. He was canonized on March 12, 1622 along with Xavier and Teresa of Avila.

CHAPTER 3

SCIENTISTS / INVENTORS

"Firmness of purpose is one of the most necessary sinews of character, and one of the best instruments of success. Without it, genius wastes its efforts in a maze of inconsistencies."

Philip Dormer Stanhope

Chapter 3 contains biographical sketches of scientists and inventors who displayed the quality of determination while making discoveries and pursuing personal goals. Their fields range from archaeology to aeronautics.

Heinrich Schliemann, the first modern archaeologist, learned on the job and made early mistakes. He earned a fortune to finance his diggings and then distinguished himself from other scientists by believing the stories of Homer. His determination permitted him to overcome the bureaucracy of Turkey and Greece and, ultimately, to uncover the secrets of Troy and Mycenae.

Louis Pasteur was a serious scientist who overcame considerable resistance and verbal abuse from other scientists about his research. He was accused of taking too long to solve biological problems and of being a "mere chemist." Nevertheless, his accomplishments are impressive, including the invention of partial sterilization (pasteurization) and vaccines. He proceeded according to his own lights and eventually achieved his research goals.

Wilhelm Röntgen benefited from an accidental discovery in the laboratory. The determination with which he followed up on an "accident" distinguished him from many other scientists. He relentlessly pursued his investigation in the laboratory, missing many meals, until he had documented and explained his discovery: X-rays. He told no one, including his colleagues, until he could explain his findings.

Thomas Edison, a self-educated inventor, was energetic in his experiments, which numbered in the thousands. In many of his experiments, he used a "try this, try that" approach to eliminate alternatives. His determination to continue with his investigations until he accomplished the desired results was notable. He persevered.

Orville and Wilbur Wright are classical examples of stick-to-it-iveness in making incremental improvements and in winning many small battles before finally winning the campaign. Samuel Langley, whose attempts to fly preceded those of the Wright brothers, made two highly publicized flights off a houseboat in the Potomac River. In both flights, the airplane crashed into the river, almost drowning the pilot on one flight. The Wright brothers made scores of flights at Kitty Hawk, North Carolina, out of the public eye. Ultimately, their determination allowed them to accomplish what no one before them had achieved: flight in a heavier-than-air craft.

These scientists and inventors were resolute in the pursuit of their objectives. Many individuals would have given up short of reaching their goals.

HEINRICH SCHLIEMANN (1822-1890) Discoverer of Ancient Troy

"With his unshakable faith in Homer, his boundless energy and enthusiasm, his organizing ability, his resolute determination, and his unfailing persistence—all backed by abundant financial resources, which he had acquired by his own efforts—with all these qualifications, Schliemann overcame numerous obstacles and difficulties and achieved a brilliant success."[112]

Carl W. Blegen, *Troy and the Trojans*

Heinrich Schliemann made a million dollars during his first four years in a responsible position in the import-export business and his second fortune, a half-million dollars, in the California gold fields. This allowed him to do what he really wanted to do with his life—discover ancient Troy. Most archaeologists thought that Troy was at Bunarbashi, Turkey. Schliemann, who believed Homer's description of the routes of Achilles, Hector, and King Priam, thought that Troy was at Hissarlik, Turkey. He was right.

Heinrich Schliemann, one of six children of a poor pastor, was born on January 6, 1822 at Neu Buckow in the German Duchy of Mecklenburg. His mother died when he was eleven. Young Heinrich did well in school, but his father was unable to pay for his continued schooling. As a teenager, he worked in a grocery store. He considered going to sea on a sailing ship, so he moved to the North Sea port city of Hamburg.

Schliemann studied bookkeeping and obtained a job as a bookkeeper until he could go to sea. He hired on as cabin boy on the brig *Dorothea*, which sailed for Venezuela on November 28, 1841. Off the coast of Holland, the *Dorothea* encountered a violent storm, and the crew had to abandon ship when the masts were lost. Many of the lifeboats were smashed. Schliemann was fortunate to hold onto an empty barrel that floated by him until he was picked up by an oarless lifeboat. Fortunately, they drifted ashore on Texel Island, one of the Frisian Islands of the Netherlands.

Schliemann walked to Amsterdam, which impressed him with its booming economy. He worked as a messenger and studied languages until 1844, when he obtained a job as a bookkeeper and correspondent with the largest import-export firm in the city. He invested successfully in indigo imported from India and accumulated substantial savings.

Schliemann's boss at Schröder Import-Export knew that his employee was making personal investments in addition to representing Schröder, but he did not want to see his star correspondent leave to go into business for himself. Schröder offered Schliemann the position of representing the firm in Russia. He learned the Russian language in six weeks and moved to St. Petersburg in January 1846. Schröder's business prospered; Schliemann branched out into spices and metals and was given a percentage of the profits.

In 1850, Schliemann was notified that his brother, Ludwig, had died of typhus in California, where he had been prospecting for gold, leaving a substantial fortune. Later that year, Schliemann left St. Petersburg for California to close out his brother's business affairs. He sailed from London to New York, where his wealth helped him obtain introductions to the financial community and to society. He met President Millard Fillmore. He sailed to Panama, and, since the Canal had not yet been dug, traveled by mule train to the Pacific Ocean and then by ship to San Francisco.

When Schliemann arrived in Sacramento, he found that the partner had vanished with his brother's fortune. He was unsuccessful in finding the missing partner. Schliemann developed gold rush fever; however, he was not motivated to mine for gold. Instead, he made short-term loans to prospectors at high interest rates and purchased gold dust and nuggets from miners for resale. He made another fortune.

Schliemann returned to St. Petersburg, became active again in business, and looked for a wife. On October 12, 1852, he married Catherine Lyschin, and they had three children. Although his business endeavors prospered, his marriage did not. Catherine had married him for his money; they had little in common. He concentrated on his businesses and multiplied his fortune by making large profits during the Crimean War.

As a young boy, Schliemann had read about Troy in Jerrer's *Illustrated History of the World,* and the memories had stayed with him. When he had sufficient wealth to finance his explorations, his thoughts returned to the stories of Homer and of adding to the world's knowledge. He wanted to walk the paths of Achilles, Hector, and King Priam and to uncover the ruins of Troy. He studied the Greek language and read books about ancient Greece.

During the summer of 1858, Schliemann visited Greece for the first time and was captivated by it. He returned to St. Petersburg for business reasons and told Catherine of his interest in living in Greece. She did not want to leave St. Petersburg, so they separated. In 1863, Schliemann sold his business interests and left Russia. He traveled around the world ending up in Paris, where he attended the Sorbonne. Courses in archaeology rekindled his interest in Troy.

In 1868, Schliemann traveled to the Island of Ithaca, Greece, where he did his first excavation. Odysseus, who ruled Ithaca, had joined Agamemnon and Menelaus in their campaign against Troy. Odysseus was shipwrecked returning from the expedition and did not arrive home for ten years. His story, and the story of Penelope's patient wait for him, is told in the *Odyssey*. Schliemann's reading and his geographic instinct led him to the site of his first dig. Initially, Schliemann broke some artifacts in digging with a pick and did not keep accurate records of the depth and orientation of the objects. As he gained experience as an archaeologist, his discipline and methods improved markedly.

Schliemann and his workers uncovered a ten-foot by fifteen-foot stone room, twenty vases, clay female figures, and a few weapons. His findings were enough to reinforce his interest in archaeology. In traveling to a possible site of Troy, he met Frank Calvert, an Englishman with experience in excavating ruins and in working with Turkish authorities. They investigated Bunarbashi, rumored to be the site of Troy, but neither man agreed with the rumors.

Schliemann and Calvert thought that a more likely site for Troy was the great mound at Hissarlik, which was closer to the sea than Bunarbashi. Calvert gave his new friend access to the part of the Hissarlik mound that he owned (where he had dug earlier), but permission to dig on the other part would have to be obtained from the Turkish owners. They had to apply for a firman (permit) before they could begin excavating. Schliemann surveyed the mound, which was 800 feet long.

Schliemann was fascinated by Hissarlik:

> No sooner has one set foot on Trojan soil than one is astonished to see the noble mound, which seems to have been intended by nature to be the site of a great citadel. If well fortified, the site would command the whole plain of

> Troy. In the whole region, there is no point that
> compares with this one. From Hissarlik, one
> can see Mount Ida, from whose summit Jupiter
> looked down on the city of Troy.[113]

The wealthy archaeologist was moved by the history of the place. It had been visited by Alexander the Great and by Caesar, who had attempted to restore the ruins.

Schliemann decided to divorce Catherine and was told that he could obtain a divorce more easily in America than in Russia or Germany. He moved to Indianapolis, where he had business interests. He bought an expensive home and established residency, which allowed him to attend to his many business holdings in the United States.

Schliemann decided not to return to the Sorbonne to complete his education. He submitted a dissertation of the story of his life written in classic Greek to the University of Rostock. They accepted his dissertation and in 1868 awarded him a Doctor of Philosophy degree.

Schliemann wrote to ask his friend, Theokletos Vimpos, in Athens to find a good Greek wife for him. Vimpos responded promptly with several descriptions and photographs. Schliemann was taken by one photograph; he set all others aside. Upon his return to Greece, Vimpos, who was a bishop and taught at the University of Athens, told him that Sophia Engastromenos was the woman whose photo he had chosen. When Schliemann met the attractive sixteen-year-old at Colonus, the home of Sophocles, he was smitten. Sophia was not concerned about the difference in their ages. She answered all of his questions and sensed his loneliness.

Schliemann and Sophia, who were very much in love, were married on September 24, 1869. After a honeymoon tour of Europe, they stopped in Paris where Sophia studied to improve her French, German, and English. Upon their return to Greece, Schliemann was told that his firman to proceed with excavation at Troy had been delayed. Sophia's enthusiasm for his work helped to keep his spirits up. He considered digging at Mycenae; however, a team of English archaeologists had been killed there by Greek bandits, and the government was reluctant to issue further permits.

In April 1870, Schliemann hired laborers and began digging at Hissarlik without waiting for the firman. The team uncovered the ruins of a stone building measuring forty feet by sixty feet, not large enough to be King Priam's palace. One of the few significant finds was a Roman coin with Emperor Commodus on one side and Hector, King Priam's son, on the other. Two Turks arrived to complain that Schliemann was digging on their land. They would not accept a reasonable price for their property but, grudgingly, let the archaeologists dig.

To spur interest in the excavations, Schliemann wrote an article about his meager findings that was read by Turkish authorities who prevented further digging. Schliemann met with Safvet Pasha, an official of the Turkish government, in Constantinople. The enthusiastic archaeologist used his negotiating skills to ask Pasha to convince the Turkish owners of the Hissarlik property to sell it at a fair price. Pasha persuaded the Turks to sell, not to Schliemann but to the Turkish government. Pasha wanted to ensure that any valuable artifacts belonged to the government.

Schliemann appealed to the American Ambassador to Turkey to assist him in his dealings with Pasha. The Ambassador, who was well-educated and had a detailed knowledge of Homer's works, was helpful. Finally, in August

1871, Schliemann received the permit to dig at Hissarlik for which he had waited so long. Sophia lived with her husband on the site and worked beside him on the excavations. Safvet Pasha sent an "observer" to ensure that no valuable artifacts were carried away by the Schliemanns, who resolved not to turn over everything that they found to Pasha.

Excavation revealed foundations of undressed stone built on older foundations. They found dressed masonry, coins, and many small terra-cotta figures of owls but nothing confirmed that it was the palace of King Priam. Schliemann did not think that the terra-cotta figures were from the time of Troy. His friend, Frank Calvert, was not able to identify them either.

Schliemann documented his findings in a German magazine article and asked for suggestions from scholars when it was published. Subsequently, he combined his notes into a book, *Trojan Antiquities*. Response from scholars was negative, ranging from suggestions that Troy was a figment of Homer's imagination to observations that Schliemann's method of excavation was not sufficiently rigorous. Many scholars continued to back Bunarbashi as the site of Troy, not Hissarlik.

During the following summer, Schliemann's diggers found marble slabs inscribed with dedications, a bas-relief of Apollo and the four horses of the sun sculpted by a master, and nine large clay jars. These findings were meager, and Pasha accused them of hiding discoveries. They distracted Pasha's man by assigning workers to dig in multiple locations; the observer could not be in several locations simultaneously. Also, Sophia engaged him in conversation when they wanted him out of the way.

Schliemann and Sophia endured many hardships; living conditions were rough, and they developed fevers. Several of their workers were caught selling stones from the excavations to nearby villagers to use in repairing their homes. The Schliemanns' hut nearly burned down because of a faulty fireplace; fortunately, all of their records were saved.

In late May 1873, Schliemann found what he believed to be the outer wall of Priam's palace. When he found shiny material near the western gate, he dismissed the men so he could investigate further. The observer followed the diggers off the site. Schliemann and Sophia dug up a large copper container filled with gold, silver, and copper artifacts. They had made one of the greatest archaeological finds until this time. It included bottles, cups, goblets, pots, vases, knifeblades, and spearheads as well as almost 9,000 gold rings and buttons. They also found gold diadems, headbands, ear pendants, and earrings that might have been worn by Helen of Troy.

Sophia bundled their findings into a shawl and took them to their hut. When the observer returned to the site, he demanded to investigate all of their packing boxes. They sent him away. During the night, they conveyed their discovery to Frank Calvert for forwarding to their home in Athens. In the morning, they allowed the observer to check all of the packing boxes and returned to Athens, where they documented their findings and buried them in multiple places for safety.

Schliemann published a detailed description of their treasure. The government of Turkey accused him of stealing their country's treasures. This grievance was the subject of many court cases. He was called a "treasure hunter" and a "gold seeker" until he told his accusers that he wanted to finance a museum to display the artifacts. He wanted to locate it in Greece, but he was not sure that the Greeks could resist the demands of the Turks.

England also wanted the museum, and Schliemann and Sophia were received by Queen Victoria; Prime Minister Gladstone believed Schliemann's concepts of Troy. The artifacts were put on display in England, silencing those who had doubted their findings. Arthur Evans, a young archaeologist who later provided the Schliemanns with professional support, made a thorough study of the treasure. Turkey settled the court cases for a payment of 50,000 francs and permitted the Schliemanns to return to Troy. The Turkish government provided no financing and agreed to a fifty-fifty split of the findings.

Schliemann had decided to excavate next at Mycenae in Greece when he read Pausanias, a second-century writer:

> In the ruins of Mycenae is a fountain called Perseia and the underground buildings of Atreus and his sons, where their treasure is buried. There is the tomb of Atreus and there are also the tombs of Agamemnon and his charioteer [Eurymedon] whom Aegisthus murdered on their return from Troy. These tombs are within the walls. A little outside the walls are the tombs of [Queen] Clytemnestra and Aegisthus for they were considered unworthy to lie in the same hallowed ground with Agamemnon and those murdered with him.[114]

The Greek government had given permission to dig at Mycenae; however, like the government of Turkey at Hissarlik, they assigned an "observer."

In August 1876, Schliemann, Sophia, and sixty workmen began digging near the Lion Gate and found the usual goblets, vases, clay animals, and figurines. Schliemann found a large rock tomb; he saw the gleam of gold under three bodies covered with clay. Sophia crawled down a narrow passageway and found a silver cup, fourteen gold laurel-leaf crosses, and fifteen gold diadems.

Schliemann found another grave under which was a burial chamber containing three more bodies; he made a significant discovery of gold crowns and scepters, goblets, jewelry, plaques, vases, wine jars, and a thousand thin pieces of gold shaped into objects. The jewelry included gold necklaces, six double crosses, and eight diadems.

Schliemann moved to an area with darker soil and found a round stone altar with a hole for offerings to those buried beneath the altar. Under the altar, he found five bodies covered in gold with gold death masks over their faces. The discoveries included a gold crown, gold breastplates, and eleven large goblets, one of which he thought was the "cup of Nestor" described in the eleventh book of the *Iliad*. Also found were gold belts, brooches, large buttons, ornaments, pins, plates, 150 gold disks, and 400 gold coins.

Schliemann reported his success to the King of Greece:

> With extreme joy I announce to Your Majesty that I have discovered the tombs which tradition, echoed by Pausanias, had designated as the sepulchres of Agamemnon, Cassandra, Eurymedon and their companions who were killed by Clytemnestra and her lover Aegisthus. They were surrounded by a double circle of stone slabs which would not have been erected unless they were great personages. In the tombs I found immense treasures of the most ancient objects of pure gold.

> These treasures alone will fill a great museum,
> the most wonderful in the world, and for cen-
> turies to come thousands of foreigners will
> flock to Greece to see them. I work only for
> the pure love of science, and accordingly I
> have no claim on these treasures. I give them
> intact and with lively enthusiasm to Greece.
> God grant that these treasures may become the
> cornerstone of an immense national wealth.[115]

In reply, Schliemann received a tersely worded note of thanks.

The Schliemanns built a large home in Athens to house the collections of a lifetime. Critics called it a marble museum, but they were happy there. He stayed home and spent time with his daughter, Andromeda, and his son, Agamemnon. Schliemann wrote a book, which was published in French and German, about his theories and his discoveries. Prime Minister Gladstone wrote a forty-page introduction to the book. Schliemann was not highly regarded in France and Germany. He had mockers and was not taken seriously by some scholars because of errors he had made with dates during his early excavations.

Schliemann's next excavation was at Tiryns, which had been documented by Homer and by Pausanias, who described its great walls. Legend declared that Proetus, King of Tiryns, built his fortress with the help of seven cyclopes. When Schliemann uncovered extensive ruins and blocks measuring six feet by three feet by three feet, he understood the basis for the legend. Unfortunately, little treasure was found.

Schliemann wanted to do his last excavation at Knossos on the island of Crete, but he could not make satisfactory arrangements with the Governor of Crete. He was still unsure where to build his museum. England and America would welcome it; he continued to have reservations about building it in Greece. One day he was visiting ruins near Mount Ida when his colleague and friend, Rudolph Virchow, mentioned Schliemann's youth in Germany. Schliemann realized that the site for his museum should be the country of his birth, Germany. Schliemann and Sophia traveled to Germany and were entertained by the Kaiser, who awarded Schliemann the Order of Merit. The museum to house the treasures of antiquity was built in Berlin.

Schliemann began to experience pains in his ears, and his health was failing. He underwent an operation in Paris to ease his headache pain, but it was not successful. He visited Pompeii and Naples on his way home to Greece. On December 25, 1890, he collapsed on the sidewalk and was taken to the office of his doctor. He could not speak, and he was partially paralyzed. The doctor notified Sophia immediately. Schliemann died in his doctor's office; his body was transported home in January.

Over time, the voices of Schliemann's detractors have been silenced. Sir Arthur Evans verified that Schliemann had, in fact, discovered King Priam's Troy. What Schliemann did not know was that he had also uncovered earlier civilizations that went back to 6000 BC. Schliemann's efforts were the foundation upon which later work was based. In some circles, he is called the "father of modern archaeology." Evans said of Schliemann:

> I had the happiness to make his acquaintance on the fields of his glory, and I still remember the echoes of his visits to England, which were his greatest scenes of triumph. Something of

the romance of his early years still seemed to cling to his personality, and I have myself an almost uncanny memory of the spare, darkly clad, slightly built man, of sallow complexion, wearing spectacles through which—so fancy took me—he looked deep into the ground.[116]

Subsequently, Evans discovered the palace of King Minos and described the Minoan civilization, which preceded the Greek civilization.

Schliemann's treasures in the museum in Berlin were buried underground at the Berlin zoo to escape Allied bombing raids during World War II. In 1945, the Russians entered Berlin, dug up the treasure, and took it to Moscow.

Schliemann's reputation suffered at the hands of the press, particularly the London *Times*. He reacted to his treatment by that newspaper, which previously had supported him:

What are my sins? ... I have excavated for many years under monstrous hardships and with an expense of upwards of 40,000 pounds [$200,000] in the pestilential plain of Troy ... and brought to light from beneath mountains of ruins, a burned city.... I have found the royal tombs of Mycenae with their treasure... I have excavated the treasures and *tholos* with wonderful ceiling in Orchomenus.... I have excavated the prehistoric palace of the kings of Tiryns, a discovery which is considered by all archaeologists even more important than ... Mycenae or Troy.[117]

In *The Walls of Windy Troy*, Marjorie Braymer comments on the long-term recognition of Schliemann's work:

Once when he was feeling most tired, the arguments about what he had or had not found seemed to hover around him like gadflies. His labors seemed thankless. He said thoughtfully, "The truth will emerge and be accepted— although perhaps it will be only after my death." Without his stubborn and passionate faith, and without his iron determination, we would be wondering to this day about the buried city of Troy and the life of the bronze age people. Our debt to him is almost beyond measuring.[118]

Schliemann's determination helped him to add to the world's knowledge and to our understanding of the origins of civilization.

LOUIS PASTEUR (1822-1895) Pioneer in Medical Science

"These three things—work, will, success—fill human exis-
tences. Will opens the door to success, both brilliant and
happy. Work passes through these doors, and at the other end
of the journey success comes in to crown one's efforts."

Louis Pasteur

Pasteur is known for his work with the process of fermentation and for the development of pasteurization, which has
saved many lives over the years. He is also known for his
knowledge of diseases that attack the human body and of the
means by which the body can be protected from those diseases or be treated for them.

Pasteur, a great scientist, was known as a crusader for
human welfare as well as a seeker of scientific truth. He advocated his ideas in public debates prior to the acceptance of
those ideas. As with many people on the leading edge of
change, he was vilified and accused of misleading the public.

Louis Pasteur was born on December 27, 1822 in Dôle
near Dijon in the Jura region of France and grew up in nearby Arbois. His father, Jean Joseph Pasteur, who had fought
with Napoleon in the Peninsular War, was a tanner. His mother, Jeanne Roqui Pasteur, came from a family of gardeners.
Pasteur had two sisters; he was the only son.

In elementary school, Pasteur was not a particularly serious student. In his teens, he developed a strong interest in
painting. He was considered talented by other artists and, to
his parents' dismay, thought that he might become a painter.

At sixteen, Pasteur enrolled in the Lycée St. Louis, a secondary school in Paris, and four years later attended lectures

at the Sorbonne, where he was impressed by the chemistry lectures of J. B. Dumas. He received a Bachelor of Science degree from the Royal College of Besançon; his studies in chemistry were considered "barely adequate." However, in 1847, he finished his dissertation on crystallography and earned a doctorate from the École Normale Supérieure in Paris. He accepted a position as Professor of Physics at Dijon before moving on to become Professor of Chemistry at Strasbourg University.

Pasteur fell in love with Marie Laurent, daughter of the Rector of Strasbourg University, and proposed two weeks after meeting her. They were married on May 29, 1848. The story circulated that Pasteur was late for his wedding because he wanted to complete the experiment on which he was working. Marie was the ideal wife for Pasteur. Their friend and Pasteur's colleague, Émile Roux, described their relationship:

> From the first days of their common life, Madame Pasteur understood what kind of man she had married; she did everything to protect him from the difficulties of life, taking onto herself the worries of the home, that he might retain the full freedom of his mind for his investigations. Madame Pasteur loved her husband to the extent of understanding his studies. During the evenings she wrote dictation, calling for explanations, for she took a genuine interest in crystalline structure or in attenuated viruses.... Madame was more than an incomparable companion, she was his best collaborator.[119]

In 1854, Pasteur joined the faculty of sciences at the University of Lille and began the study that established his reputation. Naturalists, from the beginning of recorded history, believed in "spontaneous generation"—that living matter could be produced from dead substances. Pasteur conducted a series of controlled experiments to prove that only a living thing could produce life. Other scientists mocked and scorned him, refusing to believe that microbes could cause fermentation. Pasteur observed, "A man of science may hope for what may be said of him in the future, but he cannot stop to think of the insults—or the compliments—of his own day."[120]

Pasteur was asked to save the silk industry in France. Silkworms had been infected with a disease that was destroying the industry. He interviewed silkworm cultivators in Alès and collected eggs, larvae, and moths. When he failed to suggest a quick solution, he was treated harshly and called a "mere chemist." When he suggested that diseased eggs be culled out to protect the healthy ones, his character was attacked. During a four-year period, he diagnosed the problem and ended the epidemic.

In 1859, Pasteur's oldest daughter, Jeanne, died of typhus. In 1865, his youngest child, Camille, died of a fever, and his twelve-year-old daughter, Cécile, died of typhoid fever the following year. The overworked Pasteur reeled from these multiple shocks and was temporarily paralyzed. His speech and his left arm and leg were affected by a cerebral hemorrhage. He attempted to rebound by reading *Of the Knowledge of God and of Self* by Bossuet and *Self-Help* by Samuel Smiles.

Pasteur returned to work against the advice of his doctors. In *Pasteur and Modern Science,* René Dubos comments on his determination: "This performance revealed once more that Pasteur was a man of indomitable will. It was not only his opponents that he wanted to overpower; it was also nature—

it was himself."[121]

Pasteur studied the micro-organisms that spoiled wine and beer. He developed the process of partial sterilization, which became known as pasteurization, by heating a liquid to fifty to sixty degrees Centigrade. He applied the process to many beverages including beer, cider, milk, and wine. Although he designed much of the equipment used in pasteurization, he chose not to profit from these developments.

In 1877, Pasteur began his work on anthrax. Earlier, with studies on potato blight in 1850 and silkworms in 1868, it had been shown that microbes could cause disease. Studies on anthrax showed, for the first time, that microbes caused diseases affecting higher animals and human beings. Robert Koch, the noted German bacteriologist, worked during the same period of time as Pasteur. Pasteur and Koch are considered the co-founders of the field of microbiology. Koch determined the life cycle of the anthrax bacillus and developed culture methods to determine the microbes that caused tuberculosis and cholera.

In the Auvergne district of France, from thirty to fifty percent of the sheep population had died from anthrax. Pasteur isolated the bacteria that causes anthrax and used the bacteria to cure the disease. Doctors and ministers attacked Pasteur's germ theory. In *Makers of the Modern World,* Louis Untermeyer comments:

> Nevertheless, Pasteur persisted. He surmised that a bacterial attack induced a formation in the blood of "antibodies" which attacked the germs; in fatal diseases, the invading germs multiplied so quickly as to cause death before enough antibodies could form. He experimented with the deadly, filament-shaped bacteria

and subjected them to endless tests and counter-tests. Finally, he devised a culture which was a mild form of the disease itself and, instead of killing, would build up a protection against the fever.[122]

Pasteur's success with anthrax finally brought him the recognition that he deserved. He was awarded the Legion of Honor by the government of France and was admitted to the French Academy.

Pasteur's next effort was to isolate the bacteria that caused rabies and to develop a vaccine. In July 1885, a nine-year-old boy from Alsace who had been bitten fourteen times on the hands, legs, and thighs by a rabid dog was brought to Pasteur. Pasteur's treatment had only been used on dogs, not on humans. He was not sure how strong to make the serum or what the side effects, if any, would be. However the boy was deathly ill and would not live unless Pasteur could save his life. Pasteur increased the dosage slowly, and, although a brief relapse occurred, the boy's life was saved.

On November 14, 1887, the Pasteur Institute opened. It owed its existence to contributions from many countries, including Brazil, Russia, and Turkey, as well as gifts from wealthy sponsors and many donations from the working class. Five years later, scientists gathered at the Sorbonne to honor Pasteur. Joseph Lister, representing the Royal Societies of England and Scotland, was one of many speakers. He said to Pasteur, "You have raised the veil which for centuries had covered infectious diseases. You have changed the treatment of wounds from an uncertain and too often disastrous business into a scientific and certainly beneficial art. Your relentless researches have thrown a powerful light which has illuminated the dark places in surgery."[123]

In 1889, Pasteur suffered a serious attack of uremic poisoning and almost died. He wanted to return to the laboratory but realized that he did not have the strength to go back to work. At the age of seventy-three, his health declined rapidly; he became too weak to raise his head, and he had difficulty speaking. He lapsed into a coma and died on September 28, 1895.

Pasteur was widely quoted for insights such as "change favors only the mind which is prepared." One of his more profound observations is:

> Two contrary laws seem to be wrestling for the soul of man. The one is the law of blood and death, always planning new methods of destruction, forcing nations to be constantly ready for the battlefield. The other is a law of peace, work, and health, always creating new means of delivering man from the scourges which beset him. The one seeks violent conquests; the other the relief of humanity.... Which of the two will ultimately prevail, God alone knows. But we may assert that science will have tried, by obeying the law of humanity, to extend the frontiers of life.[124]

Several years after Pasteur's death, a poll was taken in France to determine which of their countrymen they considered the greatest heroes. Napoleon was ranked fifth; Pasteur was first. In *The 100: A Ranking of the Most Influential Persons in History* by Michael H. Hart, Pasteur is ranked twelfth, before other scientists: Charles Darwin (seventeenth), Michael Faraday (twenty-eighth), James Clerk

Maxwell (twenty-ninth), and Alexander Fleming (forty-fifth). He also ranked ahead of Aristotle, Moses, Augustus Caesar, Genghis Khan, Martin Luther, Constantine the Great, and George Washington.

In *How Pasteur Changed History: The Story of Louis Pasteur and the Pasteur Institute,* Moira Davison Reynolds comments on Pasteur's personal characteristics: "In addition to his intellectual gifts, Pasteur would exhibit emotional qualities that were to his advantage. He was enthusiastic about whatever he was working on, and unsatisfactory or disappointing results did not seriously daunt him. He had patience. He also possessed a fighting spirit and the capacity to work untiringly."[125] He certainly had the will to stay with it.

WILHELM RÖNTGEN (1845-1923) Discoverer of X-rays

"The real difference between men is energy. A strong will, a settled purpose, an invincible determination, can accomplish almost anything; and in this lies the distinction between great men and little men."

Fuller

One definition of luck is the preparation of oneself to take advantage of opportunity. Wilhelm Röntgen was a highly trained, disciplined scientist and when an incident occurred in his laboratory that could be described as luck or as an accident, he knew precisely what he had to do to verify it, expand upon it, document it, and notify the scientific community of its occurrence. He had sufficient determination to continue with his efforts until they were accomplished.

On the evening of November 8, 1895, Dr. Röntgen, Professor of Physics and Director of the Physical Institute of the University of Wurzburg, was working alone in his laboratory conducting experiments. He was using a Hittorf-Crookes cathode-ray tube, an enclosed glass tube in which cathode rays—streams of electrons—were generated by applying a high voltage differential between two electrodes within the tube in a partial vacuum.

For his experiment, Röntgen had covered the tube with black cardboard so that no light could escape when he turned it on. A cardboard screen coated with barium platinocyanide crystals (a fluorescent material) was lying on a table three feet away from the tube. This screen, a standard piece of laboratory equipment used to monitor ultraviolet radiation, was not part of Röntgen's experiment; it just happened to be there. ·

When Röntgen turned on the Crookes tube, the screen on

the nearby table glowed. When he turned off the tube, the screen stopped glowing. Röntgen knew that the cathode rays themselves were stopped by the glass walls of the tube. Even a few centimeters of air stopped cathode rays. Röntgen realized that he was viewing the existence of a form of light, not visible to the eye, which had not been observed previously. He called this invisible radiation "X-rays," because X is the mathematical notation for an unknown entity.

For the next eight weeks, Röntgen worked long hours, skipped many meals, and hurried through others to return to his laboratory. He worked diligently and told no one of his efforts. The nearest he came to revealing anything was to mention to one of his closest friends, "I have discovered something, but I do not know if my observations are correct."

Röntgen experimented with moving the fluorescent object farther away from the cathode-ray tube and farther to the side of the tube and found, as he expected, a weaker glow in both cases. He made a thorough check of each item of his equipment, every procedure that he used, and each observation to ensure that his findings were factual and repeatable. He placed objects between the source tube and the screen, such as a book and a piece of wood. Various metals, such as copper, silver, tin, gold, and platinum, affected he fluorescence to varying degrees, but lead stopped it completely. He also experimented with other fluorescent materials.

Röntgen noticed that while holding his hand between the source tube and the screen, he could see the bones in it! Next he captured a picture of the bones on a photographic plate with a silver bromide emulsion. Finally, he documented his findings and submitted a paper to the Physical and Medical Society of Wurzburg entitled "W. C. Röntgen: About a New Kind of Rays (Preliminary Communication)."

Scores of scientists conducted X-ray experiments within a few months, and hundreds of papers on the subject were published within a year. Antoine Henri Becquerel was one of the scientists who pursued X-rays; his investigations led to his work on radioactivity. X-rays were found to be electromagnetic waves with a shorter wavelength than light waves.

In 1894, when Dr. Röntgen became Rector of the University of Wurzburg, he quoted a Professor who had preceded him, Althanasius Kircher: "Nature often allows amazing miracles to be produced which originate from the most ordinary observation and which are, however, recognized only by those who are equipped with the sagacity and acumen and who consult experience, the teacher of everything."[126] He could not have realized how pertinent to his own life this statement would be within a year. In 1901, Dr. Röntgen was awarded the first Nobel Prize for Physics.

THOMAS EDISON (1847-1931) Inventor Extraordinaire

"From eighteen to twenty hours a day for the last seven months, I have worked on the single word 'specia.' I said to the phonograph, 'specia, specia, specia,' but the instrument replied 'pecia, pecia, pecia.' It was enough to drive one mad. But I held firm, and I have succeeded."

Thomas Alva Edison

Thomas Edison was a determined individual throughout his career as an inventor. He conducted thousands of experiments in which he considered many alternatives until he found one that suited his needs. Even if he had not found the material or approach for which he was looking, he was eliminating the alternatives that would not work well or were not practical. Of many examples of Edison's determination, two notable ones are his efforts to perfect the phonograph and his struggle to find a practical filament for the light bulb.

While attempting to improve the transmitter used with Alexander Graham Bell's telephone, Edison had his first thoughts about inventing a device for recording the human voice. His challenge was to find a material to improve the operation of the transmitter used to transmit voice over telephone lines. He tried hundreds of materials before arriving at the choice of carbon as the optimum transmitter material.

Edison made a sketch of a device that he felt could be used to record and play back the sound of the human voice. He asked one of his associates to make a model from the sketch. The device consisted of a long, narrow cylinder on a shaft that was turned by a hand crank. A thin metal disk picked up the voice sound waves. A similar approach was used to receive sound waves in the telephone. Turning the crank caused the cylinder to rotate and a pin to move along the axis of the cylinder.

The pin in the center of the disk made a groove that modeled the voice pattern on tinfoil wrapped around the cylinder. Another pin used with a second disk picked up the voice pattern and converted it into vibrations that generated the sound. The quality of sound that this first phonograph reproduced was poor. However, Edison had proved that the voice could be recorded and then played back. He set this invention aside and went on to other things.

Ten years later, Edison decided that he should do something to improve the fidelity of the sound of his phonograph. Its principal shortcomings were in reproducing the sibilants (hissing sounds) and the higher tones of musical notes. Edison noted that, in order to overcome the defects in his phonograph design, "I worked over one year, twenty hours a day, Sundays and all to get the word 'specia' perfectly recorded and reproduced on the phonograph. When this was done, I knew everything else could be done—which was a fact."[127]

A second example of Edison's resolve was his search for a practical filament material for the electric light bulb. Electric light had been around for a long time. The first electric arc light had been developed by the English scientist, Sir Humphrey Davy, and had been improved upon by Jablochkoff, a Russian engineer. However, their arc lights generated a very glaring light and radiated considerable heat. The initial arc lamp burned for only a few minutes before the filament burned out. Improvements had been made that allowed the filament to last several hours.

Edison's challenge was to find a filament material that would heat up from the low currents and high voltages used at the time. Filaments burned out quickly when in contact with oxygen. He had to find a way to minimize the amount of oxygen in contact with the filament. In his search for a filament material, he needed a substance with a high melting point that would last considerably longer than a few hours.

The first material that Edison tried was carbon. His first carbon filaments were carbonized strips of paper. These filaments burned out in eight minutes. His next series of experiments were with threads of rare metals. He tried barium, platinum, rhodium, ruthenium, titanium, and zirconium. Of these materials, platinum worked the best. He used a double spiral of platinum for his filament. Next he investigated the problem of minimizing the amount of oxygen in contact with the filament. He asked his glass blower to make some enclosed, pear-shaped bulbs.

Edison searched for the best air pump that he could obtain. He ordered a new pump, called the Sprengel pump, and borrowed one from Princeton University until his was available. His first experiment with a pear-shaped bulb using the Sprengel pump to form a partial vacuum inside the bulb was a success. The platinum filament provided five times more footcandles of light than previous experiments. However, platinum was a rare metal and was expensive. He considered using tungsten, the material used in light bulbs today, but, unfortunately, he did not have the delicate tools required to work with it.

Edison persisted in his search for an improved filament. He experimented with various grasses, linen thread, and wood splinters. He even tried a red hair from a man's beard. His goal was to make a light bulb for fifty cents or less. He had moderate success in an experiment with a bamboo filament. He was sufficiently hopeful that bamboo was a practical filament material that he sent out three men to obtain bamboo samples for him. One went to China and Japan. A second searched across South America. The third traveled to Ceylon (Sri Lanka), India, and Burma looking for bamboo samples. Edison tried over 1,600 different materials in his search for an optimum material for his filament.

On October 21, 1879, Edison used a filament made of carbonized thread. In that experiment, the light bulb burned for thirteen and a half hours. The next day he used a different type of cotton thread, which had also been carbonized. That filament burned for forty hours. Edison and his assistants were jubilant. If they could make a filament that would burn for forty hours, they could make one that would last for a multiple of forty hours.

Edison filed the patent for his invention on November 1, 1879. Later, he was able to make a filament by carbonizing a thread of cellulose extruded from a die. This filament burned longer than the carbonized cotton filament. Also, he found that he could make a filament from carbonized cardboard that would burn for 160 hours.

On New Year's Eve 1879, 3,000 people, most of whom were from New York and Philadelphia, came to Edison's laboratory in Menlo Park, New Jersey. They were transported to Menlo Park by the Pennsylvania Railroad to witness their first view of Edison's incandescent light and to celebrate with him. Newspapers, including the New York *Herald*, gave Edison widespread coverage; the age of the electric light had begun.

ORVILLE WRIGHT (1871-1948) & *WILBUR WRIGHT* (1867-1912) Pioneers of Flight

"Vacillating people seldom succeed. They seldom win the respect of their fellows. Successful men and women are very careful in reaching decisions and very persistent and determined in action later."

L. C. Elliott

In 1903, the year of the Wright brothers successful flight, Professor of Astronomy Simon Newcomb said, "Human flight is not only impossible but illogical." He added that if a flyer managed to get an engine-powered aircraft in the air, he would crash and lose his life: "Once he slackens his speed, down he begins to fall. Once he stops, he falls a dead mass." However, the Wright brothers persevered and succeeded where others had failed "by dauntless resolution and unconquerable faith."[128]

Wilbur Wright, born on April 16, 1867 near Millville, Indiana and Orville Wright, born on August 19, 1871 in Dayton, Ohio were two of seven children of Milton Wright, a bishop of the United Brethren church, and Susan Koerner Wright. Neither Wilbur nor Orville graduated from high school. Wilbur did not graduate because his family moved from Indiana to Ohio before he finished his senior year, and Orville took advanced college preparatory courses in his junior year that prevented him from graduating with his class.

Wilbur and Orville were excellent students who took advantage of an extensive family library to expand their knowledge through comprehensive private study. They excelled in mathematics and science and benefited from growing up in an inquiring, well-educated family. In

December 1892, they opened their first shop to sell and repair bicycles. In 1895, they began to design and build their own because of increased competition in the sale and repair of bicycles.

Wilbur and Orville worked extremely well as a team, and it is unlikely that either would have achieved the success individually that they experienced together. Wilbur noted: "from the time we were little children my brother Orville and myself lived together, played together, worked together and, in fact, thought together. We usually owned all of our toys in common and talked over our thoughts and aspirations so that nearly everything that was done in our lives has been the result of conversations, suggestions, and discussions between us."[129]

In August 1896, while Orville was seriously ill with typhoid fever, Wilbur read about the death of German aviation pioneer Otto Lilienthal, whose back was broken when his kite stalled in a gust of wind and fell fifty feet. Lilienthal had added to the body of aeronautical knowledge, but his means of controlling the craft was limited—the pilot shifted his weight to control the kite.

On May 30, 1899, Wilbur wrote to the Smithsonian Institution requesting information about human flight: "My observations ... have ... convinced me that human flight is possible and practicable." He intended to "begin a systematic study of the subject in preparation for practical work." The Smithsonian's suggested reading list included *The Aeronautical Annual* for 1895, 1896, and 1897, edited by James Means; *Experiments in Aerodynamics* by Samuel Langley; and *Progress in Flying Machines* by Octave Chanute.

To test their ideas about control systems, Wilbur built a small two-winged kite with a wingspan of five feet and a chord (wing width) of thirteen inches. It used a "canard" configuration with the stabilizing surface (elevator) ahead of the wings. With this kite, they tested their concept of "wing warping" to control the craft's roll motion in the air, which in modern aircraft is accomplished by ailerons in the wings. Wilbur demonstrated the concept with an empty cardboard box that had held a bicycle inner tube. The box retained its lateral stiffness when he twisted it. He showed Orville how the idea could be applied to biplane wings.

In August 1900, Wilbur and Orville constructed their first full-sized glider capable of manned flight. The metal struts, wing ribs, and metal fittings were made in Dayton. French sateen fabric was used to cover the ash and spruce frame.

Wilbur asked Octave Chanute and the National Weather Bureau for recommendations on a site for test flights. Wilbur selected Kitty Hawk, North Carolina because of its fifteen-to-twenty-mile-per-hour winds, its lack of hills and trees, and its sandy surface. He traveled to Kitty Hawk ahead of Orville and stayed with the Tate family until he selected a site and pitched a tent. Orville arrived in September.

Wilbur had planned to buy eighteen-foot lengths of spruce en route for use as spars, but the longest he could find were sixteen-foot lengths. They modified their kite's wingspan and used a smaller wing surface area, 165 square feet instead of 200, than they had planned. Wooden bows added to the wing tips increased the wingspan to 17 1/2 feet; wing chord was five feet. The total weight of the craft was fifty-two pounds. Fabric on the 1900 glider was not sealed or varnished as it had been on the 1899 kite.

In October, they flew the tethered glider with a man on board. Young Tom Tate did most of the piloting because he weighed less than Wilbur or Orville. The brothers also flew the glider as a unmanned kite using lines to the ground to control it. In addition, They tried flying it with a fifty-pound ballast. After several days of tests, the glider was caught in a gust of wind and was severely damaged. They considered giving up, but instead they spent the next three days repairing it.

Wilbur and Orville moved the glider to Kill Devil Hills, which was four miles away, to take advantage of higher winds. On October 20, when Wilbur flew the craft, he became the first of the brothers to experience free flight. Wilbur conducted flights of 300 to 400 feet over a duration of fifteen to twenty seconds. The Wrights were disappointed with the lift of the glider, but they realized it was at least partially due to the reduced wing area. After completing the trials, they gave the glider to the Tate family to use for materials and left for Dayton on October 23 with plans to build another glider at Kitty Hawk the following summer.

The 1901 glider was a biplane with a wingspan of twenty-two feet, a chord of seven feet, and a wing area of 290 square feet. The camber (curvature) of the wing was increased. The ninety-eight pound craft was the largest anyone had flown until that time. In Dayton, they hired a machinist, Charlie Taylor, who later designed and built the engine for their 1903 aircraft. In July 1901, Wilbur and Orville traveled to Kitty Hawk, where they constructed a sixteen-foot by twenty-five-foot hangar for their glider.

Wilbur conducted the test flights. The lift and the speed of the new glider were disappointing. Control of pitch was not as responsive as they had hoped, and Wilbur experienced stalls in which the forward stabilizer assisted him in making a safe landing. The brothers sharpened the leading edge of the wing to decrease wind resistance, but the change improved lift and speed only slightly. In August, Wilbur made flights of thirteen seconds or more over distances up to 389 feet.

The wing warping mechanism worked well, but they experienced a reversal in the roll motion of the glider that they could not explain. On one flight, Wilbur was distracted when this occurred, and he did not respond quickly to the controls. He dropped onto the sand abruptly and suffered a black eye and a bruised nose. Soon afterward, they returned to Dayton. On the trip back to Dayton, Wilbur told Orville that "men would not fly for fifty years."

The brothers expanded their shop by adding a band saw and a drill press powered by a one-cylinder engine. Charlie Taylor, whose assistance was essential to their experiments, designed and manufactured their first internal combustion engine. With a machinist like Taylor and the additional equipment, the Wrights were now able to make both bicycle and airplane parts of increased complexity.

Octave Chanute invited the brothers to present a summary of their work to the Western Society of Engineers in Chicago. On September 18, 1901, Wilbur "arrayed in Orv's shirt, cuffs, cuff links, and overcoat" (Orville was a natty dresser, Wilbur a casual dresser) presented his paper, "Some Aeronautical Experiments." The paper was well-received; it became the state-of-the-art reference for aeronautical experimenters.

Wilbur and Orville built a small wind tunnel to check the coefficients required to design their aircraft. The results were so useful that they built a larger wind tunnel, a wooden box measuring sixteen-inches square by six-feet long with a glass observation window on top. They worked for a month to ensure that the thirty-mile-per-hour wind flowed through the tunnel without turbulence. It was not the first wind tunnel, but the discipline they used to apply aerodynamic data directly to the design of aircraft was new. They collected data for a variety of wing configurations to use in lift and drag formulae.

Wilbur and Orville found that the Smeaton coefficient, a factor used in their aerodynamic formula, was off by fifty percent. In addition to studying lift and drag, they also studied the aspect ratio, the ratio of the wingspan to the wing chord. The brothers learned that long narrow wings produce more lift than short wide wings with the same wing area.

In December, they discontinued their experiments and returned to the bicycle business that financed their experiments. Chanute offered to ask Andrew Carnegie to provide financial support for their aeronautical work. However, the Wrights did not want to be indebted to anyone; they chose to finance own experimental work.

Wilbur and Orville designed the 1902 glider with a wingspan of thirty-two feet and a wing chord of five feet (compared with the 1901 wingspan of twenty-two feet and a chord of seven feet) that doubled the aspect ratio. In February 1902, they added a fixed rudder to address the problem of the reversal of the direction of a roll when the wing warping mechanism was applied.

When Wilbur and Orville arrived in Kitty Hawk, they found that the force of high winds and wind-driven sand had virtually destroyed their hangar. They rebuilt a sturdier and more comfortable structure. On September 19, the 1902 glider with 305 square feet of wing area was ready for its first test. The new glider had a forward elevator of fifteen square feet and a longer, narrower rudder than the 1901 glider and weighed almost 120 pounds. The first tests were unmanned; they made fifty tests covering distances of under 200 feet during the first two days.

In the first manned flights, Wilbur encountered cross-winds that affected the lateral stability more severely than on previous models. The brothers addressed the problem by adjusting the wing trusses and causing the tips of the wings to droop about four inches. A crosswind could not catch a wingtip as easily as before. Orville began to make flights at this point. On one of his early attempts, he lost control at an altitude of thirty feet with disastrous results for the glider. Fortunately, Orville was unhurt. The craft was rebuilt in three days.

The reversal of the roll motion when the wing warping mechanism was applied, the cause of Orville's crash, was a recurring problem. It is now called a tailspin. In the middle of the night, Orville thought of a solution to the problem. In the morning, he suggested to Wilbur that they install a movable rudder to compensate for the sudden change in direction. Wilbur agreed with the solution but suggested that the rudder control be coupled with the wing warping control because the pilot already had enough on his mind.

Evolution of the controls of Wright airplanes was now complete. Three-axis motion could now be controlled; that is, the pilot could regulate pitch, roll, and yaw. The Wright Brothers had invented the first truly controllable aircraft and were ready for powered flight. On October 28, they went home to Dayton.

The Wright's first patent, which they had filed at the end of 1902, was denied because it lacked clarity. Even though they had hired a patent attorney to help them, they were not granted a patent until May 1906. It described the principles demonstrated by the 1902 glider and included no references to powered aircraft.

During the winter of 1902-03, the Wright brothers designed the aircraft that they called the "Flyer"; they calculated that the airplane would weigh 625 pounds with a pilot, assuming that the engine and propellers weighed 200 pounds. No commercially available four-cycle engine met their specifications of eight or nine horsepower with a weight of under 180 pounds. Charlie Taylor designed a four-cylinder, twelve-horsepower engine with cast-iron cylinders in a cast-aluminum crankcase cooled by a water jacket; it had no radiator or water pump because the water did not circulate.

The Wrights chose two pusher propellers mounted behind the wings, and they connected the contra-rotating propellers with the engine using bicycle sprocket and chain technology. The efficiency of existing propellers disappointed them; they realized they would have to design their own. Wilbur and Orville considered propellers to be wings that moved in a rotary motion. The propellers were 8 1/2 feet in diameter and were made from three laminations of 1 1/8-inch spruce. The 1903 craft had a wingspan of forty-four feet and four inches, a 6 1/2-foot chord, and a wing area of 510 square feet.

In September 1903, the Wrights left for Kitty Hawk. Over the next three months, they experienced bad weather, many technical problems, and some disappointing flights with the 1902 glider. The loaded weight of the 1903 aircraft had increased from 625 to 700 pounds. The engine misfired frequently, placing severe strain on the propeller shafts. The damaged shafts had to be returned to Dayton for repair. The reinstalled shafts shook loose the nuts holding the sprockets in position. Bicycle cement on the nuts solved that problem.

The steel-tube propeller shafts broke again, and Orville returned to Dayton to make new shafts out of solid spring steel. He returned on December 11, and, three days later, Wilbur won the coin toss to fly the plane on its first lift-off from the sixty-foot-long launching rail.

The "Flyer" lifted off the rail (used to guide the craft during take-off) at the forty-foot point, reached an altitude of fifteen feet, stalled, and dropped onto the sand, damaging the forward elevator and one of the skids. This 3 1/2 second flight over 100 feet was not considered a real flight. Wilbur had not anticipated the sensitivity of the elevator, and he had over-controlled the craft.

On December 17, the temperature was freezing and the wind was blowing at twenty-seven miles per hour. It was Orville's turn to pilot the airplane; the brothers shook hands as though they were not going to see each other again. At 10:35 a.m., the "Flyer" lifted off after traveling about forty feet and flew 120 feet in twelve seconds.

This flight was considered the first true flight. Orville commented: "This flight lasted only twelve seconds, but it was nevertheless the first in the history of the world in which a machine carrying a man had raised itself by its own power into the air in full flight, had sailed forward without a reduction in speed, and had finally landed at a point as high as that from which it started."[130]

Wilbur flew the second flight of the day over a distance of 175 feet, followed by Orville in a flight of over 200 feet that lasted fifteen seconds. Wilbur flew the "Flyer" on the last flight of the day—a flight of 852 feet with a duration of 59 seconds. While they were discussing the flights, a gust of wind overturned the "Flyer," breaking spars, struts, most of the wing ribs, and the engine crankcase. No more flights were conducted in 1903; however, the Wright brothers had accomplished their goal of pioneering powered flight.

In 1904 and 1905 the brothers built two more powered aircraft to continue with their experiments. However, they moved their test flights from Kitty Hawk to Huffman Prairie, eight miles from Dayton. The success of the last 1903 flight was not matched until the forty-ninth flight in 1904. On September 20, 1904, they made their first circular flight; it lasted ninety-six seconds and covered 4,080 feet. On October 5, 1905, Wilbur circled the field thirty times in thirty-nine minutes covering a distance of 24 1/2 miles.

In 1908 and 1909, the brothers successfully marketed their aircraft in the United States and Europe through sales and licensing agreements. In 1910, they established the Wright Company for manufacturing aircraft, conducting exhibitions, and training pilots. Orville ran the company while Wilbur fought patent infringement suits. Weakened by the strain of the legal process, Wilbur died on May 30, 1912, four weeks after contracting typhoid fever.

In 1914, Orville brought the suits to successful conclusion. The following year, he sold his interest in the Wright Company and retired a wealthy man. Orville lived a long, quiet life in retirement. He suffered a heart attack and died on January 27, 1948.

The Erie Canal at Schoen Place, Pittsford, NY

CHAPTER 4

ORGANIZERS / PLANNERS

"The star of unconquered will
He rises in my breast,
Serene, resolute, and still.
And calm, and self-possessed."

Henry Wadsworth Longfellow, *The Light of Stars*

Chapter 4 provides examples of individuals who were highly organized and had a plan in life. Each of these five people furnishes us with an answer to the question, "What can one person accomplish?"

DeWitt Clinton served multiple terms as Mayor of New York City and as Governor of New York. He is universally recognized as the driving force behind the building of the Erie Canal, which helped to open the Midwest to settlement and commerce. Governor Clinton convinced New York taxpayers to proceed on their own when the U.S. Government rejected a request for financing to build the Canal. The Canal was called "Clinton's folly" and "Clinton's ditch," but it was economically more successful than his wildest dreams. The Erie Canal put the word "Empire" in the Empire State.

Thomas Garrett, leader of the underground railroad in Delaware, was a Quaker who believed in being judged by what he did, not by what he said. He helped hundreds of slaves escape through Wilmington, Delaware to the North and freedom. He was indicted for his role in aiding escaped slaves, which was against the law, and had his business taken away from him. His response to this severe fine was, "If you know of any downtrodden who need help, please send them to me."

Levi Coffin, leader of the underground railroad in Ohio, used the profits of his family business to help slaves escape to the North and to Canada. On one occasion, he received a letter from a man in Kentucky who threatened to burn down the entire town in which he lived. He and his neighbors went to bed at the usual time that night and slept soundly. No fires were reported. From his strategic location on the Ohio River in Cincinnati, Coffin and his wife helped hundreds to escape from the yoke of slavery.

Andrew White was one of those fortunate individuals who had an idea, planned its implementation, successfully implemented it, and lived to see it thrive. The idea was to establish a quality university in central New York State that offered a curriculum of courses in agriculture, mechanical arts, and science balanced with courses in classics and the humanities and staffed with the best available professors. White had this idea as a young professor at the University of Michigan. He promoted his concept until Ezra Cornell provided the endowment that allowed his dream to happen.

Simon Wiesenthal suffered at the hands of the Nazis in concentration camps during World War II. He experienced firsthand one of the most horrible cases of man's inhumanity to man. After World War II, he worked with the Allied armies to track German war criminals. When the Allied armies went home, Wiesenthal continued to pursue war criminals. One of his most notable successes was tracking down Adolf Eichmann, who had planned the deaths of millions of Jews. Wiesenthal was motivated not by revenge but by the need to keep the world from forgetting. He felt that if we forget what had happened, it might happen again.

These individuals were achievers who overcame many obstacles to reach their goals.

DeWITT CLINTON (1769-1828) Father of the Erie Canal

"Has thou attempted greatness? Then go on; back-turning slackens resolution."

Herrick, *Regression Spoils Resolution*

The idea of building a canal across New York westward from Albany had been around for years in at least two versions. One alternative was to use Lake Ontario for the central and western portions of the canal route instead of digging across the entire state. The Lake Ontario route was rejected because of the possibility of giving up partial control to Canada. DeWitt Clinton may not have originated the idea of building a canal across New York State; however, as Governor of New York, he was in a position to make it happen.

DeWitt Clinton, second son of James and Mary DeWitt Clinton, was born in Little Britain, New York on March 2, 1769. DeWitt's father, James Clinton, was a Major General in the Continental Army and was second in command to Major General John Sullivan, who subdued the Iroquois Confederation in his campaign through the Finger Lakes Region in 1779.

In 1786, DeWitt graduated first in his class from Columbia College. He studied law, was admitted to the bar, and was authorized to practice before the New York State Supreme Court. After three years of legal training, he became private secretary to his uncle, George Clinton, who was the first Governor of New York. In 1797, Clinton was elected to the State Assembly and the following year to a four-year term in the State Senate.

In February 1802, Clinton was appointed to finish an

incumbent Senator's term in the U.S. Senate. He resigned in October 1803 to become Mayor of New York City. With the exception of two years, the annual terms of 1807-08 and 1810-11, he was the Mayor of New York from 1803 to 1815. As Mayor, he was the organizer of the Public School Society, patron of the New York Orphan Asylum, and chief sponsor of the New York City Hospital. While concurrently serving as Mayor, he was also a State Senator from 1806 to 1811 and Lieutenant-Governor from 1811 to 1813.

In 1815, when Clinton completed his last term as Mayor, he devoted himself to promoting the project of building a canal from the Great Lakes to the Hudson River. A short canal between the Mohawk River and Wood Creek had already been constructed, and additional canals had been discussed by Gouverneur Morris since 1803. Morris had reviewed his ideas with Simeon DeWitt, Surveyor-General of the State of New York. Both thought that building a canal across the state was feasible.

In 1807, Jesse Hawley of Canandaigua wrote and published a series of essays promoting construction of a canal from Lake Erie to Utica on the Mohawk River. In 1808, State Legislator Joshua Forman proposed that the Lake Erie canal route be surveyed. The Surveyor-General commissioned James Geddes of Syracuse to survey the route. Geddes also thought that it would be practical to build a canal across the state as far west as Lake Erie. Forman traveled to Washington, D.C. in an unsuccessful attempt to obtain federal funds for the New York canal project. President Jefferson thought that it was "a very fine project that might be executed a century hence."

Clinton read all of the material about canals that he could find, including Hawley's essays and a history of European waterways. On March 13, 1810, both houses of the State Legislature voted for the formation of the Canal Commission and for an investigation of the practicality of a New York State canal. Clinton was one of the seven members of the Canal Commission.

In 1811, members of the Canal Commission traveled along the prospective canal routes on horseback. Conditions were primitive, but they wanted to investigate personally the alternative routes. In 1812, Clinton made a strong but unsuccessful run for the presidency against James Madison on an independent ticket in an attempt to strike a balance between Democrats and Federalists.

On June 3, 1817, the Canal Commission received bids for work on the canal and selected contractors. That year, Clinton was elected Governor of New York to succeed Daniel Tompkins, who had been elected Vice President of the United States. On July 4, 1817, Clinton had the honor of digging the first spadeful of earth at Rome to initiate the construction of the middle section of the Canal. Clinton was Governor until 1822, when he lost the election to Robert Yates; he regained the office in 1824.

On April 12, 1824, as the result of maneuvering by his political opponents, Clinton was removed from his position on the Canal Commission. The maneuver backfired; the populace rebelled at the removal of the Canal's strongest supporter from the Commission. After all, the project was called "Clinton's Ditch."

In 1825, the Erie Canal was completed—two years after its original scheduled completion date and approximately $2 million over the original cost estimate. Those who had told Clinton that it would be an economic failure were wrong; it was a resounding economic success. On October 26, 1825,

Governor DeWitt Clinton presided at the opening of the Erie Canal in ceremonies from Buffalo to New York. Clinton traveled the length of the Canal on the leading canalboat, the *Seneca Chief*. Firing of cannons and cheering of crowds were heard all along the route. Two barrels of water were transported from Lake Erie to New York to be poured into the Atlantic Ocean in a "wedding of the waters" ceremony.

Clinton's crowning achievement was sponsoring the construction of the Erie Canal. He was a naturalist and a man of many accomplishments, including serving as President of the American Academy of Art and the New York Historical Society and co-founding the Literary and Philosophical Society. He was also active in the Humane Society, the Lyceum of National History, and the Society for the Promotion of Useful Arts.

On February 11, 1828, Clinton, an exhausted man, died of a heart attack. In some respects, he had the qualifications to reach high national office. He was an honest, industrious man, but his personality prevented him from achieving his potential. He could be sarcastic and tactless, and he governed in an autocratic manner. Clinton was unwilling to share the powers the his office with strong lieutenants. He sneered at those who did not share his vision of a waterway across the state to open up the Midwest and West. However, by any criteria, he achieved many goals and lived a life of accomplishment.

THOMAS GARRETT (1789-1871) Underground Railroad Leader in Delaware

> "In life's small things be resolute and great.
> To keep thy muscle trained: know'st thou when Fate
> Thy measure takes, or when she'll say to thee,
> 'I find thee worthy; do this deed for me.'"
>
> James Russell Lowell

Thomas Garrett, who helped over 2,900 slaves escape to the North, was highly regarded by his peers. Abolitionist William Lloyd Garrison expressed his feelings upon Garrett's death in a letter to one of his sons: "In view of his ... singularly beneficent life, there is no cause for sorrow, but [I would like] to express the estimation in which I held him, as one of the best men who ever walked the earth, and one of the most beloved among my numerous friends and co-workers in the cause of the oppressed and downtrodden race, now happily rejoicing in their heavenly wrought deliverance."[131]

Thomas Garrett, one of eleven children of Thomas and Sarah Price Garrett, was born in Upper Darby, Pennsylvania on August 21, 1789. Thomas, Sr. operated mills and was a scythe- and tool-maker. Young Thomas worked in his father's businesses.

Garrett's motivation to spend a lifetime supporting anti-slavery causes began when he was twenty-four-years old and still living at home with his parents. He had returned home one day to find his mother and sisters distressed. Two men had come to the house and kidnapped an African-American woman who worked for the family. He pursued their wagon following marks made by a broken wheel. He tracked them to the Navy Yard and then to Kensington, where the men had stopped at a roadside tavern. He found the kidnapped woman in the kitchen of the tavern and returned with her to Upper Darby.

During the time he was pursuing the kidnappers and while riding home, Garrett thought about the wrongs of the slavery system. It was wrong that men thought that they had a right to enter a home and carry off a woman against her will. He made a resolution to aid oppressed slaves in any way that he could.

On October 14, 1813, Garrett married Mary Sharpless of Birmingham, Pennsylvania, and, in 1822, they moved to Wilmington, Delaware, a thriving town with plenty of opportunity for an ambitious young man. Garrett opened an iron, steel, and coal business. He had early difficulties, which are described by James A. McGowan in *Station Master on the Underground Railroad*:

> A rival house ... in the iron business, sought to run him off the track by reducing the price of iron to cost, but Friend Thomas, nothing daunted, employed a man to take his place in the store, tied on his leather apron, took to his hammer and anvil and in the prosecution of the trade learned from his father prepared to support his family with his own hands as long as the run lasted. Thus, by the sweat of his brow, he foiled the purpose of his rival and laid the foundation of what after many reverses became one of the permanent business houses of the city.[132]

Garrett had few close friends and was looked upon with suspicion; his house was under constant surveillance by the police, who realized that it was a station on the underground railroad. He was not bothered by this lack of popularity or by adverse opinion because he knew that the Lord approved of his activities. Garrett believed in doing his duty. He thought that a man's duty is shown to him and that duty, once recognized, was an obligation. His approach to life was summarized by Geoffrey Hubbard a century later, "Every Quaker defines his position fully and clearly by his life."

Garrett had a powerful physique and considerable personal bravery. He had no fear of the proslavery supporters who attempted to bully him. An example of his fearlessness was his response to a supporter of slavery who told Garrett that if he ever came to his town, he would shoot him. Garrett responded, "Well, I think of going that way before long, and I will call upon thee." He called upon the man as he had promised. Garrett said, "How does thee do friend? Here I am, thee can shoot me if thee likes."[133] He was not shot.

Men confronted Garrett flourishing pistols and bowie knives. He pushed them aside and told them that only cowards resorted to such measures. On one occasion, two men were overheard planning to kill him:

> He was warned, but having a meeting to attend
> that night, he went out as usual. In the street
> two men leaped upon him, but his brawny
> hands caught them by the backs of their necks
> and brought them up standing. He shook them
> well and looked them over, then said, "I think
> you look hungry. Come in and I will give you
> supper." He forced them into his house and his
> wife prepared a warm supper, while Friend
> Thomas chaffed them about their adventure,
> and turned the enmity into friendship.[134]

On another occasion, he boarded a train in Wilmington to prevent an African-American woman from being carried off to the deep South. Several southerners attempted unsuccessfully to throw him off the train. At one point, a reward of $10,000 was offered for him in Maryland. He wrote to the parties offering the reward and told them that this was not enough. For $20,000, he would turn himself in.

On July 13, 1828, Garrett's wife, Mary, died. She had been his partner in underground railroad work. On January 7, 1830, he married Rachel Mendinhall, daughter of a Quaker merchant who was a director of the National Bank of Delaware & Brandywine. Perhaps due to her ill health, Rachel stayed in the background and was not as active a participant as Mary had been in antislavery activities.

In 1848, eight African Americans—a man, his wife, and six children—ran away from a plantation on the eastern shore of Maryland. Except for two of the children who had been born in slavery, they were free. They sought refuge at the home of a wealthy Quaker in Middletown, Delaware. Unfortunately, they had been followed. They were arrested and sent to jail in New Castle. The Sheriff and his daughter, who were antislavery supporters, notified Garrett of their plight.

Garrett visited them in jail in New Castle and returned to Wilmington. The following day, he and U.S. Senator Wales presented Judge Boothe with a writ of *habeas corpus*. Judge Booth decided that there was no evidence to hold them, and, in the absence of evidence, "the presumption was always in favor of freedom." He discharged them. Garrett said, "Here is this woman with a babe at her breast, and the child suffering from a white swelling on its leg; is there any impropriety in my getting a carriage and helping them over to Wilmington?"

Judge Boothe responded, "Certainly not."[135]

Six weeks later, the slaveholders filed a suit against Garrett in New Castle for helping fugitive slaves escape. The trial, presided over by Judge Hall and Chief Justice Taney in May 1848, lasted three days. Garrett's friends suspected that the jury had been stacked against him. He was convicted, and every dollar of his property was taken from him. He responded, "Now, Judge, I do not think that I have always done my duty, being fearful of losing what little I possessed; but now that you have relieved me, I will go home and put another story on my house, so that I can accommodate more of God's poor."[136]

Garrett's friends helped him in his time of difficulty. He was almost sixty years old, but he made the addition to his house and increased his support of escaped slaves. His activities were aided by donations from friends in England. He continued to work to help the slaves until President Abraham Lincoln freed them in 1863 by signing the Emancipation Proclamation.

Thomas Garrett died on January 25, 1871. During his lifetime, he had helped just under 3,000 slaves on their journey to the North. Not one of these slaves was captured on the road to freedom. The exception was a slave who escaped, lived in Canada for a number of years, and returned to Wilmington to preach. He was seized and returned to bondage.

Throughout his life, Garrett lived his principles: "I should have done violence to my convictions of duty, had I not made use of all the lawful means in my power to liberate those people, and assist them to become men and women, rather than leave them in the condition of chattels...."

LEVI COFFIN (1798-1877) Leader of the Underground Railroad in Ohio

"His way once chose, he forward thrust outright,
Nor stepped aside for dangers or delight."

Abraham Cowley, *Davideis IV*

The underground railroad was a risky undertaking both for the escaped slaves, who did not know whether the next door they knocked on would be opened by a friend or a foe, and the stationmasters, who were subjected to fine and imprisonment if caught. Levi Coffin in *Reminiscences of Levi Coffin,* describes the arrival of slaves at his home:

> We knew not what night or what hour of the night we would be roused from slumber by a gentle rap at the door.... Outside in the cold or the rain, there would be a two-horse wagon loaded with fugitives, perhaps the greater part of them women and children. I would invite them, in a low tone, to come in, and they would follow me into the house without a word, for we knew not who might be watching and listening. When all were safely inside and the door fastened, I would cover the windows, strike a light and build a good fire.
>
> By this time my wife would be up and preparing victuals for them, and in a short time the cold and hungry fugitives would be made comfortable.... The fugitives would rest on pallets before the fire the rest of the night. Frequently, wagon-loads of passengers from the different lines have met at our house, hav-

ing no previous knowledge of each other. The companies varied in number, from two or three fugitives to seventeen.[137]

Levi Coffin, youngest of seven children, was born in 1798 in New Garden, North Carolina. His lifelong antislavery convictions were formed at the age of seven when he watched slaves, handcuffed in pairs on each side of a long chain that extended between them, driven by a man on horseback with a long whip. Levi's father asked the slaves, "Well, boys, why do they chain you?" One of the slaves replied, "They have taken us away from our wives and children, and they chain us lest we should make our escape and go back to them."[138]

Young Levi asked his father many questions about the slaves that had just passed by. Levi Coffin, Sr. described the institution of slavery to his young son without justifying it, because he could not. Running through Levi's mind was the thought of how he, his mother, and his sisters would feel if his father were taken from them.

A second incident of his boyhood impressed Levi with the injustice of slavery. He and his father went to the shad fishery at the narrows of the Tadkin River, where rapids were formed as the river flowed over a rocky bed through wild forest growth. The shad ascended the river each spring, and fishermen from all around the region came there. Owners of the fishery permitted their slaves to fish after the other fisherman were finished and to sell the fish that they caught after hours. Levi's father bought fish from a slave the first night that they arrived.

The next morning, the slave walked up to Levi's father and asked if he would be interested in buying more fish that evening. One of the owner's nephews thought that the slave was being impertinent. The nephew picked a burning log from the fire and struck the slave a severe blow to the side of the head, baring his skull, covering his chest and back with blood, and setting his hair on fire.

Levi's father protested this brutality. Young Levi was unable to eat his breakfast that morning; he went off by himself and cried about "man's inhumanity to man." These instances inspired Coffin's hatred of slavery and made him resolve to do what he could to remedy the inequity between free people and slaves.

Coffin worked on the family farm until he was twenty-one, when he began teaching school. On October 28, 1824, he married Catherine White, a fellow member of the Society of Friends (Quakers). Levi and Catherine had grown up in the same neighborhood and had known each other since childhood. Catherine shared Coffin's interest in aiding the slaves, and she became an active supporter of the underground railroad.

In 1825, Coffin's parents and youngest sister moved to Indiana, where some of his married sisters lived. Coffin, Catherine, and their son, Jesse, followed them to Indiana early the following year. Coffin opened a mercantile business in Newport, Indiana, which he expanded during the twenty years that they lived there. In 1836, he added a linseed oil mill, but he was never too busy to participate in underground railroad activities.

Coffin was warned by friends that his underground railroad efforts put his life and his business interests at risk. He replied, "I told them that I felt no condemnation for anything that I had ever done for the fugitive slaves." Many of his pro-slavery customers left him, but new customers who moved into the area took their places.

Three underground railroad routes from the South converged at the Coffin house in Newport, Indiana: one from Cincinnati, one from Madison, and one from Jeffersonville, Indiana. Coffin had a team of horses and a wagon available at all times. Coffin received many threats because of his underground railroad activity. Pro-slavery supporters threatened to burn down his house, his store, and his pork-house.

In the spring of 1847, Levi and Catherine Coffin moved to Cincinnati. Coffin knew many abolitionists in Cincinnati and had attended many of their meetings on his trips to the city. He was not sure how much underground railroad work he would do there; however, in a short period of time, he and Catherine were even busier than they had been in Indiana. They bought a large house in Cincinnati, which was suitable for their underground railroad activities. Refugees could be hidden in the upper rooms of the house for weeks, and even boarders and visitors would not know that they were there.

Underground railroad activities were brisk in Cincinnati until the outbreak of the Civil War and for about a year afterwards, until slaves were received and protected inside Union lines. With the ratification of the Fifteenth Amendment to the Constitution stating that citizens shall not be denied the right to vote on account of race, color, or previous position of servitude, Coffin was honored at a public gathering. The attendees paid tribute to Coffin for holding the position of President of the Underground Railroad for thirty years. At the conclusion of the meeting, he resigned his position and terminated the operations of the underground railroad.

Levi Coffin died at Avondale, near Cincinnati, on September 16, 1877. He had been in ill health for over a year. The Cincinnati *Daily Gazette* described his funeral service: "The funeral of Levi Coffin, the philanthropist, drew an overflowing audience to the Friends Meeting House ... Among the congregation were several of his surviving associates in anti-slavery work, his associates in the Freedman's Aid Commission, and dusky tear-bedewed faces of members of the once oppressed race, for whose emancipation he strove so long and earnestly."[139]

The Reverend Dr. Rust, secretary of the Freedman's Aid Society, paid tribute to his friend's thorough unselfishness:

> He had too great a mission to perform to spare any time to take care of himself, and God took care of him. He was an honest, wise, and judicious man—wise in selecting the most practical and judicious methods. He was a brave and courageous man. It would take less bravery to go up to the cannon's mouth than to do the work that he did. As he walked through the streets, he was hooted at and threatened by mobs. The battlefield has no such illustrations of heroism as he exhibited every day. There is no American name more honored and revered in England than Levi Coffin. It is embalmed in the heart of every philanthropist in Britain. He has gone home.[140]

The Reverend Rust wondered if the first to meet Levi Coffin on the other side were not hundreds of those men and women whom he had helped escape from bondage to freedom.

ANDREW WHITE (1832-1918) Cornell University Founder

"You can do what you want to do, accomplish what you want to accomplish, attain any reasonable objective you may have in mind.... Not all of a sudden, perhaps, not in one swift and sweeping act of achievement.... But you can do it gradually— day by day and play by play—if you WANT to do it, if you WILL to do it, and if you WORK to do it, over a sufficiently long time."

George P. Burnham

Ezra Cornell, the benefactor for whom Cornell University is named, had a straightforward, egalitarian outlook: "I would found a university where any person can receive instruction in any subject." Andrew Dickson White, educator, historian, and diplomat, had a loftier goal in mind:

> America's future would be secure if it became more of a thoroughgoing meritocracy. If everyone had fair access to an education and if government were reserved for talented men, no further changes would be necessary. Thus, although he was a social and political conservative, White regarded himself as a reformer. As President of Cornell University, he helped to democratize higher education and to train enlightened public servants. Education was his panacea, to be used to persuade advocates of massive social change that their efforts were unnecessary and destructive.[141]

Andrew Dickson White, the first President of Cornell University, was born in Homer, New York on November 7, 1832. His parents were Horace White, a banker, and Clara Dickson White. White's grandfather was a wealthy pillar of the Homer community and a member of the State Legislature. In 1839, the White family moved to Syracuse, where Andrew attended the Syracuse Academy and later the advanced Syracuse Classical High School. He was editor of the high school magazine, *The Bee*.

Horace White insisted that his son attend Geneva College, which was the predecessor of Hobart College, because of its Congregationalist affiliation. White was not academically challenged by the school and left after one year. He was admitted to Yale University as a sophomore. In his senior year, he was editor of the *Yale Literary Magazine* and won the DeForest Prize for his oration, "The Diplomatic History of Modern Times," an early indication of his interest in diplomacy.

After graduating, White accompanied Connecticut Governor Thomas Seymour, the newly appointed Minister to Russia, to St. Petersburg as his attaché. White visited Oxford and Paris on the way to Russia; he lingered in France for several months to improve his fluency in French, the diplomatic language of Russia.

In the summer of 1855, White left Russia and enrolled at the University of Berlin in the fall. He was impressed with German scholarship and observed: "In America, the course of studies is incomplete ... the school is more splendid in England, and the scholarship is more splendid in Germany." He traveled through France, Italy, and Switzerland and added 700 books to his personal library.

In 1856, White returned to Yale to study for a Master of Arts degree. Upon receiving the degree, he accepted a position as Professor of History and Rhetoric at the University of Michigan in Ann Arbor. He was revered by his students, who were not much younger than he was. White agreed with the concepts of Henry Tappan, the President of the University of Michigan: the importance of non-sectarianism, the education of women, and the equal value of classics and the humanities compared to agriculture, law, mechanics, and medicine. Also, White liked Tappan's practice of inviting guest lecturers to the campus, such as George William Curtis, Ralph Waldo Emerson, Wendell Phillips, and Carl Shurz.

George William Curtis, while visiting Ann Arbor as a guest lecturer, was told of White's ambition to establish a great university in central New York. White envisioned a university serving a broad scope of interests. It should begin with agriculture and grow until it fulfilled the highest ideals of a university. The best teachers should be assembled from all over the world to serve it. The young scholar continued his outpouring to Curtis until the hour was late, concluding with the observation that we live in a country open to ideas and that some day his dream might be realized.

In 1860, Horace White died, leaving White $300,000 as his portion of the estate. In the summer of 1862, White obtained a leave of absence from the University of Michigan due to ill health and the need to settle his father's estate. He tried to enlist in the Union Army but was rejected for health reasons. He returned to Syracuse and busied himself with war work.

In the fall of 1862, White went to Europe to take health cures for his severe indigestion problems. After returning, he was elected to the State Senate from his Syracuse district and appointed Chairman of the Committee on Literature, which dealt with education issues. He met Ezra Cornell, the Chairman of the Committee on Agriculture, in the Senate.

One winter day, Cornell and White met on the Capitol steps and walked down Albany's State Street together.

Cornell asked White: "I have about a half-million dollars more than my family will need; what is the best thing I can do with it for the state?"[142] White told Cornell of his dream of founding a great university:

> Mr. Cornell, the two things most worthy of aid in any country are charity and education; but, in our country, the charities appeal to everybody. Anyone can understand the importance of them, and the worthy poor or unfortunate are sure to be taken care of. As to education, the lower grades will always be cared for in the public schools by the State; but the institutions of highest grade, without which the lower can never be thoroughly good, can be appreciated by only a few. The policy of our State is to leave this part of the system to the individuals; it seems to me, then, if you have a half million to give, the best thing you can do with it is to establish or strengthen some institution for higher instruction.[143]

Cornell took the young State Senator's advice. On February 7, 1865, White introduced a bill to the State Senate "to establish Cornell University, and to appropriate to it the income from the sale of public land granted to this State." On April 27, 1865, Governor Reuben E. Fenton signed the bill, and the fledgling university was born.

White wrote the University bylaws and, on October 21, 1866, submitted a Plan of Organization to the University Board of Trustees. The Honorable Andrew D. White of Syracuse was unanimously elected President of Cornell University. He observed, in a moment of self-deception: "Nothing was further from my expectations or wishes." On

October 8, 1868, the first class of students was admitted to Cornell University.

In the early years, the University's endowment had three components: Ezra Cornell's gift of $500,000, called the Founder's Fund; New York State's College Land Scrip Fund, money from the sale of land scrip by New York State to Ezra Cornell; and the Cornell Endowment Fund, which was money from the sale of land such as Wisconsin timberland.

White alternated between an academic and a diplomatic career. He served as Commissioner to Santo Domingo, Minister and Ambassador to Germany, Minister to Russia, and as head of the U.S. delegation to the Hague Peace Conference in 1899. Between 1872 and 1900, his name was frequently proposed as a candidate for Governor of New York. However, he had no aspirations to deal with the State's politics. In 1885, he retired as President of Cornell University.

Andrew Dickson White was frequently mentioned as a candidate for Secretary of State, but he was never appointed. In 1884, he was a dark horse candidate for the Republican nomination for President, but James G. Blaine was nominated. In 1900, he was proposed as the Republican candidate for Vice President, but he was sixty-eight years old and bothered by health problems, so he demurred. Theodore Roosevelt was nominated and elected Vice President. In 1901, President McKinley was assassinated at the Buffalo Exposition, and the Rough Rider became President.

White died on November 4, 1918. Cornell University was fortunate to have had a person with White's vision as its first President.

Statue of Andrew Dickson White, Cornell University, Ithaca, NY

SIMON WIESENTHAL (1908-   ) Pursuer of Nazi Criminals

"The hardest rock will yield to those who drill with determination."

Talmud: Sukhah, 53a

After World War II, Simon Wiesenthal worked to bring Nazis to trial for their war crimes. Nazis had been responsible for the deaths of at least 11 million innocent men, women, and children: 6 million Jews and 5 million Yugoslavs, Russians, Poles, Czechs, Dutch, French, and other nationalities and ethnic groups.

When asked what motivated his pursuit of Nazi criminals, Wiesenthal responded:

> My friends say: "Why do you torture yourself with these things?" My non-friends put it more succinctly: "Do you have to rake up the past, piling new hatred upon old?" Why don't I go back to my prewar profession of building houses? I could have gone to America, led a normal life, and made money. It's no use, I *have* to do it. I am not motivated by a sense of revenge.
>
> Perhaps for a short time in the very beginning. At the end of the war, when I was liberated after almost four years in more than a dozen concentration camps, I had little strength left, but I did have a strong desire for revenge. I'd lost my whole family. My mother had been taken away before my eyes. I thought my wife was dead. I had no one to live for.

> Most liberated camp inmates reacted different-
> ly. They wanted to forget so they could live
> again. They surrounded themselves with a pro-
> tective shell, trying hard not to think of what
> had happened. Even before I had time to think
> things through, I realized that *we must not for-
> get*. If all of us forgot, the same thing might
> happen again, in twenty, or fifty, or a hundred
> years.[144]

Simon Wiesenthal was born on December 31, 1908 in Buczacs, Galicia, which at that time was part of the Austro-Hungarian Empire. Two-thirds of the residents of Buczacs were Jews who lived in town; the Ukrainians lived in the countryside. Simon's father fought in the Austrian army in World War I and was killed in action in 1915. Young Simon went to Vienna to attend public school. In 1920, during the Polish-Russian War, Russian-Ukrainian Cossacks attacked Buczacs. The Poles defeated the Ukrainians, and Buczacs became part of Poland.

In 1925, Wiesenthal's mother remarried and the family moved to Dolina in the Carpathian Mountains, the location of his stepfather's tile factory. Wiesenthal applied to the Technical Institute of Lwow, the nearest large city in Poland. He was rejected because the quota for Jewish students had already been filled. He enrolled at the Czech Technological Institute in Prague, where he majored in architecture. He walked erectly and had a way of looking directly at everyone with whom he spoke. He had a good sense of humor and was well-liked by his fellow students, Gentiles and Jews.

After receiving his degree in architecture, Wiesenthal established an architectural practice in Lwow, concentrating on designing homes rather than commercial buildings. In 1936, his practice prospered sufficiently for him to marry Cyla Muller, his attractive, blond sweetheart from high school. The happy couple was aware of the changes occurring in Germany during the 1930s, but they thought that they were far enough away to be unaffected by those events.

In 1933, Adolf Hitler was named Chancellor of Germany and one year later declared himself head of the German State with dictatorial powers. In 1935, the "Nuremberg Laws" were passed in Germany, stripping Jews of all rights as citizens. They were required to register as Jews and were not permitted to marry Gentiles. Jewish students were disenrolled from colleges and universities.

In 1936, Hitler's Army invaded the Rhineland, the demilitarized zone on the border between France and Germany. France protested but took no further action. On February 12, 1938, Hitler invited the Austrian Chancellor to Berchtesgaden to threaten him. The Chancellor was told to remove the restrictions on the Nazi Party in Austria or Germany would take over Austria. On March 12, Austria had a new Chancellor, Seyss-Inquart, a Hitler appointee, and the Anschluss was announced, incorporating Austria into the German Reich.

When German troops marched into Austria, crowds cheered them yelling, "Austria awake! Judah (Jews) Perish! The Nuremberg Laws now applied to Austria. On November 9, led by the SS (Schutzstaffel—the elite corps of the Nazi Party), soldiers and civilians burned synagogues and smashed windows and destroyed Jewish-owned businesses and homes. It was called Kristallnacht, "Crystal Night," because of all the shattered glass that littered sidewalks and streets. Jews were beaten and were forced to crawl through the broken glass.

Next, Hitler marched into western Czechoslovakia, and, on September 1, 1939, his Army invaded Poland. Lwow, where the Wiesenthals lived, was in the Soviet zone. Temporarily, the Wiesenthals thought they were safe from the Germans because of the non-aggression pact Hitler had signed with Russia. However, Soviet rule was not entirely safe; businessmen and professional men were suspected of being enemies of Communism. Wiesenthal's stepfather was arrested, motivating his stepson to close his architectural practice and accept a job as a mechanic in a bedspring factory.

In 1941, Hitler broke his non-aggression pact with Russia and invaded the Soviet Union. Lwow was overrun by the Germans, who killed 6,000 Jews in the first several days of their occupation. Wiesenthal's wife and mother stayed in their apartment, but he and a friend were found hiding in a basement and taken to Brigidki prison.

With forty other prisoners, they were ordered to line up facing a wall with their hands behind their backs. A member of the German SS went down the line shooting each prisoner in the back of the neck. Each of them stood next to a wooden crate that became their coffin. When Wiesenthal's turn approached, the evening church bells rang, reminding the guards that it was time for dinner. Executions stopped for the day.

Surviving prisoners were placed in two large cells. Wiesenthal heard someone say, "Mr. Wiesenthal, what are you doing in there?" An auxiliary policeman named Bodnar who had been the construction foreman of several of the Wiesenthal-designed homes asked the question. He offered to help Wiesenthal escape by accusing him of being a Russian spy who had to be removed from the camp for questioning.

Wiesenthal and the friend who had come to the camp with him escaped as they were being moved for questioning.

Wiesenthal returned to the family apartment until all Jews were relocated to the Jewish ghetto. Several months later, Simon and Cyla were taken to a forced-labor camp at the Eastern Railroad Repair Works; his mother was left in the ghetto. Wiesenthal worked outside as a sign painter until he was noticed by a foreman named Heinrich Guenthert, who attempted to treat prisoners as fairly as he could. Guenthert moved him inside as a draftsman and technician.

Conditions worsened in 1942 after SS Gestapo Chief Reinhard Heydrich convened the Wannsee conference to determine "the final solution of the Jewish question." Adolf Eichmann, who later was responsible for all extermination concentration camps, attended the conference. The solution was the total extermination of all Jews. Wiesenthal did not hear about the Wannsee conference, but he was told where the freight cars filled with Jews that he saw moving through the railroad yards were headed.

One day, old women from the Lwow ghetto were herded to the railroad yards and pushed into boxcars. They waited for a locomotive for three days in the freight cars without water. Wiesenthal could hear their pleas, but he could not help them because the cars were surrounded by armed guards. He hesitated to search among the faces for his mother. Then he saw her with an arm outstretched, appealing to a guard for water.

Wiesenthal knew that if he took water to his mother, he would be shot before her eyes. He never saw his mother again, but he remembered the image of her looking out of the railroad car. He heard that she had died at Belzec. He was not able to help his mother, but he resolved to pursue those who had imprisoned and killed her and six million other Jews.

Wiesenthal began to plan to save his wife. With her blonde hair, she could pass as a Pole. In his job as a technician, he could move freely about the railroad yards. He knew members of a Polish underground cell. He made sketches of the most vulnerable points in the railroad yards and used them to bargain for a position for Cyla with a Polish family. The Gestapo found out about her first location; she fled as they were on their way to the house in which she was staying.

Through their contact in the Polish underground cell, Cyla met Wiesenthal at the fence surrounding the railroad yards. They held hands through the fence as she told him of her predicament. He told her to return the next night, and he would make other living arrangements for her. The Polish underground cell obtained papers for her as "Irene Kowalska" and found a position for her with a Polish family.

Wiesenthal's immediate superior at the Eastern Railroad Repair Works was Adolf Kohlrautz, who, like his boss, Heinrich Guenthert, was secretly anti-Nazi. Kohlrautz obtained two pistols for Wiesenthal, which were hidden in Kohlrautz's desk.

One day, a guard rounded up Jewish workers from the sheds and workshops and signalled Wiesenthal and two other sign painters to come with them and join a larger group of prisoners. The guard marched them two miles to der schlauch (the hose), a seven-foot-wide corridor between the barbed-wire fences that separated the concentration camp from the rest of the railroad yards. No one who had walked the length of the hose had returned.

They were marched toward a sand pit at the end of the hose that was 1,500-foot long and six-foot deep. The prisoners, thirty-eight men and six women, were told to remove their clothes, fold them neatly, and place them on a truck.

Then SS Unterscharfuhrer Kauzer began to shoot the prisoners; Wiesenthal quit counting after nine shots.

Off in the distance, they heard a whistle and someone calling, "Wiesenthal." SS Rottenfuhrer Koller told Kauzer that he had been asked to return Wiesenthal to the railroad yards. Wiesenthal was told to retrieve his clothing from the truck; he was needed to paint signs. It was Hitler's fifty-fourth birthday, and Kohlrautz had told his superiors that Wiesenthal was required to paint a large sign with the words "Wir Danken Unserem Fuhrer (We thank our Fuhrer)."

In later years, Wiesenthal cited Guenthert and Kohlrautz as examples in support of his argument against collective German guilt. Guenthert was frequently in trouble with the SS because he treated the forced laborers under his care as humans. He dismissed two members of his staff because they mistreated Jews and Poles.

Guenthert and Wiesenthal respected each other. Guenthert noted that Wiesenthal "always walked with his head up and looked me straight in the eye. The SS men said that Wiesenthal was impertinent. I didn't argue with them, but I admit I was impressed by the man's erect bearing. He had a thoughtful expression in his eyes as though he knew that we Germans would one day have to account for all this."[145]

In December 1965, Wiesenthal invited Guenthert, by then an official of the West German Federal Railroads in Karlsruhe, to the marriage of his only daughter. Guenthert observed, "When a man like Simon Wiesenthal, after all that has happened, invites a German to join his family, I feel honored."[146]

Between Kohlrautz and Wiesenthal also existed a mutual bond; Kohlrautz respected Wiesenthal's dignity and his technical ability. Kohlrautz told Wiesenthal what he had heard listening to the BBC and secretly smuggled food to Wiesenthal's mother in the ghetto. Unfortunately, Kohlrautz was transferred to the front in early 1944 and was killed in the Battle of Berlin.

When Wiesenthal heard of Kohlrautz's death he said, "Too many decent Germans died because they were ordered to fight Hitler's battles and did not try to evade what they considered their duty. And too many SS men and Party people survived because they were cowards. The SS fought a safe war in the concentration camps against defenseless men, women, and children."[147]

Wiesenthal decided not to wait any longer to make another escape attempt. He asked Kohlrautz for a pass for him and a friend to go into town to buy drafting supplies. Wiesenthal took his two pistols from Kohlrautz's desk. Kohlrautz returned with a dim-witted Ukrainian who was not familiar with Lwow. They took him to a stationery store that had a front door and a back door. When the Ukrainian was not looking, Wiesenthal and his friend went out the back door to a hiding place.

They moved around to escape detection and eventually found refuge in a ground floor apartment. The floor was sand covered with boards. They dug out enough sand so the two escapees could recline in the holes in the sand while their friends put the floorboards back in place and covered the boards with a table to avoid detection. Wiesenthal had prepared a diary and a list of the names of SS guards and the crimes they had committed that he kept under the floorboards.

On June 13, 1944, two Polish plainclothesmen entered the apartment and lifted the floorboards. They pushed Wiesenthal against the wall, confiscated his diary and list of SS guards, and took him to the police station in Smolki Square. He had one pistol with him, but, thankfully, one of the Polish guards stole it or Wiesenthal would probably have been shot. Two days later, two guards came to the jail to take him to the Gestapo prison camp.

Wiesenthal and thirty-three other Jews were brought before SS Hauptsturmfuhrer Friedrich Warzok, the camp commander, who surprised him. He said to Wiesenthal, "You thought I would have you shot, like the others, didn't you? Here people die when I want them to die. Back to your old barracks. No work, and double food rations for you."[148] Wiesenthal couldn't figure it out. Warzok, who was responsible for the deaths of 70,000 people, had spared his life and issued him double rations.

Russian aircraft flew overhead, and Russian artillery fire could be heard in the distance. The next day, Warzok informed the thirty-four surviving Jewish prisoners that he had sold them as non-German forced laborers to the Todt Organization, the state-controlled construction company. Wiesenthal said, "Now we understood why Warzok had spared us. As long as the SS had someone to guard, they might get out of front-line duty. We thirty-four Jews became the life insurance for almost 200 SS men. We were all going to be a happy family. Warzok said we would try to reach the woods off Slovakia, where we would hide until the war was over."[149]

Wiesenthal did not know that his wife, Cyla, "Irene Kowalska," had received a message from Lwow in August 1944 that he had been arrested by the Gestapo and was dead. On their way west, they stopped briefly at the Grossrosen concentration camp where Wiesenthal received terrible news from Polish prisoners from Warsaw. They described the devastating bombing there. One Pole mentioned that his street,

Topiel Street, had been completely destroyed. Wiesenthal asked him if he had known Irene Kowalska at 5 Topiel Street. The Pole knew her but said that it was certain that she was dead; no one on the street had survived.

As the Russians closed in on Grossrosen, the prisoners were marched to Buchenwald concentration camp where they were crammed into trucks for transportation to their final destination, Mauthausen concentration camp in northern Austria. Only 1,200 out of 3,000 that had marched out of Grossrosen survived the trip. On May 4, 1945, the SS guards at Mauthausen disappeared, and the crematorium ceased operating. It was whispered that Berlin had fallen, and that Hitler was dead.

The prisoners heard the rumbling of tanks and looked out and saw American tanks lumbering down the road to the camp. Wiesenthal staggered out to touch the white star on the side of the first tank, but collapsed just as he touched it. The prisoners were so starved and sick that just under 3,000 prisoners died in Mauthausen after it was liberated by the Americans.

Wiesenthal knew what he *had* to do. He went to the War Crimes Office to offer his services, which, because he had neither training nor experience, were questionable. The American Lieutenant asked him how much he weighed. His weight had dropped to 97 pounds in the camps. He responded, "Fifty-six kilos (123 pounds)." The Lieutenant chuckled and said, "Wiesenthal, go and take it easy for a while, and come and see me when you really weigh fifty-six kilos."[150] Ten days later, he returned after he had gained weight. The Lieutenant perceived that this assignment was important to him, so he assigned him to a Captain who had taught international law at Harvard University.

In 1945, when Austria was divided into four zones, Mauthausen was in the Russian Zone; the War Crimes Office at Mauthausen was moved to Linz in the American Zone. Wiesenthal spent a half-day in the War Crimes Office and the other half-day in the two-room office of the Jewish Committee in Linz, later the Jewish Central Committee of the U.S. Zone in Austria, of which he became Vice Chairman.

Wiesenthal wrote to the International Committee of the Red Cross to inquire about his wife. The Red Cross responded promptly that his wife was dead. Next he wrote to his old friend, Dr. Biener, and asked him to go to Warsaw to check the ruins of the house at 5 Topiel Street where Cyla had been staying.

As Cyla told her husband later, when the German flamethrower squads closed in on Topiel Street, she and a few others managed to escape in the darkness and confusion. She was sent as a forced laborer to a factory at Heiligenhaus in the Rhineland where they made machine guns for the German Army. She was liberated by the British on April 11, 1945. Cyla returned to Poland on the chance that her husband was still alive.

In Cracow, she recognized a man on the street from Lwow, who suggested that she talk with Dr. Biener. She was surprised to learn that Dr. Biener of Lwow now lived five minutes away in Cracow. She walked to his house and knocked on the door. Dr. Biener opened the door, looked as though he had seen a ghost, and quickly closed the door. Cyla called out and knocked again. Dr. Biener said, "But you're dead. I just got a letter ... Come in. You don't understand. Yesterday I had a letter from your husband. Simon writes that you died under the ruins of a house in Warsaw." It was now Cyla's turn to be shocked. "Simon? But he's dead. He's been dead for a year." Dr. Biener said, "No, no, Cyla. Simon is alive, in Linz, Austria. Here, read the letter."[151]

Their reunion was a joyous one made more poignant by the fact that both thought that they had lost the other. They moved into a larger apartment in Linz, where Wiesenthal worked for various U.S. agencies: the War Crimes Commission, the Office of Strategic Services (OSS), and the Counter-Intelligence Corps (CIC). The following year, their daughter, Paulinka, was born in Linz.

In the pursuit of Nazi war criminals, the Americans went from one extreme to the other. Initially, they followed a policy of "automatic arrest," interning large numbers of people while their interrogators separated the criminals from the hangers-on.

As long as the Americans who had seen the conditions in the concentration camps were still around, the denazification process was done impartially; however, when they were replaced by others who had been stationed elsewhere, the new officers did not have the same knowledge of the Nazi problem. One of the new American Captains told Wiesenthal: "There'll always be people with different viewpoints. At home we had the Democrats and Republicans. Here you have Nazi and anti-Nazis. That's what makes the world go round. Try not to worry too much about it."[152]

The best-known Nazi that Wiesenthal pursued to bring to justice was Adolf Eichmann, SS Gestapo head of Nazi Bureau IV. Eichmann was responsible for building the concentration camps, determining how they would function, selecting the gas chambers, and transporting people to the camps. He personally killed no single individual; however, he planned the murders of over six million people. Eichmann once commented that Jewish death lists were his favorite reading mate-

rial before going to sleep. For sixteen years, Wiesenthal hunt-
ed Eichmann, who was never out of his pursuer's mind.

In 1945, Wiesenthal uncovered his first clue about
Eichmann. One evening, Wiesenthal's landlady noticed the
name Eichmann on a list that he was reading. She said,
"Eichmann. That must be the SS General Eichmann who
commanded the Jews." She asked if he knew that Eichmann's
parents lived at 32 Landstrasse down the street. Wiesenthal
notified the War Crimes Office and two investigators were
sent to search the house. They learned nothing except that the
last message the Eichmanns had from their son came from
Prague.

The OSS asked Wiesenthal to concentrate on finding
Eichmann and issued him a special pass enabling him to
move freely within the American Zone of Austria. In 1947,
Wiesenthal opened a Documentation Center in Linz. He continued to work with the Americans and with the Jewish
Committee, but he concentrated on collecting information
about war criminals, particularly Eichmann.

One day, one of Wiesenthal's assistants told him that he
had heard that Eichmann was hiding at 8 Fischerdorf in the
village of Altausee. Wiesenthal passed the information on to
the U.S. Counter-Intelligence Corps, who asked the Austrian
police to search the house. The police went to 38 Fischerdorf
instead of 8. Wiesenthal contacted the CIC again, who sent an
American to check out 8. Living there was Frau Veronika
Liebl, who told the investigator that she was the "former"
wife of Eichmann, whom she had divorced in Prague in
March 1945. She said that she had not seen Eichmann and had
no photographs of him. Frau Liebl was kept under observation.

In late 1947, Frau Liebl applied to the district for a decla-

ration of death for Eichmann "in the interest of the children."
A man called Karl Lukas sent an affidavit to the judge assert-
ing that he had seen Eichmann shot and killed in Prague on
April 30, 1945. Karl Lukas was married to Maria Liebl
Lukas, Eichmann's wife's sister.

Wiesenthal proved that Eichmann had been seen alive
since that date; otherwise, his name would have been dropped
from all lists of war criminals. During the summer of 1948,
Wiesenthal found two photographs of Eichmann in
Nuremberg, one in uniform and one in civilian clothes.
However, the pictures had been taken in 1936; his appearance
had changed considerably since then.

On December 20, 1949, an Austrian police official told
Wiesenthal that they suspected Eichmann was hiding in the
village of Grundlsee. He had also heard that Eichmann
intended to spend New Year's Eve with his family in
Altausee. They planned to raid the house and asked
Wiesenthal to come with them.

Wiesenthal met a young Israeli who had visited the
Documentation Center. He and his parents had emigrated
from Germany to Palestine when he was a child. He had
fought in the Israeli Army in the war of independence and was
now visiting Germany. He was fascinated by the Eichmann
case. Foolishly, Wiesenthal told him that Eichmann might
soon be in captivity. The young Israeli begged to go along for
the capture.

They registered on December 30 in a hotel in Bad Ausee,
about two miles from Altausee. Wiesenthal warned the Israeli
not to walk around and particularly not to talk to people. That
evening, the young man became restless and went to a night-
club where he told the girls he was an Israeli. The capture was
planned for the following night, and Wiesenthal met with

police officials to make final arrangements. When Wiesenthal returned to the hotel that evening, he was appalled to find the young Israeli in the hotel tavern drinking with the local people and talking about exploits of the Israeli Army.

Late that evening, two men were walking toward Altausee from Grundlsee when a third man ran from Altausee and warned them off. Apparently, the presence of the Israeli had alerted Eichmann's friends. About a week later, the Austrian police heard that Eichmann had left the area. They called off their search; another opportunity had been lost.

In January 1951, Wiesenthal heard that Eichmann had been seen in Rome during the previous summer. Apparently, he had stayed in a monastery while making arrangements to travel with a group to South America; Brazil and Argentina were the most likely destinations.

In 1948, Wiesenthal had decided that he needed a hobby to take his mind off war crimes; he became a stamp collector. Late in 1953, an Austrian Baron from the Tyrol offered to show him his stamp collection. The Baron listened closely when Wiesenthal told him of his efforts to bring Nazi criminals to justice. He knew some ranking Nazis who now had responsible positions in banking and industry "as though nothing had happened." The Baron was shocked by it.

The Baron mentioned that he had just received a letter from Argentina from a former Lieutenant Colonel in the German Army who was serving as an instructor to Peron's Army. The Baron had asked him if he had seen any of their old friends in Argentina, and his friend had replied:

> There are some people here we both used to
> know. You may remember Lieutenant
> Hoffman from my regiment, and Hauptmann

> Berger from the 188th Division. A few more
> are here whom you never met. Imagine whom
> else I saw—and even had to talk to twice: this
> awful swine Eichmann who commanded the
> Jews. He lives in Buenos Aires and works for
> a water company.[153]

Wiesenthal tried to contain his excitement while asking to see the letter to check out the stamps. He reread the letter and memorized the part about Eichmann. Wiesenthal realized that he could not proceed on his own. He prepared a report of everything that he knew about the case including photographs, examples of Eichmann's handwriting, copies of personal letters, and the information that he had obtained from the Baron. He sent copies of the report to the Jewish World Congress in New York and to the Israeli Consulate in Vienna.

Wiesenthal heard from Rabbi Kalmanowitz in New York requesting Eichmann's address in Buenos Aires. When Wiesenthal offered to send an investigator to Argentina if the Jewish World Congress would pay his expenses, he was told that no money was available for this purpose. Wiesenthal was surprised not to hear from the Israelis. In March 1954, he closed the Documentation Center and forwarded boxes weighing 532 kilos to the Yad Vashem Historical Archives in Jerusalem. The only file that he retained was the Eichmann file.

In 1959, Israel's interest in the case resumed. An investigator visited Frau Eichmann's mother. Frau Liebl was not friendly to her visitor, but she mentioned that her daughter had married a man named "Klement" or "Klemt" in South America. She said that she did not have their address and asked to left alone.

On February 6, 1960, the Linz newspaper printed the obituary of Eichmann's father, Adolf Eichmann, listing Veronika Eichmann as a daughter-in-law. Eichmann did not attend the funeral, but his four brothers did. Wiesenthal asked a photographer to stay out of sight and to photograph Eichmann's brothers at the gravesite with a telescopic lens. Many people had told Wiesenthal that Eichmann resembled his brother Otto. He was amazed at the resemblance. From Otto's picture, they now had a good idea of what Eichmann's facial features looked like at the time.

The Israelis knew that they could not get papers to extradite Eichmann from Argentina, so they planned to do the next best thing—kidnap him. However, they had to be sure of their man. The recent photograph increased their level of confidence. On May 23, 1960, Prime Minister David Ben Gurion notified the Israeli Parliament that Eichmann had been captured and was in an Israeli prison. One of Wiesenthal's clients, a former high-ranking SS officer, visited Wiesenthal's office to say, "Nice work." He meant it.

On August 1, 1944, fifteen-year-old Anne Frank, who had been hiding from the Gestapo in an attic in Amsterdam for two years, made her last entry in her diary: "If I'm watched to that extent, I start by getting snappy, then unhappy, and finally I twist my head around again, so that the bad is on the outside and the good is on the inside, and keep on trying to find a way of becoming what I would so like to be, and what I would be if ... there were not other people living in the world."[154]

Three days later, the door was broken down, and five German soldiers led by an SS Underscharfuhrer entered the building. A Dutch informer had told the SS about them. Of the eight people in the attic—Anne, her parents and her sister, another couple and their son, and a dentist—were arrested and transported to concentration camps. Anne's father, Otto Frank, was the only one who survived. Anne died of typhus in the concentration camp at Bergen-Belsen in March 1945. In the spring of 1945, Otto Frank returned to the Amsterdam house. The diary was still lying on the floor where the SS men had thrown it.

Otto Frank permitted it to be published. *The Diary of Anne Frank* is the story of a young girl who admitted her concerns: "I'm very afraid that we will be discovered and be shot." It was translated into thirty-two languages and was made into a play and a motion picture. Millions of people were moved by it.

In October 1958, a performance of *The Diary of Anne Frank* at the Landestheater in Linz was disrupted by an anti-Semitic demonstration. Young people, most of whom were between fifteen and seventeen, shouted, "Traitors! Toadies! Swindlers!" From the gallery, the youths threw leaflets that read "This play is a fraud. Anne Frank never existed. The Jews have invented the whole story because they want to extort restitution money. Don't believe a word of it! It's fake!"[155]

Two days later, Wiesenthal was at coffee house in Linz with a friend when some high school students sat down at the next table. His friend called over a boy whose parents he knew well. When asked what he thought about the disruption of the play, the youth responded, "Well—it's easy. There is no evidence that Anne Frank lived. The diary may be a clever forgery. Certainly it does not prove that Anne Frank existed." When reminded that she was buried in a mass grave a Bergen-Belsen, the boy shrugged and said, "There is no proof."

Wiesenthal asked him, "Young man, if we could prove to you that Anne Frank existed, would you accept the dairy as genuine?" He inquired, "How can you prove it?" Wiesenthal asked, "Suppose the Gestapo officer who actually arrested Anne Frank were found. Would that be acceptable as proof?" The youth answered, "Yes, if the man himself admitted it."[156]

The trail was fourteen-years old. The only information that Wiesenthal had was the recollection of Paul Kraler, who had hidden the Frank family, that the SS man was from Vienna and his name was Silvernagl. Silvernagl was not an Austrian name; the little information that Kraler had probably was not going to be very helpful. Silbernagel was a more common Austrian name, but investigating that name was unproductive. Years later, Dutch officials provided Wiesenthal with the 1943 telephone directory of the SS in Holland. In the section of the directory headed IV, Sonderkommando, was an entry "IV B 4, Jews" was the name Silberbauer.

The 1963 Vienna telephone directory contained a dozen Silberbauers. Many former German officers, after a grace period, joined the police force. Wiesenthal gambled that his Silberbauer was a member of the police department in Vienna. He called Polizerat Dr. Joseph Wiesenger, head of the section that dealt with Nazi crimes, to tell him that the man who arrested Anne Frank was a member of the police force in Vienna. Wiesenger asked for Silberbauer's first name, informing Wiesenthal that they had six Silberbauers on the force. Wiesenthal asked him to check their service records for someone who was with Section IV B 4 in Amsterdam in 1944. After a long delay, Wiesenthal was told that the files were "still being examined."

On November 11, Austria's Communist Party newspaper

published the story that Inspector Karl Silberbauer of the Vienna police force had been suspended "pending investigation and possible prosecution" for his role in the arrest of Anne Frank. Wiesenthal called Dr. Wiesenger, who was embarrassed. He told Wiesenthal that they had instructed Silberbauer to keep quiet, but he had informed the Communist Party newspaper. They had intended to have the discovery announced by Wiesenthal, who subsequently notified a newspaper editor in Holland. It received front-page coverage around the world.

In addition to Adolf Eichmann, the list of war criminals brought to justice by Wiesenthal include:

- Dr. Karl Babor—judge and executioner at Grossrosen concentration camp
- Martin Borman—Hitler's chief deputy and designated successor
- Dr. Joseph Mengele—chief doctor at Auschwitz concentration camp who performed medical experiments on inmates
- Franz Murer—the "butcher of Vilnius," who oversaw the murder of 80,000 Jews in Lithuania
- Franz Stangl—commander of Treblinka concentration camp
- Kurt Wiese—murderer of over two hundred Polish Jews

Of the 22,500 names on the list, Wiesenthal helped to bring to justice over 900 in the first twenty years after World War II. Wiesenthal was embarrassed by those who considered him an international detective and, as such, a romantic figure. He realized that although he had a few flashes of brilliance, his success was due primarily to hard work and a certain amount of plodding. He had the will to stay with it. He is an outstanding example of what can be accomplished when determination supports moral convictions.

CHAPTER 5

LUMINARIES / NOTABLES

"Everything depends on will in this world."

Portuguese Proverb

Chapter 5 provides examples of literary, artistic, and human-itarian role models of determination.

Elizabeth Barrett Browning was an invalid who never left her home except to move to another house. Her only social life was having friends visit her and vicariously, through her husband, Robert Browning. She had hesitated to marry Browning, even though she was in love with him, because she thought that she would pull him down socially. She was a talented poet who overcame her struggle with ill health to write widely acclaimed poetry. She advised her husband on improving his poetry with great success.

Paul Gauguin was a leader of the Impressionist movement but was unsuccessful selling his art during his lifetime. He began his professional career as a stockbroker who painted in his spare time. Ultimately, HE HAD TO PAINT, so he gave up his job and his family. Some of Gauguin's personal characteristics were not admirable; nevertheless, he is an example of a highly determined individual. His resolve to paint caused his family to leave him and resulted in his living in poverty. However, he did what he had to do—PAINT.

F. Scott Fitzgerald knew at a young age that he wanted to write. However, he received 122 rejection slips for his first novel. Only one editor saw a spark of writing ability in Fitzgerald, who wrote advertisements displayed in public transportation to earn living expenses while writing short stories that did not sell. Eventually, he totally rewrote the novel, writing only on weekends while on active duty in the U.S. Army during World War I. Finally, the editor who liked his work convinced his employer to publish the book. As with Gauguin, Fitzgerald's personal characteristics were not all those of a role model; nevertheless, he is another good example of determination.

Frederick Douglass was an effective antislavery speaker because he had escaped from slavery himself. He became well-known as the publisher of an abolitionist newspaper, *The North Star,* and as a determined supporter of reform causes, including the women's rights movement. Because of his speaking ability, he was popular on the lyceum circuit. Later in his life, he had several responsible positions in the U.S. Government. He was relentless in speaking out on reform issues.

Harriet Tubman was a successful conductor on the underground railroad, motivated by her own escape from slavery. She conducted nineteen trips on the underground railroad that caused her to return to areas of the South where she could be recognized. At one time, she had a price on her head of $12,000. During the Civil War, she served the Union as a nurse and spy. Her accomplishments were the result of her personal qualities of grit and determination.

All of these men and women were driven individuals, who had to overcome obstacles to achieve their goals. Their strong resolve assisted them in accomplishing what they set out to do.

ELIZABETH BARRETT BROWNING (1806-1861) Poet Who Overcame Illness

> "How do I love thee? Let me count the ways.
> I love thee to the depth and breadth and height
> My soul can reach, when feeling out of sight
> For the ends of Being and ideal Grace.
> I love thee to the level of every day's
> Most quiet need, by sun and candlelight.
> I love thee freely, as men strive for Right;
> I love thee purely, as men turn from Praise.
> I love thee with the passion put to use
> In my old griefs, and with my childhood's faith.
> I lived with a love I seemed to lose
> With my lost saints,—I love thee with the breath,
> Smiles, tears, of all my life!—and, if God chooses,
> I shall love thee better after death."

Elizabeth Barrett Browning, *Sonnets from the Portuguese*

Elizabeth Barrett's reputation as a poet exceeded that of Robert Browning when they met. She was an invalid who rarely left her room in her parents' home. Initially, they corresponded, and then Robert arranged their meeting through a mutual friend. Each had a strong respect for the other's poetry, and they found that they had much in common emotionally. Elizabeth's father had forbidden his children, both sons and daughters, to marry. Since Elizabeth was chronically ill, she wasn't concerned about this parental edict until she met Robert. Her health improved as their love for each other developed.

Elizabeth and Robert were married secretly, eloped, and moved to Italy. Elizabeth was disowned by her father, but she had a small annuity on which to live. Robert's income was not sufficient to support them. They remained deeply in love and had an idyllic marriage. They had no serious arguments, and each was strongly supportive of the other's writing. In her opinion, she had not begun to live until she met Robert. Ultimately, with her advice and editing, Robert's poetry gained a wider acceptance than his earlier works, and her poetry was also improved by his advice and suggestions. Elizabeth's story cannot be told without also telling the story of Robert.

Elizabeth Barrett, the oldest child of Edward Moulton Barrett and Mary Graham-Clarke Barrett, was born on March 6, 1806 in Durham, England. Edward Barrett was a wealthy merchant whose family owned a plantation in Jamaica. Elizabeth received no formal education, but she read widely and, to a large extent, was self-educated. She learned Greek by participating in her brother Edward's lessons. Her first poems, including "The Battle of Marathon," were published when she was thirteen. Her father paid for a private printing of her early poems.

In 1832, the Barrett family moved to Devon and three years later moved to London. In 1838, they moved into 50 Wimpole Street, which was popularized in Rudolf Besier's play, *The Barretts of Wimpole Street*. She published *The Serafim and Other Poems* that year and suffered a serious health problem that affected her respiratory system, which possibly involved abscesses in the lungs. Her health deteriorated to the point that she was considered an invalid.

For health reasons, she was sent to Torquay, where her brother, Edward, drowned. Elizabeth and Edward had been close. Because he had accompanied her to Torquay, she considered herself at least partially responsible for his death. In 1841, she returned to London as a complete invalid. She spent her days reclining on a sofa and rarely left her room. She received few visitors and did not envision much of a future for herself. However, she wrote many letters and stayed current in the literary world by corresponding with scholars and writers of the day.

In 1844, her reputation as a poet was enhanced by the publication of her new book of poems, which included "A Drama of Exile" (about the exile of Adam and Eve from Paradise), twenty-eight sonnets, some romantic ballads, and miscellaneous other poems. These poems elevated her standing with the critics and brought her to the attention of a fellow poet, Robert Browning.

Robert Browning, oldest child of Robert Browning, Sr. and Sarah Weidemann Browning, was born at Camberwell, England on May 7, 1812. Robert's sister, Sarianna, was born two years later. Robert Browning, Sr. was a bibliophile and scholar who worked for the Bank of England for fifty years. Young Robert grew up in a home with thousands of books. He attended private schools in his neighborhood, but most of his education was received at home with his father serving as one of his tutors. His education was almost exclusively literary and musical.

Father and son were very close throughout their lives. Robert was also close with his mother, even to the extent of sharing illnesses with her when he was growing up. He frequently displayed his temper as a young man; his tolerant parents provided an environment that was "sheltered, enclosed, dependent." He lived at home until he married at the age of thirty-three.

When he was sixteen, Robert attended classes in Greek at London University and decided that writing poetry was his life's work. The generous father was willing to finance his son's writing. Robert was never bothered by financial problems; he was grateful to his father for his support.

When he was twenty-one, Robert published, anonymously, "Pauline, a Fragment of a Confession." Mr. W. J. Fox of *The Monthly Repository* gave it a favorable review, but it was not well-received by other critics. In later years, Robert was ashamed of this early work and destroyed all copies that he could find. At this stage of his development as a poet, he was strongly influenced by Shelley.

For the next twelve years, Robert was a prolific author, writing "Paracelsus," "Sordello," "Pippa Passes," "Bells and Pomegranates," and five plays—*King Victor and King Charles, The Return of the Druses, Columbe's Birthday, Strafford,* and *A Blot in the 'Scutcheon.* The last two had very short runs on the stage, and the other dramas were not produced. He was not considered a successful playwright.

Robert had a full social life, and he had many literary friends including John Forster, literary critic of *The Examiner.* Initially, Forster was the only critic to perceive the merit of "Paracelsus." Thomas Carlyle became a lifelong friend. Robert had many women friends but had no close attachments with women. That was about to change.

Elizabeth was ambitious and wanted to break out of the shell that her illness had imposed on her. She did not think of love and sexual passion, but she wanted to find another person with whom she could share poetic passion. When she read "Paracelsus," she suspected that Robert Browning might be that poet. Most of what she knew of Robert was from his poetry and her interpretation of it. She knew a few facts about Robert, the man, from her distant cousin, John Kenyon.

In late December 1844, Robert returned from a trip to Italy and read Elizabeth Barrett's collection of poems which had been published the preceding August. He admired her poetry and heard more about her from his friend and her cousin, John Kenyon. Robert wrote to Elizabeth to tell her how much he enjoyed her poetry.

In his first letter to her, Robert said, "I love your verses with all my heart, dear Miss Barrett." He did not attempt to analyze her poetry; he said that "into me it has gone, and part of me it has become, this great living poetry of yours, not a flower of which but took root and grew ... I do, as I say, love these books with all my heart—and I love you too."[157]

Elizabeth replied that she was delighted with "the sympathy of a poet, and such a poet!" She asked him for criticisms of her writing and offered some comments on his efforts: "'Misty' is an infamous word for your kind of obscurity. You are never misty—not even in 'Sordello'—never vague. Your graver cuts deep sharp lines, always—and there is an extra-distinctness in your images and thoughts, from the midst of which, crossing each other infinitely, the general significance seems to escape."[158]

They corresponded frequently. Over 600 of their letters survive, providing a wealth of personal information for biographers. In one of her letters to him, she offers her views on writing: "Like to write? Of course, of course I do. I seem to live while I write—it is life, for me. Why, what is to live? Not to eat and drink and breathe—but to feel the life in you down all the fibers of being, passionately and joyfully. And thus, one lives in composition surely—not always—but when the wheel goes round and the process is uninterrupted."[159]

Initially, their letters were about their craft, but soon the relationship deepened. On May 20, 1845, they met for the first time. After that meeting, Robert wrote to her, concluding his letter: "I am proud and happy in your friendship—now and forever. May God bless you!" He followed that letter with one declaring his love. He was moving too fast for her. She responded, "You do not know what pain you give me by speaking so wildly ... you have said some intemperate things ... fancies—which you will not say over again, nor unsay, but forget at once."[160] He replied that she had misunderstood him; she accepted his explanation.

Robert's letters give the impression of a man attempting to control an overwhelming emotion. Her letters in response provide a recurring theme; she is unworthy, and she fears that she will encumber him because her poor health will limit his social activity.

Elizabeth had another problem in addition to her health concerns. Her autocratic father refused to allow any of his children, either sons or daughters, to marry. No rational explanation exists for this behavior. Several biographers have conjectured that some Negro blood had entered into the family genealogy in Jamaica, and that Barrett did not want to pass it on to subsequent generations of the family.

Elizabeth, the oldest child in the family, had been left a modest legacy on which she could live. Her sisters, Henrietta and Arabel, did not have a comparable annual stipend. They were entirely dependent on their father for support, or on a husband if they chose to go against their father's wishes and marry. Henrietta married, but Arabel remained single and was always financially dependent upon her father.

Elizabeth held Robert off. She viewed him as the giver and herself as the taker; she felt that she was not good enough for him. Ultimately, Elizabeth and Robert acknowledged to each other that they were very much in love; they began to plan their marriage. Only two months before their wedding, she told him that he would be better off if he left her.

They planned to be married in secret and then wait for a time when her father was away to leave for a honeymoon in Italy. Elizabeth told her sisters of her plans, but would not allow them to attend the wedding ceremony because it would upset their father. She did not tell her brothers or most of her close friends about her wedding plans.

The deception during the two months before their wedding upset Elizabeth. She was not used to being devious. "I am so nervous that my own footsteps startle me ... To hear the voice of my father and meet his eyes makes me shrink back — to talk to my brothers leaves my nerves trembling."[161] They were married in St. Marylebone parish church on September 12, 1846. Elizabeth lived another week in her father's house before embarking for France en route to Italy. She said, "I did hate so, to have to take off the ring."

On September 19, accompanied by her maid, the Brownings left for Italy. Elizabeth had almost fifteen years of happy married life and creative professional life ahead of her. She gave birth to a son in 1849, and in 1861, after a flurry of loving kisses, died peacefully in Robert's arms.

Their letters provide a comprehensive look at the complexity of their relationship. They even corresponded when Robert was away on a short trip, for example, to find a place to stay for the summer away from the heat of Florence. Both correspondents were able to express their feelings superbly in writing. When Elizabeth died, Robert exclaimed, "How strange it will be to have no more letters."

While living at the Casa Guidi in Florence after the birth of their son, Weidemann ("Pen"), Elizabeth showed Robert the poems that she had written during their courtship but had never let him read. She had traced their courtship from hesitation, doubt, and reservation to the happiness of reciprocated

232

love. They were personal poems, and she suspected that he would object to their being published.

To the contrary, Robert considered them among the best sonnets in the English language. "When Robert saw them he was much touched and pleased—and thinking highly of the poetry he did not let ... could not consent, he said, that they should be lost to my volumes [of 1850] and so we agreed to slip them in under some sort of veil, and after much consideration chose the 'Portuguese.'"[162] The collection of forty-three sonnets was entitled *Sonnets from the Portuguese*.

Robert completed two volumes of poetry entitled *Men and Women* while living in Florence. At the same time, Elizabeth worked on *Aurora Leigh*, a novel in verse that she described as "the novel or romance I have been hankering after for so long." She described it to her brother, George, as "beyond question my best work."

In Elizabeth's verse novel, Aurora Leigh is born in Italy to an English father and an Italian mother, from whom she is orphaned at the age of thirteen. A disciplinarian aunt in England, who raised her, wants her to marry her cousin, but Aurora wants to become a poet. Elizabeth addresses the question in her work of whether women can be happy with just their art or if they need men to feel fulfilled. Her cousin proposes to a poor girl who jilts him. Elizabeth uses an intricate plot to tell her "thoroughly modern" story.

Elizabeth told her sister Arabel, "Robert and I work every day—he has a large volume of short poems which will be completed by the spring—and I have some four thousand, five hundred lines of mine—I am afraid six thousand lines will not finish it."[163] To protect their work schedule, they did not receive visitors before three o'clock. Elizabeth wrote in the drawing room, and Robert worked in the sitting room. The doors to the dining room in between these two rooms remained closed. She wrote in an armchair with her feet raised; he worked at a desk.

Although Elizabeth and Robert edited each other's completed work, they did not review each other's daily effort nor did they discuss their work every day. Elizabeth, in particular, had strong feelings about this. She thought that no matter how close two people are to each other, that closeness should not extend to their work. She said, "An artist must, I fancy, either find or make solitude to work in, if it is to be good work at all."[164] Until her work was completed, she kept the details to herself.

The Brownings visited London to oversee the printing of Robert's *Men and Women*. Elizabeth pitched in and read the proofs as they came off the press. The effort was very exhausting for her, but she was convinced that this work would enhance her husband's reputation. Her own effort to complete *Aurora Leigh* was postponed.

Men and Women was successful initially; the first edition sold out immediately, and American publishers requested the rights to reprint it. Elizabeth had helped Robert to be clearer in expressing his artistic feelings. Critics were no longer calling his work obscure. Elizabeth had also helped him to think less of financial concerns and to place more emphasis on writing poems. She considered *Men and Women* a brilliant collection and hoped that his genius would be acclaimed by his peers.

As soon as Elizabeth had completed *Aurora Leigh*, Robert made arrangements to have it published; in effect, he acted as her business manager. Both Elizabeth and Robert read the proofs and prepared the manuscript for the press. He discontinued the promotion of his last collection and postponed work on his next book of poems. Sales of *Men and Women* began to slip; it could have used additional promotion.

Robert took drawing and sculpting lessons in Florence. While they lived in Italy, he was not as dedicated to writing as Elizabeth was. During their fifteen-year marriage, his poetic output was not nearly as great as hers. Before their marriage, he had lived at home where his sister and his parents had ministered to his needs. He had no responsibilities that diverted him from writing. After he was married, he had to look after Elizabeth, whose health continued to be delicate.

Their son, Robert Weidemann Browning ("Pen"), was born on March 9, 1849. Elizabeth wrote poetry while she was pregnant; she completed the first part of "Casa Guidi Windows" during this time. Early in their marriage, Robert learned from Elizabeth; her reputation was greater than his at that stage of their careers. She encouraged him to concentrate on dramatic monologues in poetry and to give up playwriting. She was concerned that he was not measuring up to his potential because of his reduced productivity. He was not concerned; he looked upon it as a temporary condition.

After the birth of their son, Robert began work on a long double poem entitled "Christmas Eve and Easter Day." Elizabeth was a strong influence on the choice of a theme for this work. She suggested that he write from the heart, not the head, and that he convey his own thoughts using a minimum of dramatic devices. She encouraged him to write about his hopes and fears, particularly those of a religious nature, in his poetry.

On January 1, 1852, Elizabeth was pleased to hear that Robert had made a New Year's resolution to write a poem every day. He began with "Love Among the Ruins," "Women and Roses," and "Childe Rolande." However, his writing was not sustained. They were staying in Paris at the time, and he resumed his contacts with society. Elizabeth encouraged this, even though she was unable to accompany him. However, she experienced social activity vicariously through him and stayed current with the Paris social scene.

Attending social events provided an outlet for Robert at a time when Elizabeth's poor health restricted her mobility. However, talk continued to be an important factor in the couple's relationship. They knew that as long as they could be together and communicate freely, Elizabeth's delicate health would not ruin their marriage. This openness extended to instances of minor disagreement. Elizabeth wrote to Robert's sister, Sarianna, that "the peculiarity of our relation is that even when he's displeased with me, he thinks out loud and can't stop himself."

The Brownings' marriage was solid and enduring. The few disagreements that they had involved viewing some of their friends from different perspectives and Elizabeth's practice of keeping their son in curls and frilly clothes until he was twelve years old. Elizabeth could learn from Robert about the nature of people, but she tended to stay with her own evaluation of friends.

Their principal difference of opinion was Elizabeth's belief in spiritualism and in communicating with the dead in seances. They attended sessions with the seer Daniel Douglas Home. Robert remained unconvinced of the value of seances; he wrote a spoof of spiritualism entitled "Mr. Sludge, the Medium."

Elizabeth and Robert retained their own identities. They thought independently and were exciting conversationalists. Neither tried to convert the other to their image of an ideal partner in marriage. Robert wrote to his brother-in-law

George, "I shall only say that Ba [Elizabeth] and I know each other for a time and, I dare trust, eternity—We differ ... as to spirit-rapping, we quarrel sometimes about politics, and estimate people's characters with enormous difference, but, in the main, we know each other, I say."[165]

Elizabeth's health deteriorated during the last three years of her life. When she seemed to be slipping away, the doctor was summoned. She appeared to be sleeping; Robert whispered in her ear, "Do you know me?" She murmured, "My Robert—my heavens, my beloved!" She kissed him repeatedly and said, "Our lives are held by God." He laid her head on the pillow. She tried to kiss him again but could no longer reach him, so she kissed her own hand and extended it to him. Robert asked, "Are you comfortable?" She responded, "Beautiful."[166]

She began to fall asleep again, and Robert realized that she should not be in a reclining position when a cough was coming. He raised her up to ease the cough. She began to cough up phlegm but then stopped. Robert was not sure if she had fainted or fallen asleep. He saw her brow contract as though in pain and then relax. She looked very young. Their servant Annunciata, who realized that she was dead, said in Italian, "Her last gesture a kiss, her last thought of love."[167]

Robert's friends expected him to break down completely after the loss of one so close. However, he remained in control, partly because Elizabeth had died so peacefully in his arms. Robert knew that his friends felt sorry for him in his loss. He was extremely grateful for the fifteen years that he and Elizabeth had together. He knew that she had more to give, but he appreciated the rare union that they had.

Friends were also concerned about Pen, who had been as close to his mother as a son and a mother can be. He, too, held up well and, in fact, was a consolation to his father. Robert told his sister, Sarianna, that Pen was "perfect to me."

Elizabeth's place in literary history is summarized by essayist and poet Alice Meynell:

> The place of Elizabeth Barrett Browning in English literature is high, if not on the summits. She had an original genius, a great heart, and an intellect that was, if not great, exceedingly active. She seldom has composure or repose, but it is not true that her poetry is purely emotional. It is full of abundant, and often overabundant thoughts. It is intellectually restless ... she "dashed" not by reason of feminine weakness, but as it were to prove her possession of masculine strength. Her gentler work, as in the *Sonnets from the Portuguese*, is beyond praise. There is in her poetic personality a glory of righteousness, of spirituality, and of ardor that makes her name a splendid one in the history of incomparable literature.[168]

Although Elizabeth was only fifty-five when she died, she had accomplished the goal that she had set as a young girl: to produce lasting poetry that made a significant contribution to her era. She influenced other poets, including Emily Dickinson, even before she died.

Elizabeth was not sure that marriage was for her; she knew that the goals of husband, home, and children, by themselves, were not enough. To have found Robert to love and to have her love reciprocated was more that she had hoped for. Having a son at the age of forty-three added to her joy. She never stopped appreciating her good fortune to be poet, wife, and mother. Her remaining goal was for Robert to make the mark in poetry of which she knew he was capable.

Robert and Pen left Florence on July 27, 1861. In September, they arrived in London where Robert lived for the next twenty-five years. He visited Italy, but he never returned to Florence. Initially, he was lonely, but eventually he resumed his literary connections in society. He published *Dramatis Personae* in 1864, which led to his being lionized. In 1867, Oxford University awarded him a Master of Arts degree "by diploma" and Balliol College elected him an honorary Fellow.

The Ring and the Book, generally regarded as his masterpiece, was published in four volumes in 1868-69. Elizabeth's dreams were at last realized when he was hailed as "a great dramatic poet." In *The Ring and the Book*, which was based on Guido Franceschini's court case in Florence, Browning told the story of a gruesome murder twelve times. He versified the arguments of the counsels for the prosecution and the defense as well as the gossip of busybodies. The story was told with the detail of a court recorder.

In 1881, the Browning Society was formed by Dr. Furnival and Miss E. H. Hickey. Browning received additional honors: a LL.D degree from Cambridge University in 1879, the D.C.L. from Oxford University in 1882, and a LL.D degree from Edinburgh University in 1884. In 1886, he became foreign correspondent to the Royal Academy.

During his twenty-eight-year widowhood, privacy was important to him. He destroyed all of the letters of his youth and all of the letters to his family. He could not destroy his wife's letters to him, nor could he destroy his letters to her. However, he was not sure what to do with them. He left them to his son to decide; Pen published them in 1899. Robert never ceased promoting Elizabeth's work. He realized that part of his popularity was because he was the widower of Elizabeth Barrett Browning.

Robert died on December 12, 1889, while visiting Pen in Venice. His body was transported to London for burial in Westminster Abbey. It was proposed that Elizabeth's body be disinterred from the cemetery in Florence and buried alongside her husband. However, Pen decided that her grave should not be disturbed.

PAUL GAUGUIN (1848-1903) Artist Who Emphasized the Primitive

"Different generations can find in Gauguin the examples and lessons which they demand of the past to guide them in the future. Gauguin's life was neither constant nor unified. It reflects struggles, continual waverings, and an opposition between the man and his work that make it one of the most dramatic of all time. It is, however, these contradictions and incessant conflicts between inclination and development that finally resolved the artist's life into a complete unity entirely dedicated to the fulfillment of personality. Continually, passionately pursuing his ideal and never wholly satisfied with his work, Gauguin was nevertheless sufficiently sure of his genius to sacrifice his whole existence to it."[169]

Raymond Cogniat, *Gauguin*

Paul Gauguin was a stockbroker in Paris until he was thirty-five years old. Drawing and painting began as a hobby. By 1882, painting evenings and weekends in his spare time was no longer enough. He had a wife and four children when he began painting full time. In December 1882, a fifth child was born. Eventually, his wife moved with the children to Denmark, her native country, when it became apparent that Gauguin could not support them as an artist.

In *The Moon and Sixpence,* W. Somerset Maugham's protagonist, Strickland, a Gauguin-like artist, responds to the question, "What makes you think you have any talent?" with the reply "I've got to paint." Upon being questioned further and asked "Aren't you taking an awful chance?," Strickland again replied "I've got to paint." When Gauguin informed his wife that he had quit his job as a stockbroker, he told her, "From now on, I paint every day." He had to paint.

241

Unfortunately, Gauguin was never able to sell enough paintings during his lifetime to escape constant financial worry. He endured poverty and ill health but continued to paint. He is considered by art historians to have influenced the direction of modern painting more than any artist except Cézanne.

Paul Gauguin was born in Paris on June 7, 1848. His father, Clovis Gauguin, a political journalist from Orleans, died when Paul was very young. His mother, Aline Marie Chazal, the daughter of a Spanish-Peruvian nobleman, shared her father-in-law's home in Orleans with her brother-in-law. Paul attended the parochial school in Orleans and later attended the lycée.

At the age of seventeen, Gauguin shipped out as an apprentice on the *Luzitano,* a 1,200-ton sailing ship that carried passengers and cargo between LeHarve and Rio de Janeiro. After three years in the merchant service, he entered the French Navy and was assigned to the cruiser *Dessaid* patrolling the Cattegat. His mother died before he completed his military service in 1871.

Gauguin moved in with a friend of his mother, Gustav Arosa, in Paris. Gauguin's artistic interests were awakened while he lived with Arosa, who owned a substantial collection of contemporary artists and had painted reproductions of Courbet and Delacroix. Gauguin painted with the guidance of Arosa's daughter, Marguerite. Arosa arranged a job for him at Bertin's, a banking firm. Gauguin learned fast and was given the responsibility of closing the day's business for the bank on the Bourse. He made a good salary at Bertin's.

In 1873, Gauguin married Mette Sofie Gad of Copenhagen whom he met in Paris while she was traveling with a friend. Mette, daughter of a magistrate, was a level-headed young woman who had been governess for the children of the Danish Prime Minister when she was seventeen.

Gauguin's co-worker and friend, Emile Schuffenecker, was also a part-time artist. They spent occasional evenings sketching at the Academie Colarassi. Gauguin began to collect Impressionist works, including paintings by Cézanne, Manet, Pissaro, Renoir, and Sisley.

One of Gauguin's favorite artists when he began to paint was Millet, who influenced some of his early works. Although Gauguin was to become the foremost colorist, his early paintings gave no indication of this direction. The artist who had the greatest influence on his early efforts was Camille Pissarro, who had worked in business until he was twenty-five.

Edouard Manet gave Gauguin early encouragement. When Gauguin told him that he was only an amateur who painted in his spare time, Manet responded, "Oh, the only amateurs are those who paint bad pictures."[170] Gauguin contributed paintings to the Impressionist Exhibition; he received critical acclaim for his *Study of the Nude,* but not for his landscapes that were considered too similar to Pissarro's.

In 1883, Gauguin resigned from Bertin's and painted full time. Mette, a very practical person, was astounded. She did not understand her husband's motivation; in fact, she never really fully reconciled herself to his decision. Even Pissarro was surprised at its abruptness.

In *Hommage a Gauguin,* Victor Segalen wrote about the influence of Pissarro on Gauguin:

> It was this master who taught him to choose
> the tones to put on his canvas: the elimination
> of waxy blacks, stucorous browns, earthy col-

ors and thin ochres, and the naive resolution to stick to the three primaries and their immediate derivatives. Pissarro, a Dane born in the Antilles, forced by his family into business, who without instruction taught himself the elements of drawing.... Far more than the division of colors, Pissarro first taught Gauguin how to get out of the clutches of one's family, how to avoid a commercial fate, with its ledgers of income and outgo and its balance sheets and banknotes: how not to become a businessman.[171]

In early 1884, Gauguin, Mette, and the five children moved to Rouen where they could live more cheaply and be closer to Pissarro. This did not work out because Gauguin was not able to sell his paintings. In August 1884, Mette returned to the relative security of Copenhagen. Gauguin joined the family there and, partly to please his in-laws and partly for the income, became an agent for a manufacturer.

Gauguin's exhibition at the Society of Friends in Copenhagen was closed by the Academy. He was out of his element, and he offended Mette's family and friends. Mette taught French to young Danes who were preparing for foreign service. In June 1885, Gauguin returned to Paris, where he experienced real poverty. Later in life, he said,

I have known the direst poverty, I mean hunger and all the rest of it. This is nothing, or almost nothing. One gets used to it, and with a bit of will power, one laughs it down in the end. But there is another "suffering" which stimulates genius, although too much of it is liable to kill you.... Having a great deal of con-

ceit, I ended up with a great deal of energy and
I DESIRED DESIRE.[172]

In early 1886, Gauguin's works were displayed at the
Eighth Impressionist Exhibition in Paris. His paintings were
beginning to be more original and to look less like those of
other Impressionists. Art critic Felix Fineon wrote a less than
glowing review of his work: "Monsieur Gauguin's tones are
very close to one another; hence the muffled harmony of his
pictures."[173]

In June 1886, Gauguin moved to Pont-Aven in Brittany,
where he could live less expensively. His friend, Daniel de
Monfried, thought that Gauguin went to Brittany to find "an
atmosphere and environment different from our civilized
milieu, so that, in his works, he could return to primitive
art."[174] This quest for primitive art was a lifelong search.
Gauguin was looking for a pure cerebral art, such as the primitive art of Egypt. He met young artist Emile Bernard on this
visit to Brittany. In the fall of 1886, Gauguin returned to Paris
where he met Vincent Van Gogh in Montmartre.

In his search for a more primitive way of life, Gauguin
traveled to Panama. He worked for several months as a laborer on the Panama Canal and then moved to Martinique to
escape the dysentery and fever associated with the Canal. In
Martinique, some of the techniques that evolved over the
remainder of his life began to take shape. His paintings
showed the arrangement of substantial colors that became
part of his mature works. Also, the works done at this time
contain bands or contour lines, frequently blue, which framed
the forms in the painting. In this, he was influenced by Emile
Bernard.

In February 1888, Gauguin returned to Pont-Aven. In

October of that year, he had a show at the branch of the Goupils Gallery run by Theo Van Gogh, Vincent's brother. Vincent Van Gogh moved to Arles in southern France, where he hoped to establish an artists' colony with himself and Gauguin at its center. Theo Van Gogh convinced Gauguin to move to Arles, where he stayed with Van Gogh for two months at the end of 1888. The visit ended with Van Gogh attacking Gauguin with a razor. He caused no injury, but Van Gogh went home and cut off part of his right ear. Gauguin returned to Paris, and Van Gogh was placed in an asylum.

In early 1889, Gauguin returned to Brittany. He stayed in Poulder, a small fishing village more isolated than Pont-Aven, where his work departed even further from the Impressionists. He wrote to his friend Schuffenecker: "Do not copy nature too much. Art is an abstraction; draw it out of nature in a dream when you are thinking more about the act of creation than the result."[175] His works "La Belle Angele" and "The Yellow Christ" were painted at this time. He said, "I love Brittany; there I find the wild and primitive. When my wooden shoes ring on the stony soil, I hear the muffled, dull and mighty tone I am seeking in painting."[176]

In 1891, Gauguin moved to Tahiti. To raise money for the trip, he had a show of thirty paintings that earned him 9,860 francs. Octave Mirbeau wrote a commentary on the exhibit in the *Echo de Paris* making collectors aware that this was "a man fleeing from civilization, voluntarily seeking silence and oblivion in order to become more conscious of himself and better able to hear those inner voices which are stifled in the uproar of our passions and disputes."[177]

Before leaving for Tahiti, Gauguin visited his family in Copenhagen. It was not a satisfactory visit; the younger children did not remember him, and they were all struck by the unusual way that he dressed. The visit was short.

Gauguin was given the official but unpaid mission to "study the customs and landscapes of the country" in Tahiti by the French Director of Fine Arts, Ary Renan. After his ship docked in Tahiti, Gauguin paid his respects to the Governor-General, who was impressed by the papers that Ary Renan had obtained from the Ministry of Public Instruction. Gauguin's initial impression of Papeete was: "Here was the Europe from which I had thought to escape, masquerading under the irritating form of colonial snobbery, childish imitation, grotesque to the point of caricature. That was not what I came here to seek."[178]

Once Gauguin left Papeete and moved into the interior, he was more at ease with his decision to move to Tahiti and found something closer to what he had been seeking. In his manuscript, *Noa-noa,* he described what he found in the interior: "I have all the joys of a free existence, animal and human. I have escaped from the artificial into the natural world. With the certainty of tomorrow as free and beautiful as today, peace descends upon me. I develop naturally and have no more vain cares."[179] His paintings from his first stay on Tahiti include "When are you to be married?" and "The Market."

After two years, Gauguin returned to Paris, where he exhibited his works at the Galerie Durand-Ruel without much success. Degas was the only painter who perceived Gauguin's large talent. His acceptance by the public was still in the future. He expressed his concern: "Oh, if the good public would learn to understand a little bit, how I would love it! When I see them examine one of my pictures and turn it upside down, I am terrified they may spoil it.... And then someone in the crowd calls out to me, 'Why do you paint? For whom do you paint? For yourself alone?' That hits me. I crawl away ashamed."[180]

Gauguin returned again to Pont-Aven to paint. While out for a walk, he fought with a group of sailors who had spoken rudely to a woman. He received a kick that broke his shin bone, requiring him to be hospitalized.

In 1895, Gauguin visited his family in Copenhagen before leaving Paris for the last time. He returned to Tahiti, where he settled in a thatched hut surrounded by flowering shrubs at Punaauia. His art continued to evolve. Unfortunately, his health began to slip, and his leg bothered him.

In 1897, Gauguin painted two of his better-known works, "Nevermore" and "Whence come we? What are we? Whither go we?" He described his intent with "Nevermore": "I have tried to suggest a certain bygone barbaric luxury in a simple nude. The whole picture is bathed in deliberately somber colors. It is neither silk nor velvet nor batiste nor gold that creates this luxurious quality, but simply a richness of texture due to the hand of the artist. There is no fooling here ... [but] the imagination of man alone with himself."[181]

Gauguin was going through a particularly difficult time when he painted "Whence come we? What are we? Whither go we?" He applied for a loan from the Bank of Tahiti to pay his living expenses. He received news of the death of his daughter, Aline, from pneumonia, and Mette stopped writing. He summed up his motivation to paint this work in a letter to a friend in July 1901: "I wanted to die and full of despair, I painted it at one go."[182] It was a large work done on a piece of burlap measuring fourteen feet, nine inches by five feet, six inches. It is an example of symbolism; from left to right, it proceeds from birth with several women near a baby, through representatives of adult life, to death depicted by older women on the right. The figure in the center of the work is plucking an apple from a tree.

Gauguin's health continued to decline. His eyesight worsened, and he developed eczema on his legs. In July 1901, he wrote to a friend, "I'm at the end of my rope ... I'm going to make the final effort and am off next month to Fatu-Iva in the Marquesas, an island still almost cannibalistic. I think that the savage element there, together with complete solitude, will revive the fire of enthusiasm before I die, give new life to my imagination, and bring my talents to a fitting conclusion."[183]

In Paris, Gauguin's friend, Daniel de Monfried, continued to search for a market for his work. Ambroise Vollard, a dealer in Paris, was beginning to take an interest in his paintings and to find customers for them. Gauguin considered returning to France, but Monfried advised against it in December 1902: "You would do best not to come back.... You now enjoy the immunity of the honored dead.... Your name has passed into art history."[184]

On May 8, 1903, Gauguin's native servant found him dead in bed. Interest in his work increased when news of his death reached France. Ambroise Vollard arranged a show in his memory. Public acceptance of his work was slow in coming, partly because the public did not understand it. Of his own work, Gauguin had written, "the essential part of work is precisely that which is not expressed: it is implicit in the lines, without either colors or words, and has no material being."[185]

Of his place in art history, Gauguin had written, "You have known for a long time what I wanted to accomplish; the right to dare anything.... The public owes me nothing, since my pictorial work is only 'relatively' good, but the painters who, today, are profiting from this freedom, do owe me something."[186] Gauguin's niche in art history is difficult to evaluate because a considerable portion of his work was purchased by Russian collectors and could only be seen at the Hermitage in St. Petersburg and at the Public Museum in Moscow.

In 1988, Gauguin's work went on view in the West for the first time since 1906. The Paul Gauguin Retrospective, comprised of eleven paintings, was displayed at the National Gallery of Art in Washington and the Art Institute of Chicago; his paintings were shown at the Grand Palais in Paris the following year.

Gauguin has a reputation as a writer as well as a painter. Richard Breitell, an American curator who helped to organize the 1988-89 retrospective of Gauguin's works, commented that his writing was the "largest and most important body of texts, illustrated and otherwise, produced by any great artist in France since ... Delacroix.... That he has always been treated as a businessman-turned-artist rather than an artist shows the extent to which his literary achievement has been undervalued."[187]

Gauguin was determined to make a mid-career change. He made a decision to do what he was created to do; this forced him to live in poverty and suffer from the rejection of his family. However, a case can be made that he rejected them. In her later years, Mette's views of her husband's actions mellowed. Shortly before she died, she gave Gauguin's letters to their youngest son, Paul (Pola), with the comment:

> Read them and they will give you a fairer estimate of your father; publish them if you think fit. He was a strong man both in his disposition and in his actions, without malice or suspicion. Perhaps he was rather inconsiderate in his candor and in acting according to his convictions,

but he was always calm and consistent, without fanaticism. I could not understand his taking up art, though now I understand that he had a right to act as he did. But surely no one can be surprised that I refused to accompany him and bear him more children in an existence which to my mind was a mad and hopeless adventure.[188]

Gauguin's accomplishments are more fully understood today than they were during his lifetime. He was determined to paint and, furthermore, to paint in a primitive style that the public did not understand. His place in art history confirms that he was right on both counts.

F. SCOTT FITZGERALD (1896-1940) Overcame 122 Rejection Slips for His First Novel

"It is not easy to get a clear view of Fitzgerald's career and of his talent; it is not even easy—despite its pervasive influence—to define his achievement. There are many good reasons for this blurring, but perhaps the most important is Fitzgerald's curious ability to get close to the reader. He was, as a person, probably no less odd and alone than most people, but he had a talent for intimacy.... He created an air of interest in those he was with, when he chose to, which is rarely provided for anyone except by himself. He did so because, with his quick imagination, he always saw what others were feeling and sympathized with them...."[189]

Arthur Mizener, *The Far Side of Paradise*

F. Scott Fitzgerald's desire to write was within him from an early age. Growing up in St. Paul, Minnesota and attending the St. Paul Academy, he began by writing detective stories and stories about the Civil War. His father was an American history buff and encouraged him to write Civil War stories. While in high school, Fitzgerald wrote plays and a few football stories. Although he did not have the stature for football, he enjoyed playing the sport.

In an attempt to impose additional academic discipline upon Fitzgerald when he was fifteen, his parents sent him to the Newman School, a small Catholic preparatory school near Hackensack, New Jersey. The Newman School was forty minutes from New York, which made it convenient for him to go into the city to see Broadway plays and musical comedies. However, when his grades began to slip because he was doing the things he wanted to do instead of studying, his pleasures were denied him.

During Fitzgerald's summers home from the Newman School, he participated actively in a St. Paul drama group. While at the Newman School, Fitzgerald wrote feature stories for the newspaper, composed several musical comedies, and served as editor of the *Newman News*.

In his last summer at home before entering college, Fitzgerald studied for the entrance exams to Princeton University. He had time left over to write another play for the St. Paul drama group, a play about the Civil War called *The Coward*. It was a success, and he became known as a young man with writing talent.

Fitzgerald realized early in his first year at Princeton that football was not going to be one of his college activities. He went out for the freshman football team and was cut at the end of the first day. However, there were other potential outlets for his talents: *The Princetonian*, the student newspaper; *The Tiger*, the humor publication; and the Triangle Club, founded by Booth Tarkington, which produced catchy musical comedies that toured the United States every year. Fitzgerald concentrated on *The Tiger* and the Triangle Club. He persisted in sending articles to *The Tiger* until they relented and published some of them. He was less successful with the Triangle Club, so he compromised by working as a stagehand for their productions.

At the end of his freshman year, a musical comedy Fitzgerald had submitted to the Triangle Club was a finalist in their competition. However, when he returned to Princeton in the fall, he had two disappointments waiting for him. The first was that although his musical comedy had won the competition, another student had rewritten the music and Fitzgerald was only given credit for the lyrics. Also, because of his poor grades, he was not permitted to participate in the production of the play. However, later in his college career, he was elected secretary of the Triangle Club and member of the board of editors of *The Tiger*. His reputation as a writer was increasing and some of his work was published by the *Nassau Lit,* whose editor at the time was Edmund Wilson. Wilson became a well-known literary critic and was an important influence in Fitzgerald's literary career.

Eventually, Fitzgerald's lack of attention to his classwork caught up with him again. He was prohibited from participating in extracurricular activities; he lost the presidency of the Triangle Club and had to drop back a year academically. In 1917, many of his classmates volunteered for the army. In October 1917, the fall semester of his senior year, Fitzgerald took an examination for an appointment as Second Lieutenant and received his commission. He reported to infantry officers' training camp at Ft. Leavenworth, Kansas in November.

Fitzgerald's foremost goal was to finish a novel that he had started, *The Romantic Egoist*. Weekends were the only time he could work on his novel. He wrote at the officers' club from one o'clock Saturday afternoon until midnight and from six o'clock in the morning until six o'clock in the evening on Sundays. He wrote his novel of 120,000 words in three months of weekends, an accomplishment that indicated his drive and determination.

In March 1918, Fitzgerald sent his novel to Scribners, who returned it to him in August with the recommendation that he revise it extensively. He made the suggested revisions and resubmitted it. Again, they rejected it. Maxwell Perkins was the only editor on the review board who recommended its acceptance.

On November 11, 1918, the armistice ending World War I was signed, frustrating Fitzgerald's goal of going to Europe and becoming a hero. He was discharged in February 1919 and moved to New York, the writers' Mecca. He applied to and was turned down by all seven New York newspapers. The only job he could find was at the Baron Collier Advertising Agency writing advertising slogans for trolley car ads. Instead of living in Greenwich Village as he had hoped, he rented a room on Claremont Avenue in the Bronx.

Fitzgerald spent all of his spare time writing short stories, poems, and scripts for movies. He completed nineteen stories between April and June. The longest time he spent on any one story was three days. At the end of three months, he had posted 122 rejection slips on the walls of his cramped room. They included not a single word of encouragement from an editor. Finally, he sold a novelette for $215 to *Smart Set*, a magazine edited by H. L. Mencken. He had written the piece for the *Nassau Lit* in 1917.

Fitzgerald returned to St. Paul to revise the manuscript for his novel while living at home. He completed the revisions and additions to his manuscript in early September and forwarded it to Maxwell Perkins at Scribners. Perkins mailed a special delivery letter to Fitzgerald in mid-September notifying him that Scribners would publish his novel, now renamed *This Side of Paradise*. Fitzgerald was fortunate to have been accepted by Scribners, a conservative publisher not particularly known for catering to young authors.

After having a manuscript accepted, Fitzgerald found that his other work began to sell. He sold two stories to *Scribners Magazine*. Harold Ober became his literary agent; Ober's first act was to sell his story "Head and Shoulders" to the *Saturday Evening Post*. The next sale was of the movie rights for "Head and Shoulders" to MGM. He was on his way as an author. Unfortunately, he was not able to handle success; he was extravagant and was unable to control his drinking.

Fitzgerald's later works include *The Great Gatsby* and *Tender Is the Night*. Most readers view *The Great Gatsby* as his greatest novel. No line of work interested Fitzgerald other than writing; he was determined to become a successful author. Fitzgerald is known as the novelist of the Jazz Age of the 1920's. Biographer Arthur Mizener comments in *The Far Side of Paradise* on Fitzgerald's place in American literature:

> Fitzgerald loved reputation, the public acknowledgment of genuine achievement, with the impersonal magnanimity of a Renaissance prince. He lived, finally, to give that chaos in his head shape in his books and to see the knowledge that he had done so reflected back to him from the world. He died believing that he had failed [in his opinion, "a first-rate writer who has never produced anything but second-rate books"]. Now we know better, and it is one of the final ironies of Fitzgerald's career that he did not live to enjoy our knowledge.[190]

FREDERICK DOUGLASS (1817-1895) Abolitionist Leader and Publisher

"It rekindled the few expiring embers of freedom and revived within me a sense of my own manhood. It recalled the departed self-confidence, and inspired me again with a determination to be free.... He can only understand the deep satisfaction which I experienced, who has himself repelled by force the bloody arm of slavery. I felt as I never felt before. It was a glorious resurrection, from the tomb of of slavery to the heaven of freedom. My long-crushed spirit rose, cowardice departed, bold defiance took its place, and I now resolved that, however long I might remain a slave in form, the day had passed forever when I could be a slave in fact."[191]

Frederick Douglass (upon winning a fight with a "slave breaker")

Historian George L. Ruffin observes the position of Frederick Douglass at the height of his career:

> Frederick Douglass stands upon a pedestal; he has reached this lofty height through years of toil and strife, but it has been the strife of moral ideas; strife in the battle for human rights. No bitter memories come from this strife; no feeling of remorse can rise to cast their gloomy shadows over his soul, and Douglass has now reached the meridian of his life.... We rejoice that Douglass had attained unto this exalted position—this pedestal. It has been honorably reached; it is a just recognition of talent and effort; it is another proof that success attends high and noble aim.[192]

257

Frederick was born in February 1818 in Talbot County on the Eastern Shore of Maryland; he was not sure of the actual date of his birth. His mother, Harriet Bailey, was a slave and his father, whom he never met, was a white man. His master was Captain Aaron Anthony.

In March 1826, Frederick was sent to live with a member of Anthony's family, Hugh Auld, in Baltimore. Initially, Hugh's wife, Sophia, was kind to Frederick. He asked her to help him learn to read and write; she did so willingly until her husband heard what she was doing. Then the lessons stopped, and Sophia was no longer friendly to him. However, living in Baltimore was a good experience for him; he had many opportunities to learn.

Thomas Auld, Frederick's legal owner, brought him back to rural slavery in 1833. Frederick did not like Auld or Auld's wife, Rowena. He was not completely obedient, so Auld hired him out to Edward Covey, who had a reputation as a "slave breaker." After Frederick had endured six months of flogging and other mistreatment, he turned on Covey in a two-hour fight that Frederick won. After that, Covey did not bother him, but Frederick was even more committed to winning his freedom. He helped his fellow slaves with reading lessons.

In April 1836, Frederick and five other slaves made plans to escape. However, one of them told authorities of their plans, and they were jailed in Easton. Instead of selling Frederick, Thomas Auld sent him back to Hugh and Sophia in Baltimore. Frederick became an experienced caulker in a boatyard, where competition for jobs was fierce between poor white immigrants and slaves. Frederick was badly beaten because he was thought to have taken a job from a white immigrant.

Frederick continued his self-education by joining the East

Baltimore Mental Improvement Society, a debating club. He met Anna Murray, a freed slave who was barely literate, at one of their meetings. In 1838, they became engaged and began to save money and make plans to escape to the North. An argument with Hugh Auld motivated Frederick to board a northbound train and escape. The conductor asked to see his free slave papers, which he did not have; Frederick showed him his seaman's papers instead. Despite some tense moments when he saw two local men who could identify him as a slave, he arrived in Philadelphia safely and then continued on to New York City.

Frederick stayed with David Ruggles, publisher of the antislavery quarterly, *The Mirror of Slavery.* He sent for Anna Murray, and they were married on September 15, 1838. Ruggles, who was active in the underground railroad, suggested that they move farther north.

They traveled to New Bedford, Massachusetts, where Frederick hoped to find work as a caulker, and lived with Nathan Johnson and his wife. Johnson suggested that because Frederick was an escaped slave, he should change his name. Johnson had just finished reading Sir Walter Scott's *Lady of the Lake*; he suggested the surname of "Douglass," the name of the Scottish lord and hero. Frederick Bailey became Frederick Douglass.

When Douglass looked for work as a caulker, he found that prejudice existed in the North as well as the South. White caulkers did not want to work with African Americans. He was forced to take odd jobs as a common laborer. Anna helped by doing domestic work. One day he found a copy of William Lloyd Garrison's antislavery newspaper, *The Liberator,* and it changed his life.

Garrison was a strong-willed abolitionist. In addition to

being an editor, Garrison had helped to establish the New England Anti-Slavery Society. Douglass subscribed to Garrison's paper and was moved by it.

Douglass attended the annual meeting of the New England Anti-Slavery Society in New Bedford on August 9, 1841 and a meeting the next day on the Island of Nantucket. At the second meeting, Douglass was asked to speak. Although he was nervous, he spoke movingly about his life as a slave and was well-received. Historian Oscar Handlin comments on the impression of an audience who had not previously encountered a slave:

> Hence the impression Frederick Douglass made upon the audience to which he spoke at the Nantucket Atheneum in August 1841. Here a man, not an abstraction but a creature of flesh and blood. Not long before, he had been a chattel, a thing bought and sold. But the escape to freedom had restored his manhood so that now he addressed the meeting in meaningful terms using the intellectual equipment acquired through his own efforts.

> The abolitionists took up Douglass, who seemed the crowning evidence to complete their case; then for years he labored in the effort to persuade others. In doing so, he entered into the mainstream of the reform movements that occupied increasing attention in the decades before 1860.[193]

Douglass was asked to become a full time lecturer for the organization. He reluctantly accepted a three-month assignment and then stayed for four years. He improved his oratorical skills and became one of the Society's most popular lecturers. The life of an abolitionist was not easy; Douglass had to learn to overcome hecklers. On September 15, 1843, he was severely beaten in Pendleton, Indiana. He escaped with a broken wrist and bruises.

Abolitionist newspaper editor Elijah Lovejoy was killed in Alton, Illinois while defending his press from an incensed mob. William Lloyd Garrison was dragged through the streets of Boston with a rope around his waist and almost lost his life. During the winter and early spring of 1844-45, Douglass left the lecture circuit to write an autobiography, *The Narrative of the Life of Frederick Douglass, an American Slave.* In August 1845, he went on a successful lecture tour of England, Ireland, and Scotland.

One month after Douglass's return to America, Anna and Ellen Richardson of Newcastle raised money and negotiated for his freedom. They contacted American agents to buy his freedom from the Aulds for $711.66. The deed of manumission was filed at the Baltimore Chattel Records Office on December 13, 1846, and Douglass was a free man.

Douglass returned to England for another lecture tour in 1847. Upon his return to America, he proceeded with plans to publish an antislavery newspaper. His British friends raised $2,000 to help him get started. He was surprised when Garrison advised against it. Garrison, who did not want competition for his newspaper, *The Liberator,* said that there were already too many newspapers of that type.

Douglass started his newspaper despite Garrison's counsel against it. He knew that he would have to choose a base far from Garrison's in New England. Douglass chose Rochester, a booming city of 30,000 on the Erie Canal, where he had been well-received on the lecture circuit in 1842 and

1847. The leading abolitionist of central New York, Gerrit Smith, supported him and gave him the deed to land near Rochester. Douglass moved his family there on November 1, 1847.

On December 3, 1847, the first edition of his newspaper, *North Star*, was published. He named the paper *North Star* because the North Star was the guide that the slaves used when escaping from the South to freedom. In 1851, the *North Star* merged with the *Liberty Party Paper,* which was financed by Gerrit Smith; the resulting paper was called *Frederick Douglass's Paper.* In 1858, he began publishing *Douglass's Monthly* for British readers. The weekly ran until 1860; he stopped printing the monthly in 1863, thus ending a sixteen-year publishing career.

Douglass served as a Rochester stationmaster on the underground railroad. He hid hundreds of escaping slaves at the *North Star* printing office, at his first house on Alexander Street, and later at his home on South Avenue near Highland Park.

Douglass wrote about this effort: "On one occasion I had at least eleven fugitives at the same time under my roof— until I could collect sufficient money to get them to Canada. It was the largest number at any one time, and I had some difficulty in providing so many with food and shelter. But they were content with very plain food and a strip of carpet on the floor for a bed or a place in the straw in the hayloft."[194]

Douglass received financial assistance from friends in England. He had many assistants in raising funds for the fugitives' escape. The production foreman for the *Daily Democrat* was a principal aide. He hid slaves in his press room in the Tallman building, where Douglass's printing office also was housed, and solicited money for underground railroad efforts from downtown Rochester business offices.

Douglass supported the Woman's Rights Movement. On July 14, 1848, his *North Star* carried the announcement: "A convention to discuss the Social, Civil, and Religious Condition and Rights of Women will be held in the Wesleyan Chapel at Seneca Falls, New York, the 19th and 20th of July instant." The masthead that Douglass used for the *North Star* was: "RIGHT IS OF NO SEX — TRUTH IS OF NO COLOR."[195]

During the Civil War, Douglass was among the earliest to suggest the enlistment of Negro troops in the U.S. Army. Two of Douglass's sons served in the Union Army. After the war, Douglass was a popular public speaker and traveled widely.

In January 1871, President Grant appointed Douglass to a commission to Santo Domingo (Dominican Republic). He moved to Washington. D.C. because he thought that more federal appointments would be offered. In 1877, President Rutherford Hayes appointed him United States Marshal for the District of Columbia. He served in that position until 1881, when President James Garfield appointed him Recorder of Deeds for the District of Columbia. He held that office until 1886.

Douglass's wife, Anna, died in August 1882. In January 1884, he married Helen Pitts, his secretary in the Office of the Recorder of Deeds. The mixed marriage caused controversy, but Helen said, "Love came to me and I was not afraid to marry the man I loved because of his color." Douglass's response to critics was that his first wife "was the color of my mother and the second the color of my father."[196]

In September 1889, President Benjamin Harrison appointed Douglass Minister-Resident and Consul-General to the Republic of Haiti, where he served until July 1891. Douglass, one of the strongest antislavery voices of his time, died of a heart attack in Washington, D.C. on February 20, 1895.

Statue of Frederick Douglass, Highland Park, Rochester, NY

Harriet Tubman House, Auburn, NY

HARRIET TUBMAN (1820-1913) Conductor on the Underground Railroad

"When I found I had crossed that [Mason-Dixon] line, I looked at my hands to see if I was the same person. There was such glory over everything; the sun came like gold through the trees, and over the fields, and I felt like I was in heaven."[197]

Harriet Tubman

William Still, Philadelphia abolitionist leader, commented on Harriet Tubman's role in the underground railroad:

> Her success was wonderful. Time and time again she made successful visits to Maryland on the underground railroad, and would be absent for weeks at a time, running daily risks while making preparations for herself and passengers. Great fears were entertained for her safety, but she seemed wholly devoid of personal fear. The idea of being captured by slavehunters or slaveholders never seemed to enter her mind.[198]

She was resolved to do her part to free those members of her race still in captivity.

Harriet Ross Tubman, one of eleven children of Harriet Greene and Benjamin Ross, was born in 1820 on a plantation in Dorchester County on the Eastern Shore of Maryland. The plantation on Big Buckwater River, which was owned by Edward Brodas, was 100 miles south of the Mason-Dixon Line and sixty miles from Baltimore. Harriet's parents were full-blooded Africans of the Ashanti, a West African warrior people.

Harriet, who was called Araminta at birth, was born in a slave cabin with an open fireplace and without windows or furniture. The family slept on a clay floor. When she was five years old, Harriet was hired out to a family named Cook. Mrs. Cook used Harriet to wind yarn.

Because she was slow at the job, Harriet was turned over to Mr. Cook, who put her to work tending his muskrat traps. She waded in the cold water of the river with a thin dress and no shoes and eventually developed bronchitis and a high fever. Mr. Cook thought she was faking illness and returned her to her home plantation, where she recovered from bronchitis and a case of measles.

Harriet was hired out again, this time as a baby nurse and housekeeper. She said, "I was so little that I had to sit on the floor and have the baby put in my lap. And that baby was always on my lap except when it was asleep or when its mother was feeding it."[199] When the baby awakened during the night, Harriet was expected to rock it in its cradle to prevent it from crying. If the baby's crying awoke Mrs. Cook, she would beat Harriet with a cowhide whip that left permanent scars on her back and neck.

Harriet was fed scraps from the table and was hungry most of the time. When she was seven, she took a lump of sugar from the sugar bowl. Mrs. Cook saw her take it and got out her whip. Harriet fled the house and lived with pigs in the pigpen for five days, competing with them for potato peelings and other scraps of food. Finally, she returned to the Cook's home, where she was given a severe beating and sent home to the Brodas plantation.

Harriet was then hired out to split fence rails and load wagons with lumber. The heavy work was difficult for her, but she preferred it to being under the thumb of the mistress of the house. In her early teens, she worked as a field hand and saw many examples of cruelty to slaves on the plantation. Later in life, she said of the owners and overseers, "They didn't know any better. It's the way they were brought up ... with the whip in their hand. Now it was not that way on all plantations. There were good masters and mistresses, as I have heard tell. But I did not happen to come across any of them."[200]

In 1835, when she was fifteen years old, Harriet saw a slave sneak away from the plantation. The tall African American was followed by the overseer with his whip and by Harriet. The overseer soon caught the runaway slave and asked Harriet to hold the man while he tied him up. She refused. The black man ran away, and Harriet stood in the way to prevent pursuit. The overseer picked up a two-pound weight and threw it at Harriet. It struck her in the middle of her forehead, fractured her skull, caused profuse bleeding, and gave her a severe concussion.

Harriet was in a coma for weeks. For the rest of her life, she was affected by severe headaches and "sleeping fits," during which she would fall asleep for a few minutes—sometimes in the middle of a conversation. She was left with a depression in her forehead and a disfiguring scar. While she was in bed recovering, her master brought prospective owners to her bedside in attempts to sell her. No one wanted to buy her, even at the lowest price; "They said I wasn't worth a penny."[201]

When Harriet had regained her strength, she was hired out to John Stewart, a local contractor. Initially, she worked as a maid in Stewart's home, but she begged him to let her work outdoors with the men. She cut wood, drove a team of oxen, and plowed. Soon she was swinging an ax to cut timber for the Baltimore shipbuilding industry. When work was slack on the Stewart farm, she was allowed to hire herself out to cut and haul wood for neighboring farmers. For this privilege, she paid Stewart fifty dollars a year and was permitted to keep everything she earned above that amount. She put away a small nest egg from this work.

While Harriet toiled at heavy outdoor work, she dreamed of being free. She thought, "I had reasoned this out in my mind; there was one of two things I had a right to, liberty or death; if I could not have one, I would have the other. For no man would take me alive; I should fight for my liberty as long as my strength lasted, and when it came time for me to go, the Lord would let them take me."[202]

In 1844, Harriet married John Tubman, a free African American who lived nearby. John Tubman had been born free because his parents had been freed when their master died. Her husband's freedom did not change Harriet's slave status. Furthermore, her children would belong to the plantation. The constant threat to slaves in Maryland was to be "sold South," that is, sold to plantation owners from Alabama, Georgia, Louisiana, or Mississippi, where conditions for slaves were much harsher than in states closer to the Mason-Dixon Line.

One day, Harriet heard that two of her sisters had been sold and were being transported south in chains. She knew of the underground railroad and of people who helped slaves escape. She did not know geography, but she knew enough to follow the North Star to freedom.

Harriet tried to convince three of her brothers to come with her, but they were afraid of being captured and punished. She knew that her husband did not want to travel to the North; in fact, he would have turned her in if he had known that she was leaving.

Tubman left the plantation in the middle of the night with a loaf of cornbread, some salt herring, and her prized possession—a patchwork quilt. As she left, she sang an old spiritual:

> I'll meet you in the morning,
> When I reach the promised land,
> On the other side of Jordan.
> For I'm bound for the promised land.

Tubman went to the house of a woman who was known to help slaves escape. The woman took her in and gave her a slip of paper noting her next stop on the way to freedom. Tubman was so grateful that she gave the woman her quilt. She was tired when she arrived at the next stop early in the morning. The woman opened the door and handed her a broom and told her to start sweeping the yard.

At first, Harriet was suspicious; then she realized that no one would question a slave working around the house. The woman's husband put her in his wagon, covered her with vegetables, and took her to the next stop that evening, generally following the course of the Choptank River.

Tubman finally crossed the Mason-Dixon Line and entered Pennsylvania. She was free, but she did not have any contacts to help her find a job and a place to live. In her words, "I was a stranger in a strange land."

Tubman traveled to Philadelphia, where she found a job in a hotel kitchen cooking and washing dishes. She met two founders of the Philadelphia Vigilance Committee, James Miller McKim, a white clergyman, and William Still, a free-born African American. They needed someone to guide a slave family north from Cambridge, Maryland. Harriet volunteered, but they hesitated letting her go because she might be retained in the South as a slave. When she heard that the family was her sister, Mary, and her brother-in-law, John Bowley, she insisted on going. She brought them to safety in Philadelphia.

In the spring of 1851, Tubman made her second trip south to guide fellow slaves northward. This time she guided her brother, James, and two of his friends to freedom. The overseer and the hounds were on their trail. Tubman evaded the dogs by crossing an ice-cold river. None of them could swim, and the men opposed the crossing. She waded out into swift-flowing water up to her chin to prove that they could make it across. If she had not changed their route on a hunch, they would have been captured.

On her next trip to Dorchester County, Maryland, Tubman stopped at her husband's cabin. She found that he had remarried and had no interest in traveling north. She brought several slaves back to Philadelphia, being very careful in country in which she was known.

Tubman traveled northward through Delaware, waiting until the last moment to cross into Maryland because Delaware was the site of the headwaters of many rivers that drained through the Eastern Shore into Chesapeake Bay. Also, the State's African-American population in 1860 contained only 1,798 slaves out of a total of 21,627. Delaware was the only southern state in which an African American was assumed to be free until proved to be a slave.

When she approached a stop on the underground railroad, Tubman hid her "passengers" before she rapped on the door. Then she would announce that she was "a friend with friends." Many of her trips north were through Wilmington, Delaware, the home of Thomas Garrett, a leader of the underground railroad movement.

On September 18, 1850, the passage of the Fugitive Slave Act made helping escaped slaves riskier. U.S. Marshals were empowered to catch runaways and return them to their owners. Anyone assisting a fugitive could be fined $1,000 and sent to jail. Slavecatchers were hired to pursue runaway slaves who had thought that they were safe in the North.

More slaves were now going to Canada, which was beyond the reach of the Fugitive Slave Act and the slave-catchers. Tubman said, "I wouldn't trust Uncle Sam with my people no longer."[203] Eventually, she moved from Philadelphia to St. Catharines, Ontario, where she lived for five years.

In December 1851, Tubman made her fourth trip south. On her return, she guided another of her brothers and his wife to freedom. When she reached Garrett's home in Wilmington, she added nine more passengers, including a baby. From this trip onward, she carried a sedative to keep baby passengers quiet.

Between 1851 and 1857, Tubman made a spring trip and a fall trip to Maryland's Eastern Shore each year. On these trips, she met many of the leaders of the underground railroad movement, including John Brown, Frederick Douglass, J. W. Loguen, and Gerrit Smith. Brown called Tubman "General Tubman."

On one of her trips, Tubman had a nervous passenger who panicked and wanted to turn back. She knew that if he were captured, he would be tortured to describe escape methods and "stations" on the road north. She pointed a gun at his head and told him to keep walking, while reminding him that if he were dead he could not reveal any information. This occurred more than once on her trips on the underground railroad.

Tubman frequently stopped at Cooper House in Camden,

Delaware and hid her passengers in a secret room above the kitchen. In Odessa, Delaware, they hid in a concealed loft over the sanctuary in a Quaker meeting house.

On many farms, slaves hid in a "potato hole," a rough vegetable cellar with few amenities. On one occasion, Tubman pretended to be reading a book when the slavecatchers passed by. One of the men said to the other, "This can't be the woman. The one we want can't read or write."

People began to call Tubman "the Moses of her people." A $12,000 reward was offered for her capture. She made her last journey on the underground railroad in 1860. In nineteen trips, she led over 300 slaves to their freedom.

During the Civil War, Tubman worked with slaves who had been left behind when their owners joined the Confederate Army. Major General David Hunter was pleased to have her help with the slaves at Beaufort, South Carolina. She also served as a nurse at Hilton Head, South Carolina and in Florida. For three years of service to the federal government, she was paid only $200, most of which was spent to build a washhouse where she instructed slave women in doing laundry to support themselves.

During the summer of 1863, Tubman worked as a scout for Colonel James Montgomery, who commanded an African-American regiment. Harriet assembled a network of spies, who notified her which slaves were ready to leave their master and serve in the Union Army. She was supposed to receive a reward for recruiting slaves to the Grand Army of the Republic. She was owed at least $1,800 for her efforts, but she was never paid.

In 1864, Tubman was exhausted, and her seizures were occurring more frequently. She went to Auburn, New York to rest and recuperate. In 1867, Harriet's friend, Sarah Bradford, wrote a biography about her and turned over the proceeds of the book, $1,200, to her. Some of the money went to African Americans who needed food and clothing.

While living in Auburn, she heard that her husband, John Tubman, had died. On March 18, 1869, Tubman married Nelson Davis, whom she had met in South Carolina during the war. William H. Seward, Secretary of State in the Lincoln and Andrew Johnson administrations, attended her wedding. Seward had obtained property for Tubman when she first moved to Auburn; they maintained their friendship until he died in 1872.

In 1888, Tubman purchased a 25-acre property at a public auction to establish a home for African Americans who were ill and needy. She lacked the money to build the home, so she deeded the property to the African Methodist Episcopal Zion Church. The church built the home, but Tubman was unhappy when she heard that it cost $100 to enter it.

Tubman's second husband died in 1888. In 1890, Congress approved pensions for widows of Civil War veterans. Since Davis had served in the Union Army, she was entitled to eight dollars a month, which was increased to twenty dollars a month in 1899. Except for $200, this was the only money she received from the government; she was never fully paid for her efforts during the Civil War.

On March 10, 1913, Tubman died of pneumonia at the age of ninety-three, after living two years in the home that she had helped to establish. The Auburn post of the Grand Army of the Republic gave her a military funeral at which Booker T. Washington spoke.

Tubman was truly the Moses of her people; she was also an abolitionist, a humanitarian, a nurse, and a spy. Today, she is mainly remembered for her underground railroad activities, about which she said, "I never ran my train off the track, and I never lost a passenger."[204]

CHAPTER 6

VICTORS / LEADERS

"Confidence is conqueror of men;
     victorious both over them and in them;
The iron will of one stout heart
     shall make a thousand quail:
A feeble dwarf, dauntlessly resolved,
     will turn the tide of battle,
And rally to a nobler strife
     the giants that had fled."

Tupper, *Proverbial Philosophy of Faith*

Chapter 6 provides examples of individuals who were victors in battle and successful leaders. They displayed firm resolve and are excellent role models of determination.

Horatio Nelson was given significant responsibility as a junior Admiral because his senior officers knew that he was aggressive and determined to win. He was outnumbered and outgunned at the Battle of the Nile and at Trafalgar, but he won both battles decisively. His winning strategy was to be bold and to bring superior firepower to bear on a portion of the enemy line. Losing the sight of an eye in action at Calvi, Corsica and his right arm in an attack at Santa Cruz in the Canary Islands did not slow him down.

Brigham Young succeeded founder Joseph Smith as head of the Church of Jesus Christ of Latter-Day Saints. He was the highly organized natural leader who directed the Mormon's move to the Salt Lake Valley after being persecuted in New York, Ohio, Missouri, and Illinois. Other than the knowledge gained by Lewis and Clark, little was known about routes to the West. Young organized wagon trains of several thousand men, women, and children across primitive country. He was not only an effective leader of the rapidly growing Mormon Church but also one of the most successful colonizers in the history of the United States.

Ulysses S. Grant sustained an admirable personal effort to complete the writing of his memoirs. He was in constant pain dying of throat cancer, but he knew that he had to complete his memoirs to earn money to pay off debtors after the failure of the Grant & Ward investment firm. His partner, Ward, had misled investors and then absconded with the funds of the partnership. Many of Grant's family members and friends lost their savings in the business failure. At times, Grant had to take a break from his writing because of recurring pain. He died shortly after finishing his two-volume work.

Mustafa Kemal, Atatürk, as a junior lieutenant colonel was the principal actor in the Battle of Gallipoli won by the Turks and their German allies in World War I. Kemal was unable to convince his superiors in the Turkish Army and their German staff advisors of the anticipated landing site of Australia / New Zealand forces. He repeatedly responded to landings by moving his division around to address the latest point of attack. Rarely has one person contributed so dramatically to a military victory. After World War I, Kemal westernized Turkey and brought the country into the twentieth century. He changed the alphabet and dress code and freed Turkish women from centuries of bondage.

Benjamin O. Davis was determined to succeed in his Army career. When he was denied entrance to the Army as a commissioned officer, he signed on as an enlisted man with the goal of earning a commission. His assignments during his career were not typical. Although he served in line duty in the American West and in the Philippines, many of his assignments were as a Professor of Military Science and Tactics at African-American colleges. When African Americans entered the military service in large numbers during World War II, integration was evolving but not without growing pains. The U.S. Army was extremely fortunate having an officer like Brigadier General Benjamin Davis to address and to ease these growing pains.

These victors and leaders led lives of impressive accomplishment. We can all gain by emulating their strong personal qualities.

HORATIO NELSON (1758-1805) Victor of the Battles of the Nile and Trafalgar

"Morale is a state of mind. It is steadfastness and hope. It is confidence and zeal and loyalty. It is élan, esprit de corps, and determination."

Douglas MacArthur

Admiral Lord Horatio Nelson's illustrious career was noted for three major battles: the Battle of the Nile, the Battle of Copenhagen, and the Battle of Trafalgar. *Staying With It: Role Models of Perseverance* highlights the Battle of Copenhagen, a sea fight in which Nelson persevered amid adversity and was victorious. These battles are represented by three stripes on the collar of the Royal Navy sailor's uniform.

One of Nelson's mentors, Captain William Cornwallis, advised him, "When in doubt, to fight is to err on the right side." Later, Nelson advised his captains, "No captain can do very wrong if he places his ship alongside that of an enemy."[205] Nelson always advocated attack, even when he was outgunned or was at a strategic disadvantage such as at Copenhagen, where he was opposed by Danish forces on dry ground that could replace their casualties. He was determined to win even if it was no more than refusing to admit defeat.

The Battle of the Nile

In March 1798, during Britain's long and painful war with France, Nelson left England in his flagship, *Vanguard,* bound for the Mediterranean. With him sailed Captain Troubridge in *Culloden,* Captain Foley in *Goliath,* Captain Hood in *Zealous,* and Captain Miller in *Theseus* in a squadron that would later go into battle with fourteen ships. Lord St.

Vincent, his commander-in-chief, was pleased to welcome the aggressive Nelson, whose arrival gave his commander "new life."

Napoleon wanted to attack England, but he realized that the French Navy was no match for the Royal Navy. Instead, he carried the war to the Mediterranean by attacking and sacking Malta, which was listlessly defended by the Knights of St. John, a shadow of their former selves when they had fought the infidels in Palestine during the Crusades. Napoleon, who was General of France's Army and Admiral (assisted by Admiral De Brueys) of France's Navy, loaded Malta's treasures on his flagship, *L'Orient,* and sailed for Egypt.

Nelson arrived in Egypt, but because he was short of frigates, the eyes of the fleet, he did not know the location of the French fleet. Napoleon off-loaded his army from his ships at Marabout. Nelson had used the time looking for Napoleon to train his already highly trained fleet. British seamen may not have been well paid, well fed, or well treated, but they were well trained and when they were asked to fight, they fought well. England was justifiably proud of their "hearts of oak."

The French fleet of seventeen ships, which included the flagship (120 guns), three ships of the line (80 guns each) and nine ships of the line (74 guns each), and four frigates (two with 40 guns and two with 36), outmanned Nelson's ships. Nelson had fourteen ships of the line, all with 74 guns except the smaller *Leander,* and no frigates. The difference in weight of metal was significant; a French seventy-four carried heavier guns than a British seventy-four. However, the level of discipline and training was much higher in the British ships.

Admiral De Brueys had anchored at Aboukir Bay, near

the mouth of the Nile, because of excessive silt in the bay at Alexandria. De Brueys felt secure because he had shoals on one side of his ships, breakers on the other side, and he had positioned his frigates on the flanks. Furthermore, French artillery on Bequier Island provided additional cover for his ships, and sunset was only a few hours away when the British fleet was sighted.

Nelson, who had been restless while searching for the French fleet, was eager for a fight. He said, "Before this time tomorrow, I shall have gained a peerage, or Westminster Abbey."[206] Nelson took a substantial risk by attacking a fleet anchored so close to shore; he assumed that the typically conservative French fleet would not risk anchoring too close to the shoreline.

The battle began at 6:30 p.m., at sundown. Early in the battle, Captain Troubridge's *Culloden* went aground on a shoal. Each of Nelson's ships mounted four lights in a line at the top of the mizzen mast to distinguish them from French ships. Realizing that he was facing an enemy with superior firepower, Nelson's plan of battle was to bring an overpowering force to bear on part of the French line (the van).

Captain Foley, the most experienced of Nelson's captains, in *Goliath*, took the initiative by leading *Zealous*, *Theseus*, *Orion*, and *Audacious* between the first ship in the French line, *Le Guerrier*, and the French battery on Bequier Island to position themselves between the shoreline and the French line of ships. These ships brought concentrated fire to bear on the French line, destroying the French ships in the van within two hours of the start of the battle. Captain Darby's ship, *Bellerophon*, had her masts and cables shot away by *L'Orient* and drifted out of control. *Majestic* had many casualties; her Captain, Westcott, was killed.

Admiral De Brueys in *L'Orient* fought on after receiving three wounds, two in the body and one in the head, before being virtually cut in two by the fourth shot. Commodore Casabianca assumed command until *L'Orient,* with all of Malta's treasures, blew up at ten o'clock. The explosion was heard at Alexandria, fifteen miles away.

During the battle, Nelson was struck in the forehead by a piece of iron shot, causing a flap of skin to hang down over his right eye, his blind eye. He had lost the sight of that eye in 1793 in a raid on the French garrison at Calvi in Corsica when shot striking the ground near him drove sand and gravel into the eye. The three-inch wound in his forehead, which bared his skull, bled profusely, and he was temporarily blinded. Although he was in great pain, when the doctor left the sailor he was treating to attend the admiral, Nelson said, "No, I will take my turn with my brave fellows."

Nelson drafted a report of the battle for Lord St. Vincent and the Lord Commissioners of the Admiralty that included the comments:

> Nothing could withstand the Squadron your Lordships did me the honor to place under my command. Their high state of discipline is well known to you, and with the judgment of the captains, together with their valor, and that of Officers and Men of every description, it was absolutely irresistible. Could anything from my pen add to the character of the Captains I would write it with pleasure, but that is impossible.[207]

Lord Howe wrote to Nelson that he thought it notable that *every* captain had done his duty. Howe had experienced naval battles in which that statement could not have been made. Nelson felt that he owed a description of the battle to Howe, whom he thought was the "first and greatest sea-officer the world has ever produced": "I had the happiness to command a Band of Brothers ... Each knew his duty, and I was sure each would feel for a French ship. By attacking the enemy's van and center, the wind blowing directly along their line, I was enabled to throw what force I pleased on a few ships.... We always kept a superior force to the enemy."[208]

Of the seventeen ships in Admiral De Bruey's fleet, all but four were either on fire or flying the British Union Jack the next morning. Nelson had not lost a single ship; it was the most complete victory that the Royal Navy had ever experienced. The French had six times the casualties, 5225, of the British, including men who were missing or captured. The Admiralty, which had been criticized for choosing a young Admiral like Nelson for such an important command, was justified in its choice. England was overjoyed with Nelson's victory; he was raised to the peerage with the title Baron Nelson of the Nile.

The Battle of Trafalgar

In the fall of 1805, Nelson prepared for what would be his last battle. Under his command were twenty-seven ships of the line, four frigates, a schooner, and a cutter. His squadron included Admiral Collingwood (his second in command) in *Royal Sovereign,* Captain Berry in *Agamemnon* (one of Nelson's previous commands), Captain Harvey in *Téméraire,* and Captain Freemantle in *Neptune.* Captain Hardy, Nelson's close friend, commanded *Victory,* his flagship.

Admiral Villeneuve, in command of the combined French and Spanish fleet at Trafalgar, instructed the Captains under his command of Nelson's intentions: "He will try to double our rear, cut through the line, and bring against the ships thus isolated groups of his own, to surround and capture them. Captains must rely on their courage and love of glory, rather than the signals of the Admiral, who may already be engaged and wrapped in smoke. The Captain who is not in action is not at his post."[209]

Nelson's written instructions to his captains were similar to what Villeneuve had expected:

> The order of sailing was to be the order of battle ... The second in command, Admiral Collingwood, after Nelson's intentions had been made known by signal, would have entire direction of the line. If possible he was to cut through the enemy about the twelfth ship from the rear. The remainder of the combined fleet was to be left to the management of the commander-in-chief, whose endeavor would be to see that, while the rear was pulverized by Collingwood, no interference should be encountered from the van.[210]

Villeneuve commanded thirty-three ships of the line (eighteen French and fifteen Spanish), five French frigates, and two brigs. During the evening of October 19, the brig *Argus* notified Villeneuve on the French flagship, *Bucentaure,* that eighteen British ships had been sighted.

Prior to going into battle, Nelson thought of his family. He wrote a document asking his country to provide for his beloved Emma Hamilton "that they will give her an ample provision to maintain her rank in life,"[211] and he also left "to the beneficence of my country my adopted daughter,

Horatia."

At six o'clock the following morning, Nelson signaled his fleet from his flagship, *Victory,* to form into two columns while sailing toward the combined French and Spanish fleet. Nelson's officers on the *Victory* convinced him that the flagship should not be the first ship to go into action. He seemed to agree to let *Téméraire* go into action ahead of *Victory;* however, *Victory* did not give way, and Nelson hailed *Téméraire* from the quarterdeck, "I'll thank you, Captain Harvey, to keep your proper station, which is astern of the *Victory.*"

Nelson signalled his squadron, "England expects that every man will do his duty," followed by the signal for close action. Collingwood in *Royal Sovereign* went into action well ahead of his squadron, cutting the line of the combined fleet just astern of the *Santa Anna,* Admiral Alava's flagship.

Gunfire from the topmasts of the combined fleets' *Redoubtable* rained down on the deck of *Victory* until *Téméraire* came up to support *Victory*. At 1:15 p.m., Hardy saw Nelson, on his knees, fall to the deck. He told Hardy, "They have done for me at last, Hardy." A shot from the fighting tops of *Redoubtable* had shattered Nelson's left shoulder, penetrated his chest, and lodged in his spine. Nelson was carried below. Hardy visited Nelson to give him status of the battle: "We have got twelve or fourteen of the enemy's ships in our possession but five of their van have tacked, and show an intention of bearing down on *Victory*. I have therefore called two or three of our fresh ships around us, and have no doubt of giving them a drubbing."[212]

Hardy returned to his duty station to send Collingwood a message about the severity of Nelson's wound. He visited Nelson about an hour later. Nelson asked Hardy to "take care of my dear Lady Hamilton, Hardy; take care of poor Lady Hamilton. Kiss me, Hardy." After Hardy had kissed his cheek, Nelson said, "Now I am satisfied. Thank God, I have done my duty."[213] Before returning to the deck, Hardy bent down again and kissed his dying friend on the forehead. Nelson died at 4:30 p.m.

Nelson had won another overwhelming victory. Villeneuve was a prisoner, his combined fleet was scattered, and no British ships had been lost. Nelson was mourned by an appreciative nation. Nelson's body was shipped home and on December 23 was transported up the Thames River to Greenwich, where it lay in state in Christopher Wren's Painted Hall in a coffin made from timber from *L'Orient*. The body was taken to Whitehall and the Admiralty and finally, on January 9, to St. Paul's Cathedral for burial.

Collingwood became a peer, and Hardy was made a baronet. *Victory* was repaired and saw further service in the war against Napoleon. *Victory* was restored and then restored again after being struck by a bomb during World War II; the ship is a popular attraction for visitors to England.

BRIGHAM YOUNG (1801-1877) Led the Mormons to the Salt Lake Valley

"Dreamers and doers—the world generally divides men into those two general classifications, but the world is often wrong.... Dreaming is just another name for thinking, planning, devising—another way of saying that a man exercises his soul. A steadfast soul, holding steady to a dream ideal, plus a steady will determined to succeed in any venture, can make any dream come true. Use your mind and your will. They work together for you beautifully if you'll only give them a chance."

B. N. Mills

Historian Oscar Handlin describes the role of Brigham Young in opening up the West:

> When a furious mob murdered [Mormon founder Joseph] Smith, Young assumed the leadership of the Mormon survivors and redirected their vision toward new goals. Far beyond the Mississippi, in heretofore unsettled territory, lay the Great Basin to which he led the remnants of the Church and its followers. There Young supervised the building of a new society that soon attracted thousands of newcomers from other parts of the Union and from Europe as well.
>
> The account of this life is thus an American success story, a rise from poor beginnings to power and wealth. But ... it is also a story that illuminates important features of the social history of the United States—religious enthusiasm, the pioneering spirit, and the encounter with the American West.[214]

Brigham Young, the sixth child and third son of John and Abigail Howe Young, was born on June 1, 1801 in Whitingham, Vermont. John Young was a farmer who moved frequently because of increasingly worn-out soil. Abigail Young was a relative of Elias Howe, one of the inventors of the sewing machine, and Samuel Gridley Howe, an eminent nineteenth-century reformer. She suffered from tuberculosis and had difficulty caring for the children and doing the chores around the house.

In 1802, John Young moved the family to Smyrna, New York. John cleared land for farming and built a log dwelling in an area known as Dark Hollow. The family's next move was to Genoa, east of Cayuga Lake. Brigham was introduced to hard work at an early age, including logging and driving a team of horses. The family was poor and hired Brigham out to neighbors to earn additional income. He attended the Drake School House and was tutored by his mother.

The Youngs were Methodists who originally had been New England Congregationalists. In Brigham's opinion, his parents were "the most strict religionists that lived upon the earth." The children were not allowed to use words such as "devil" and "I vow." Brigham held back from joining the Methodist church or any other church. He said a prayer to himself: "Lord, preserve me until I am old enough to have sound judgment, and a discreet mind ripened on a good, solid foundation of common sense."

Abigail Young died on June 11, 1815, just after Brigham's fourteenth birthday. He had been close to his mother; in his words, "Of my mother—she that bore me—I can say no better woman lived in the world."[215] His older sister, Fanny, who had helped care for him as a child, returned home and became the stabilizing influence in the family. Brigham developed into an independent individual with a deliberate manner.

In 1815, the family moved again—to the Sugar Hill area near Tyrone. Their farm had many maple trees, and they went into maple sugar-making to supplement their income. Maple sugar could be bartered for flour and other necessities. In 1817, John Young married Hannah Dennis Brown, a widow with several children of her own. He broke up his household and moved in with his new wife. Sixteen-year-old Brigham's father told him: "You now have your time; go and provide for yourself."

Young moved to Auburn, where he became an apprentice to learn the trades of carpentry, glazing, and painting. An early project was the finish carpentry and painting of the new home of Judge Elijah Miller, the father-in-law of William H. Seward, a future Governor, U.S. Senator, and Secretary of State. The Seward Mansion, which Seward inherited from Judge Miller, has an ornate fireplace mantel crafted by Young. Young also worked on the construction of the Auburn Theological Seminary.

In 1823, Young moved to Port Byron, a fast-growing town on the new Erie Canal. He worked in a furniture repair shop, a wool carding mill, a pail factory, and a boatyard. One of his employers observed that he "would do more work in a given time and secure more and better work from his help without trouble than any man they have ever employed."[216] In 1824, Young joined the Methodist church. He insisted on being baptized by immersion, although that was not the usual Methodist practice at the time.

On October 5, 1824, Young married Miriam Works, a beautiful blonde whom he had met while working at the pail factory. Their daughter, Elizabeth, was born in Port Byron. In 1828, the family moved to Oswego, where he worked on the construction of a large tannery. When the tannery was finished the following year, he moved his family to Mendon, where his father and several of his sisters had settled. Young built a house in Mendon and constructed a large undershot waterwheel on the creek that flowed through his property; it provided power for grindstones, lathes, and saws.

In June 1830, their second daughter, Vilate, was born. The childbirth temporarily incapacitated Miriam, who suffered with tuberculosis—the same ailment that had afflicted her mother-in-law. Young took part-time jobs so he could do more of the household chores while Miriam was bedridden. The family remained poor and contracted small debts.

While living in Port Byron, Young heard "rumors of a new revelation, to the effect of a new Bible written upon golden plates ... at Palmyra. I was somewhat acquainted with the coming forth of the Book of Mormon ... through ... the newspapers [and] many stories and reports ... circulated ... as the Book of Mormon was printed and ... scattered abroad."[217] In June 1830, Young saw a copy of the Book of Mormon when Samuel Smith, a brother of Joseph Smith who had found the golden plates on Hill Cumorah, visited Mendon to preach about Mormonism and to sell copies of the "golden Bible."

In January 1830, Young, his brother, Phineas, and his good friend and neighbor, Heber Kimball, traveled to Columbia, Pennsylvania, the location of the nearest Mormon church, to observe Mormons interpreting their religion, prophesying, and speaking in tongues. Young returned to Mendon and then visited his brother, Joseph, a Methodist minister in Canada, to ask his opinion of the new religion. In early April, John, Sr., Joseph, and Phineas were baptized into the Mormon religion.

On April 14, Young was baptized by Elder Eleazer Miller

in the stream behind his home. He said that before his clothes "were dry on my back [Elder Miller] laid his hands on me and ordained me an Elder, at which I marveled. According to the words of the Savior, I felt a humble, childlike spirit, witnessing unto me that my sins were forgiven."[218] Ordination as an Elder gave Young the authority to preach the gospel. The rest of the family followed him in joining the new religion.

Four things that Young liked about Mormonism were its similarities to Puritanism, with its emphasis on common sense; its espousal of "Christian Primitivism," the restoration of Christianity as it existed at the time of Jesus Christ; its authoritarianism, which required unquestioning loyalty to the Mormon prophet Joseph Smith; and its lay priesthood, which provided a path to status and influence.

On September 8, 1832, Miriam Young died of tuberculosis. Young and his two daughters moved in with his friend, Heber Kimball. That fall, Young and Kimball traveled to the main Mormon settlement in Kirtland, Ohio, just east of Cleveland, to meet Joseph Smith—founder of the Church of Jesus Christ of Latter-Day Saints. Upon meeting the charismatic Mormon prophet, Young spoke in tongues and asked the Latter-Day Saints leader's opinion of his gift of tongues. Smith "told them that it was of the pure Adamic language.... It is of God, and the time will come when Brother Brigham Young will preside over this church."[219]

Young returned to Mendon to preach Mormonism and traveled around upstate New York and Canada baptizing converts. In September 1833, he moved to Kirtland to be near Joseph Smith and the center of Mormon activity. He courted Mary Ann Angell, a former Baptist from Seneca, New York. In February 1834, Young and Mary Ann were married by Sidney Rigdon, an influential Mormon leader. Early the following year, Smith appointed Young one of the Council of Twelve Apostles, modeled on the Apostles of the New Testament, who were responsible for overseeing Mormon churches and missionary activity.

From 1835 through 1837, Young traveled around upstate New York, New England, and Canada spreading the word of Mormonism. On a return visit to Kirtland during this time, he supervised the completion of the Kirtland Temple. Smith encountered difficulties in Kirtland when he attempted to establish his own bank. Because of his indebtedness and his plan to print his own money, Smith was denied a state banking charter. He established the bank anyway; unfortunately, it was adversely affected by the Panic of 1837.

In 1838, Young was drawn into the conflict between Mormons and non-Mormons in Missouri. Non-Mormons were concerned about the Mormons' economic and political control of the region. A series of armed clashes began in Gallatin, Missouri when non-Mormons attempted to prevent Mormons from voting. Three Mormons were killed at Crooked River, Caldwell County and seventeen Mormons were killed and fifteen wounded seriously at Haun's Mill, Caldwell County by an unruly mob of over 200 men.

The Governor of Missouri, Lilburn Boggs, called out the Missouri militia and issued the order that Mormons "must be exterminated or driven from Missouri, if necessary, for the public good." Joseph Smith turned himself in to the authorities and his brother, Hyrum, and Sidney Rigdon were arrested. Young was the only senior member of the Council of the Twelve Apostles who was not in captivity. He appealed to the Missouri Legislature for compensation for Mormon property that had been seized. The Mormons received a token payment and, due to threats to their lives, left Missouri for Illinois.

In 1839, Young made his last visit to upstate New York while en route to a successful mission that more than doubled church membership in England. He promoted the increase in the number of English Elders and the immigration of English Mormons to the United States. During the next six years, over 4,000 Mormons immigrated to the United States from Great Britain. He also established a Mormon periodical, the *Millennial Star,* in England. Young clearly established a reputation as an efficient administrator and organizer.

Smith escaped from his six-month captivity and established the center of Mormon faith in Nauvoo, Illinois. In July 1841, when Young returned to Nauvoo, he found that it had become a rapidly growing city of 3,000; it would expand to 10,000 by the end of 1841. The Nauvoo Charter gave Mormons comprehensive powers of self-government, although they could not pass any laws contrary to the Illinois and U.S. Constitutions. The Mayor and city council formed their own municipal court, and the city controlled its own militia, the Nauvoo Legion.

Young was elected to the Nauvoo city council and was appointed editor of the Nauvoo newspaper, *The Times and Seasons*. His commitment to Mormonism was severely tested in 1841, when Joseph Smith endorsed the practice of polygamy for the Latter-Day Saints. Smith may have been influenced by the practices of the Oneida Community in New York State when he supported the concept of plural marriage. Initially, Young was appalled by the practice. He said that it "was the first time in my life that I had desired the grave." When he expressed his views to Smith, he was told, "Brother Brigham, the Lord will reveal it to you."

Young was faced with the dilemma of either practicing polygamy or defying the prophet Joseph Smith. Eventually, he accepted plural marriage. In June 1842, he married 20-year-old Lucy Ann Decker Seeley. On November 2, 1843, he married Augusta Ann Adams and Harriet Cook. In May 1844, he took his fourth plural wife, Clarissa Decker, the sister of his first plural wife. His wives lived in their own houses.

The practice of polygamy was the greatest source of difficulty for the Mormons, both within and outside of the church. Nauvoo was envied as the most prosperous city in Illinois, but its self-government was not easily accepted by non-Mormons. Smith realized that he must look to the Far West as "a place of refuge" where "the devil cannot dig us out." In February 1844, Smith asked the Council of Twelve to send a delegation westward toward California and Oregon to build a temple and to establish a government of their own.

The delegation to the West was delayed by Smith's decision to run for the Presidency of the U.S. in 1844 as an independent candidate. Young and other Mormon leaders did much of the campaigning for the candidate. Smith had problems of his own back in Nauvoo, however. A group of dissidents led by William Law split off from the Latter-Day Saints due to disagreements with Smith's policies, particularly polygamy. Law and his associates established a competing newspaper, the Nauvoo *Expositor*. Smith asked the city council to destroy the press and all copies of the newspaper, a blatant violation of freedom of the press.

Anti-Mormon feeling intensified around Nauvoo, and Smith, his brother, Hyrum, and two other Mormon leaders gave themselves up to county authorities in Carthage. On June 27, 1844, a large, organized mob entered the jail at Carthage and killed Smith and his brother, and wounded another of the Mormon leaders. Young, who was campaigning for Smith in Massachusetts at the time, returned to

Nauvoo by a roundabout route to avoid assassination.

Young's only serious rival for the Mormon presidency was Sidney Rigdon. Young's forceful speech, his alignment with the Council of Twelve, and his confidence that the Church would make the right decision made him the clear choice. Although Smith's brother, William, supported Young's election to the presidency, later he attempted to replace him. Anti-Mormon sentiment continued to run high, and Illinois Governor Thomas Ford repealed the Nauvoo charter, which disfranchised both the city police and the Nauvoo Legion. Earlier, he had ordered the Nauvoo Legion to return their state-supplied weapons.

In late 1844 and early 1845, Young married fifteen additional wives, five of whom had been plural wives of Joseph Smith. Only five of these wives bore offspring. It was thought that Young merely provided many of them with financial aid and the protection of his name. He had a strictly platonic relationship with one wife, Eliza R. Snow, who founded the Mormon Relief Society and was known as the church's "First Lady of Letters."

Illinois justice was unable to convict the killers of Joseph Smith and his brother, and anti-Mormon mobs burned barns and crops on farms around Nauvoo. Young realized that they would have to abandon Nauvoo and settle in a frontier sanctuary. Texas was considered a possible site, as were California, Oregon, and the Island of Vancouver. Young ruled out the latter two because they were involved in ongoing boundary disputes between the United States and Great Britain. He favored the Great Basin of Utah because it was remote and virtually uninhabited by whites.

In February 1846, the main body left Nauvoo. Young organized twenty-four companies of 100 each and personally selected the leader of each company. Mormons sold most of their property for a fraction of its value. Utopian Robert Owen and the Catholic Church looked at the property, particularly the Temple, but decided not to purchase it. Before leaving Nauvoo, Young was continually threatened with arrest. The Mormons' trek to the West was the largest and best-organized of all migrations.

They spent the first winter on Potawatomi Indian lands just north of Omaha, Nebraska. Young supervised the building of 538 log houses and 83 sod houses for 3,483 people. In early 1847, he assumed personal responsibility for the pilot company of 159 pioneers, seventy-two wagons, sixty-six oxen, and ninety-two horses. The company, whose goal was to chart the path to the Great Salt Lake Valley for others to follow, used artificial horizons, a circle of reflection, and sextants. They did not employ professional guides.

Initially, they traveled the Oregon Trail along the Platt River. They averaged ten miles a day. Dry buffalo dung was used as fuel for their fires. On the trail, they encountered hostile Pawnees and friendly Sioux Indians. On July 7, 1847, they reached Fort Bridger on the Green River. John C. Fremont's description of the Great Salt Lake Region was favorable; however, Jim Bridger, the famous scout, told them that the Indians in the area were unfriendly, and that the area's cold nights would prevent the growth of crops. When they got within fifty miles of the Great Salt Lake (near Ogden, Utah), another scout gave them a favorable report of their destination, including its agricultural potential.

On July 24, 1847, Young saw the Great Salt Lake Valley for the first time, from the mouth of Emigration Canyon, and said, "This is the place." Compared with Nauvoo, the Salt Lake Valley was dry and remote. It was forty miles long from north to south and twenty-five miles wide and bounded by majestic snow-capped mountains. Young laid out the city with streets eight rods wide in a perfect grid.

During the winter of 1847-48, Young reorganized the First Presidency of the Church and appointed Heber Kimball First Counselor and his own cousin, Willard Richards, Second Counselor. Also, he assumed the designation of prophet, seer, and revelator that had been held by Joseph Smith. By the spring of 1848, the settlement had grown from 300 to over 5,000 people.

The first crop was severely reduced by an invasion of crickets, which they could not get rid of. Their prayers were answered when seagulls came from the Great Salt Lake to consume them. Mormons benefited economically during 1849, when wagonloads of gold prospectors passed through on their way to California. Mormons repaired the travelers' harnesses and wagons and sold supplies to them.

During 1849 and 1850, Young sought statehood for Utah and sent two representatives to Washington, D.C. to lobby for it. He did not want territorial status because it would involve federal observers that could limit his control. President Taylor denied the request for statehood; however, upon Taylor's death, President Fillmore granted territorial status to Utah, which was named for the Ute Indians in the region. Mormons had named it Deseret. Young was chosen as Utah's first Territorial Governor, and Mormons were appointed as Associate Justice of the Territory's Supreme Court, U.S. Marshal, and U.S. Attorney.

Young counseled keeping on friendly terms with the Ute Indians in the area. He asked Mormons to "feed them and clothe them ... never turn them away hungry" and "teach them the art of husbandry." In his opinion, "It was cheaper to feed the Indians than to fight them." From 1850 to 1855, the number of Mormons in the Salt Lake Basin grew from 5,000 to 60,000, mainly from the East but including 15,000 from Great Britain.

In May 1857, President Buchanan sent 2,500 federal troops to Utah to remove Young as Territorial Governor. As had occurred earlier, anti-Mormon sentiment was rampant, principally due to their practice of polygamy. The original commander of federal troops was replaced by Colonel Albert Sidney Johnston, who later distinguished himself as a Confederate General during the Civil War. The winter weather caused hardship for Colonel Johnston's contingent. As a goodwill gesture, Young sent 800 pounds of salt to Johnston who responded that he would "accept no favors from traitors and rebels."

Young accepted President Buchanan's appointed Governor, Alfred Cumming, but refused to let Colonel Johnston's men enter Salt Lake City. Young threatened to burn every structure built by the Mormons if the army entered the city. The Mormons vacated the city until July 1858, when peace was made with the federal government.

The settlement continued to expand. Young was a good businessman and by the late 1850s had an accumulated wealth between $200,000 and $250,000, earned from lumbering, lumber mills, real estate, and a tannery. He married more plural wives until, ultimately, he had fifty-five, with whom he had fifty-seven children.

On August 23, 1877, Young became very ill and was diagnosed with cholera. His condition worsened, and he died on August 27 exclaiming "Joseph! Joseph! Joseph!" John Taylor, senior member of the Council of Twelve, became President of the Church in 1880.

Brigham Young provided leadership for the Mormon Church at a critical period in its history, enabling it to become the largest religion founded in the United States. Also, he contributed heavily to the growth of the American frontier and is considered one of the great colonizers in the history of the United States.

ULYSSES S. GRANT (1822-1885) While Dying, Finished His Memoirs to Pay Off His Debts

"Everyone has his superstitions. One of mine has always been when I started to go anywhere, or to do anything, never to turn back or to stop until the thing intended is accomplished."

Ulysses S. Grant

Ulysses S. Grant could never have been mistaken for a savvy financial person. His reputation was established at an early age. His father sent him to buy a colt for his Ohio farm. Ulysses was open with the owner of the colt, "Papa says I may offer you twenty dollars for the colt, but if you do not take that, I am to offer you twenty-two and a half, but if you would not take that, to give you twenty-five."[220] Obviously, he paid twenty-five dollars for the colt.

In 1877, when President Grant completed his second term in office, he did not know what occupation to pursue, but he knew that he needed a source of income. He and Senor Romero, Mexican Minister to the United States, organized a company to build a railroad in Guatemala. That project and others failed.

Jay Gould, John Mackay, and William H. Vanderbilt raised $250,000, yielding an annual income of $15,000, for Grant by public subscription with the help of George W. Jones, proprietor of the New York *Times*. Grant had additional income of approximately $5,000 a year. The government provided him with two houses, and he bought a house off Fifth Avenue in New York. All of this would have been sufficient to live on if he and his wife, Julia Dent Grant, had not decided to live in New York.

Their son, Ulysses S. Grant, Jr. ("Buck"), formed a partnership with Ferdinand Ward that was returning substantial profits. General Grant joined the partnership and maintained an office at Grant & Ward. He and Ward's father-in-law, who was President of the Marine Bank of Brooklyn, were silent partners. Ward, a smooth talker, also persuaded Buck's father-in-law, a Colorado millionaire, to invest in Grant & Ward. Ward used the influence of Grant's name to attract investors.

On May 4, 1884, Ward told General Grant that the Marine Bank of Brooklyn was in difficulty, and that if Grant could raise $150,000, he would raise another $150,000 to help the bank out of its temporary problems. Grant obtained the money from William H. Vanderbilt, who told him that the money was for him, personally, not for Grant & Ward.

On May 6, when Grant arrived at the offices of Grant & Ward, Buck told him that Ward had disappeared with the $150,000, nothing had been deposited with the Marine Bank, and that Grant & Ward had failed. General Grant lost about $350,000 in the failure of Grant & Ward. Grant was not the only notable duped by Ward. The President of the Erie Railroad lost a million dollars, and other captains of industry lost hundreds of thousands of dollars investing with Ward.

Grant had convinced his wife, his sons, his nieces, and war cronies to invest in Grant & Ward, and he had pulled them all down. To William Vanderbilt, Grant gave the deeds to his house in Manhattan, a house in Philadelphia, and the Dent farm in Missouri, as well as all of his trophies from the Civil War. Vanderbilt tried unsuccessfully to return the deeds to Grant, and subsequently gave all of the war relics, including Grant's sword, to the national museum.

Few options were available to Grant to repay debts to his family and friends. He decided to write his memoirs, an effort that resulted in the two-volume *Personal Memoirs of General*

Grant with 1231 pages and 295,000 words. Its sales earned $450,000 for the Grant family within two years of its publication, a record for a nonfiction book.

Earlier, Richard Watson Gilder of *Century Magazine* had contacted Grant and had asked him to contribute to his periodical. Grant declined, responding that he was a soldier, not a writer. After the failure of Grant & Ward, Robert Underwood Johnson, associate editor of *Century Magazine,* wrote to Grant:

> The country looks with so much regret and sympathy upon General Grant's misfortune that it would gladly welcome the announcement and especially the publication of material relating to him or by him concerning a part of his honored career in which everyone takes pride. It would be glad to have his attention diverted from his present troubles, and no doubt such diversion of his own mind would be welcome to him.[221]

Johnson visited Grant at the cottage in Long Branch, New Jersey, where Grant and Julia were staying. Their initial contract was for $2,000 for four articles, including descriptions of the Battles of Shiloh, Chattanooga, and Vicksburg. Johnson was disappointed with the first article about the Battle of Shiloh; it read like the official army report of the battle and contained little of Grant's feelings or opinions. He visited Grant to ask him details about the battle and about the reasoning behind the decisions that he had made. Johnson embellished the article, and the circulation of *Century Magazine* increased by 50,000 copies. Grant saw what the editor had done and employed similar techniques in his later writing. Subsequently, *The Personal Memoirs of General*

Grant was compared with *Caesar's Commentaries.*

Roswell Smith, President of the Century Company, visited Grant at Long Branch to ask if he would expand his initial articles into a book. In *General Grant's Last Stand*, Horace Green describes Grant's reply: "The General said naively, for he was entirely free from affectation: 'Do you really think anyone would be interested in a book by me?' Mr. Smith replied, 'General, do you think the public would read with avidity Napoleon's personal account of his battles?'"[222] Grant agreed to write the book, a task that literally became his "last stand."

During the spring of 1884, when Grant began writing the article about the Battle of Shiloh, he experienced throat pains and noticed that his throat was particularly sore when he ate fruit. Grant ignored this soreness until he began to have stabbing pains. Julia Grant convinced him to visit a doctor. He consulted Dr. DaCosta in Philadelphia, who referred him to Dr. Fordyce Barker in New York. Unfortunately, Dr. Barker was in Europe until mid-October. Upon his return, Dr. Barker referred him to Dr. John Hancock Douglas, the foremost throat specialist in New York. Because Grant observed professional etiquette and did not visit Dr. Douglas until he was referred to him, his throat cancer went untended for three months.

On October 22, 1884, Grant was examined by Dr. Douglas, who found that the soft palate was inflamed and of a "dark, deep congestive hue, a scaly squamus inflammation, strongly suggestive of epithelial [membranous tissue] trouble." Grant asked, "Is it cancer?" Dr. Douglas told him, "General, the disease is serious, epithelial in character, and sometimes capable of being cured."[223]

One evening in November 1884, Mark Twain, flushed

with the success of *The Adventures of Huckleberry Finn,* lectured at Chickering Hall. Coming out of the hall, he overheard
Gilder of the Century Company telling someone about
Grant's decision to write his memoirs. Twain visited Grant the
next morning to inquire about the nature of the contract with
the Century Company. Grant showed him the contract for ten
percent royalty, no advance, and anticipated sales (with no
guarantee) of 25,000 copies.

Twain, a master of overstatement, was incensed:

> The thing that astounded me was that ... it
> never seemed to occur to him [the *Century* edi-
> tor] that to offer General Grant five hundred
> dollars for a magazine article was not only the
> monumental injustice of the nineteenth centu-
> ry, but of all centuries. He ought to have
> known that if he had given General Grant a
> check for ten thousand dollars, the sum would
> have been trivial; that if he had paid him twen-
> ty thousand dollars for a single article, the sum
> would still have been inadequate, that if he had
> paid him thirty thousand dollars for a single
> magazine war article, it still should not be
> called paid for; that if he had given him forty
> thousand dollars for a single magazine article,
> he would still be in the General's debt.[224]

Twain offered to publish Grant's memoirs through his
own publishing house, Webster & Company of Hartford,
Connecticut and to provide a $25,000 advance royalty for the
first volume and a similar amount for subsequent volumes.
Grant hesitated; he told Twain that he felt an obligation to
those who had first suggested the book. Twain replied that in
that case he should publish it because he had much earlier

suggested to Grant that he write his memoirs.

Grant began writing his memoirs while still living in Manhattan. His gentle nature showed in his writing, the quality of which improved as he wrote. His use of humor was subdued. He described walking with a stranger in the rain to a reception in his honor. The stranger, who shared his umbrella with Grant, said, "I have never seen Grant, and I merely go to satisfy a personal curiosity. Between us I have always thought that Grant was a very much overrated man." Grant replied, "That's my view also."[225]

After an examination the following January by Dr. Douglas and Dr. William A. Schrady, assisted by Dr. Henry B. Sands and Dr. Barker, Grant realized that he was not going to recover. When Grant was depressed, sometimes to the point of being unable to write, he was quiet. Reporters and curiosity seekers gathered outside of his home. He issued a frequently quoted statement: "I am very much touched and grateful for the (prayerful) sympathy and interest manifested in me by my friends—and by those who have not hitherto been regarded as my friends. I desire the goodwill of all, whether hitherto friends or not."[226]

Grant's throat began to bother him more, so he started to supplement his dictation with writing. He finished volume I, 180,000 words, by midwinter of 1885 and made a good start on volume II. The pains in his throat occurred more frequently and even talking in a whisper was painful. He began to have difficulty breathing. By the spring of 1885, his throat was hemorrhaging, and he was in severe pain. Doctors gave him what later would be called "comfort care."

In April 1885, doctors thought that Grant was dying so he was baptized, and they gave him brandy to stimulate his heart. However, his memoirs were not done. The iron will for which he was known took over. Grant bounced back from this brush with death. He lived in fear of choking to death. He could take short walks inside the house and go for short rides in the park with Dr. Douglas. One day, Dr. Douglas entered the house and asked his patient how he was doing. Grant was unable to speak his reply, so he wrote a short note: "I said that I had been adding to my book and to my coffin. I presume every strain of the mind or body is one more nail in the coffin."[227]

Dr. Douglas offered Grant the use of his family's cottage near Saratoga Springs at Mount McGregor, New York, which was known for its crystal-clear air. Grant, with a woolen cap on his head, a scarf around his neck, and a shawl on his lap, sat on the porch in a chair and wrote continually.

During the last week of Grant's life, he was visited by Robert Underwood Johnson of *Century Magazine,* who commented:

> I did the talking ... merely conveying the sympathy of my associates and the assurance that we should gladly do anything for the success of the book in Mr. Clemens's hands, adjusting our (magazine) plans to his. He smiled faintly and bowed his acknowledgment, and as I rose gave me his hand. I could hardly hold back the tears as I said made my farewell.... The story may well be taught in all our schools as a lesson of fortitude, patriotism, and magnanimity.[228]

On June 28, Grant wrote a note about the book: "I feel much relieved this morning. I had begin to feel that the work of getting my book together was making but slow progress. I find it about completed.... It can be sent to the printer faster than he is ready for it. There are from one hundred and fifty to two hundred pages more of it than I intended. I will not cut out anything of interest."[229]

On July 10, Grant wrote, "Buck has brought up the last of the first volume in print. In two weeks if they work hard they can have the second volume copied ready to go to the printer. I will then feel that my work is done." He said this two weeks before he died.

On July 16, Grant noted:

> There never was one more willing to go than I am. I know most people have one thing and then another to fix up, and never quite get through. I first wanted so many days to work on my book so authorship would be clearly mine. It was graciously granted to me ... and with a capacity to do more work than I ever did in the same time.... There is nothing more I should do to it now, and therefore I am not likely to be more ready to go than this moment.[230]

On July 22, Grant asked to be put to bed. The end was near, and the family members were all at Mount McGregor to be with him. His last request was for a drink of water, which he could not swallow. About eight o'clock the following morning, General Ulysses S. Grant slipped away quietly without a sigh or a gasp. He just stopped breathing.

General Grant was buried in Manhattan across the Hudson River from the palisades of New Jersey. The granite tomb, inscribed with "LET US HAVE PEACE," has a dome supported by six Doric columns.

MUSTAFA KEMAL (1881-1938) Victor at Gallipoli and Father of Modern Turkey

"The hero in history is the individual whom we can justifiably attribute preponderant influence in determining an issue or an event whose consequences would have been profoundly different if he [or she] had not acted as he [or she] did."

Sydney Hook, *The Hero in History*

Mustafa Kemal played such a vital role in winning the Battle of Gallipoli that is difficult to think of another military officer who influenced the outcome of a campaign to the extent that he did. He assumed responsibility beyond his rank and kept going without sleep despite bouts of malaria. When he became the leader of modern Turkey, he brought his country reluctantly into the twentieth century by the force of his will.

Before Mustafa Kemal (Atatürk, father of all the Turks), Turkey was the decadent, down-trodden "sick man of Europe," with its mixture of races and religions and its poor and uneducated populace. It was burdened by sultans who ruled as despots, by participation in foreign wars that it could not afford, and by foreign exploitation. Its government was disintegrating, and the past glories of the once-powerful Ottoman Empire were memories.

Kemal virtually dragged Turkey into modern times. When he became President in 1923, he abolished the sultanate and the Islamic caliphate (the Moslem secular and religious head of state), outlawed the Arabic alphabet, installed the Latin alphabet, and emancipated Turkish women. He knew that Turkey would not reach its full potential if women were held down. "Kemal campaigned against ... customs that restricted women, maintaining that if they did not share in the social life of the nation, we shall never attain our full development.'"[231]

He encouraged western dress, passed a law that forbade Turkish men to wear the fez, and discouraged the wearing of veils in public by women. His reforms were sweeping. He began a movement to elevate national pride and rewrite Turkish history to place less emphasis on past accomplishments of the Ottoman Empire.

Mustafa Kemal's reputation was made defending the Gallipoli Peninsula from the attacking Allies, principally British Commonwealth forces, in early World War I. Lieutenant Colonel Kemal was assigned to command the 19th Division by Enver Pasha, the Minister of War. When he asked about the location of the division, he was referred to the offices of the General Staff; no one seemed to know much about the 19th Division.

Finally, since Turkey was allied with Germany in World War I, it was suggested that he speak with the German Chief of Staff, General Liman von Sanders. The General said that no such division existed, but that the Third Army Corps stationed at Gallipoli might be planning to form the 19th Division. Kemal was advised to go to Gallipoli and ask about the new unit being formed.

In February 1915, the British Army pounded the forts at the entrance to the Dardanelles, and the Royal Navy and supporting French naval units bombarded other defensive locations. The Royal Navy failed to break through the Narrows in March. This attack was not followed up; the British waited until they could support their navy by an attack on land. Enver Pasha assigned General von Sanders to command the Fifth Army defending the Dardanelles. The headquarters of the 19th Division, an element of the Fifth Army, was located at

Maidos.

Maidos and the Gallipoli Peninsula were familiar to Lieutenant Colonel Kemal since he had been assigned to Maidos during operations against the Bulgarians in the Balkan War. Kemal's fellow officers thought that barbed wire defenses on the beaches would prevent the British from landing. Kemal knew otherwise from his experience in opposing the landing of the Italians at Tripoli with their supporting naval fire. Kemal realized that since the British would have considerable covering fire from their ships, his division would need strong defensive positions to fire down upon the attackers to keep them on the beaches.

Von Sanders had six divisions in the Fifth Army to cover the fifty-two-mile coastline of the peninsula. His assessment of potential landing spots differed from Kemal's. He assigned two divisions to the field of Troy and two divisions to the northern end of the peninsula at Bulair. Another division was directed to Cape Helles, and Kemal's 19th Division was held in reserve to move to the area of greatest need.

Kemal moved his headquarters to the village of Boghali, within easy reach of both coasts. Kemal thought that the British would land either at Cape Helles at the southern end of the peninsula, where they could use their naval guns most effectively, or at Gaba Tepe on the western coast to allow ease of movement to the Narrows on the eastern coast.

Early in the morning of April 25, 1915, the Allies landed in force at the two locations Kemal had anticipated. The British landed at Cape Helles, and the Australians and New Zealanders landed at Ariburnu, just north of Gaba Tepe. These landings were accompanied by two diversions, a raid by the French on the Asiatic coast and a Royal Naval Division at Bulair. Von Sanders fell for the diversionary maneuver at

Bulair and sent a third division to join the two he had already located there.

Kemal was awakened at Boghali that morning by naval guns and found that he was near the center of the action. He sent a cavalry unit to Koja Chemen, a crest on the Sari Bair range, a ridge that ran parallel to the western shoreline. Kemal received a report that a small enemy force was climbing the slope to the Chunuk Bair crest and received a request from the division on his flank to send a battalion to halt their advance. He realized immediately that this was the site of the major offensive. He knew that the Sari Bair ridge, particularly the Chunuk Bair crest, was crucial to the Turkish defense. Kemal ordered his best regiment, the 57th, and a battery of artillery to move to the Chunuk Bair crest.

It was a bold move that committed a significant portion of von Sander's reserve division and exceeded Kemal's authority as a division commander. If he were wrong, and the major offensive was at a different location, only one Turkish regiment would be available to oppose it. However, he was confident that he was right. In fact, he had acted correctly, and the Australians and New Zealanders (Anzacs) landed in force at Ariburnu, which became known as Anzac Cove.

Kemal personally led the 57th regiment up the hill to Chunuk Bair. As they neared the crest, the Turkish unit that had been located there came running down the slope. Kemal asked them why they were running away. They said the English were coming, and they were out of ammunition. He ordered them to fix bayonets and to lie on the ground. The Australian troops, which were closer to the crest than the Turks were, lay down also. Then, as the 57th regiment came up the slope, Kemal ordered them to take the crest and to set up a mountain battery on the highest ground. His orders were,

"I don't order you to attack, I order you to die. In the time it takes us to die, other troops and commanders can come and take our places."[232] By the end of the day, most of the 57th regiment had taken his orders literally.

Although the Turks experienced heavy casualties, they prevented the Anzacs from moving off the beaches. During the day, Kemal ordered a second regiment into the line to reinforce the 57th. Again, he acted without authority, but, as before, he notified the corps commander, Essad Pasha, of his actions. He urged Essad Pasha to commit the last regiment of the 19th division to defend the Sari Bair front. Essad agreed, gave him the remaining regiment, and, in effect, put him in charge of the entire Sari Bair front. General von Sanders continued to think that the main Allied attack would be at Bulair and telegraphed that he would not commit any additional troops to the Sari Bair front.

By midnight, General Birdwood, the Anzac commander, requested permission from Sir Ian Hamilton, the British commander-in-chief, to return to the ships. Sir Ian denied them permission to evacuate the beaches and ordered them to dig in. He reasoned that the British forces at Cape Helles had established a beachhead and would take pressure off of the troops at Anzac Cove.

On the morning of April 26, Kemal led the remnants of the 57th regiment and the regiment that reinforced them down the slopes in a attack on the Anzacs. He recklessly exposed himself to fire and had three horses shot out from under him. His reputation as a fearless leader of men was reinforced daily. His orders to his men were: "Every soldier who fights here with me must realize that he is in honor bound not to retreat one step. Let me remind you that if you want to rest, there may be no rest for the whole nation throughout eternity.

I am sure that all our comrades agree on this, and that they will show no signs of fatigue until the enemy is finally hurled into the sea."[233] General von Sanders was aware of Kemal's role in the defense of Chunuk Bair. In June, Kemal was promoted to Colonel.

Kemal tried in vain to convince Essad Pasha of the importance of the Ariburnu area in the coming offensive. Essad visited Kemal and was given a personal tour of the defenses. Kemal attempted to persuade Essad that the next attack would be on the beaches along Sulva Bay, up the Sazlidere ravine to Chunuk Bair. Essad disagreed with Kemal. He thought that the terrain was too difficult, and that the Allies would not attempt to move any forces other than small raiding parties through it.

Heavy Allied bombardment continued both from naval guns and shore-based artillery. One day Kemal was sitting on a rocky outcropping calmly smoking a cigarette and talking with his men. An artillery shell landed about one hundred yards away from him. The next shell, obviously from the same battery, burst fifty yards away. The third shell struck twenty yards away, sending pieces of rock flying. His men pleaded with him to take cover, but he remained seated where he was. He said that he did not want to set a bad example for his men. After waiting for the fourth shell, which never came, Kemal observed that there must have been only three guns in that battery.

On August 6, the Allies shifted their main offensive to the Ariburnu front. They planned an assault along the Sari Bair ridge. One advance was planned to go up the Sazlidere ravine to Chunuk Bair, precisely as Kemal had predicted, and a second to attack the Koja Chemen summit. Both of these planned advances were supported by the landing of fresh troops at

Sulva Bay. Again, von Sanders expected the main attack to come against Bulair or at the southern end of the Sari Bair range, not at the center where Kemal's forces were located. In fact, the Allies landed a diversionary force at the southern end of the range, which caused Essad Pasha to commit most of his reserves to the wrong location.

Belatedly, von Sanders realized his mistake and ordered units from Bulair and Helles to Anzac Cove and Sulva Bay; however, it took them twenty-four hours to reach their destinations. Allied forces scaled the slopes during the night and attacked at dawn. The attack was ferocious. Allied forces climbed to the crest of Chunuk Bair and found it defended by one machine gun crew—and they were asleep. For some inexplicable reason, the Turkish infantry had left the crest.

Turkish defenders were confused. Kemal was aware from an early stage of the attack of disorder on his right. Casualties mounted. The German commander of the division adjacent to the 19th Division sustained a severe chest wound. Two division commanders of the division holding the ridge were killed, and it was now commanded by a lieutenant colonel who was more experienced in running a railway than directing a battle.

Kemal appealed to von Sanders to place all available forces under a unified command or be faced with catastrophe. He asked to be appointed as commander of the unified forces. Von Sanders had confidence in Kemal's ability. He promoted him to General, which entitled him to be addressed as "Pasha," and appointed him commander of the Anafarta front. Kemal's energy level was incredible. The first three nights of his unified command he went without sleep, even though he suffered from severe bouts of malaria.

The battle became a race for the crest of the Anafarta

ridge, particularly the Tekke Tepe summit. The Turks won the race by a half hour. They continued down the other side of the crest once they reached it and inflicted murderous fire on the British forces. In fact, the Turkish fire was so intense that the surrounding brush caught fire. The Sulva offensive was not successful; nevertheless, the Anzacs were still hanging on at Chunuk Bair.

After a fourth night without sleep and while feverish with malaria, Kemal personally led a attack on Chunuk Bair. His instructions to his troops were, "Soldiers, there is no doubt that we are going to defeat the enemy in front of you. But do not hurry. Let me go ahead first. As soon as you see me raise my whip, then you will all leap forward." The Turks over-whelmed the men in front of them and drove them back to the beaches.

Kemal was struck in the chest with a bullet as he led fresh troops from Bulair to drive the Anzacs off Chunuk Bair. He moved his left hand cautiously over the painful spot in his right ribs, but observed no blood. He opened his tunic and found an ugly blue and red bruise about three inches in diam-eter in his lower right ribs. He reached into the small inner pocket of his tunic and took out the pocket watch that he had carried since military school. The bullet had struck close to the center of the dial. This experience added to Kemal's rep-utation for indestructibility. After the battle, Liman von Sanders asked for and received the watch as a souvenir. In return, von Sanders gave him an expensive chronometer engraved with the von Sanders coat of arms.

The Allies tried another attack on Tekke Tepe and were again beaten back. Finally, Sir Ian Hamilton realized that they had failed. He thought that the Turks had superior numbers, more reserves, and higher morale than his men. Without the element of surprise, 100,000 additional troops were needed to resume the offensive. He observed: "We are now up against the main Turkish army, which is fighting bravely and is well commanded." By December, all Allied forces were withdrawn from the Gallipoli Peninsula.

The official British historian wrote, "Seldom in history can the exertions of a single divisional commander have exercised ... so profound an influence not only on the course of a battle, but perhaps on the fate of a campaign and even the destiny of a nation."[234] Some of the withdrawn Anzac forces were sent to Salonika to fight Germans in the Balkan campaign. Since the Gallipoli defense also protected the Dardanelles and the Bosporus, the Russians were locked into the Black Sea and blocked off from their allies. The repercussions in England over the Gallipoli defeat forced the resignation of the First Lord of the Admiralty, Winston Churchill, who had been one of the major architects of the Dardanelles campaign.

BENJAMIN O. DAVIS (1880-1970) First African-American General in the U.S. Army

"I did my duty. That's what I set out to do—to show that I could make my way if I knew my job."[235]

Brigadier General Benjamin O. Davis, Sr. in an interview, June 2, 1968

Benjamin O. Davis displayed determination throughout his career, initially, to become an officer and then to perform his duties to the best of his ability. Biographer Marvin E. Fletcher observes:

> Benjamin Davis was a unique individual. As a member of two minorities [the black middle class], he worked most of his life in isolation. In his own mind, he was first of all an army officer, and then a black man. For the black community, he was first of all a black. These different viewpoints led to different approaches to problems, and Davis at times took positions that did not please other blacks. To the army, Davis was also a minority, and his points of view were ones that few other officers espoused. Davis's career followed a pattern different from that of most army officers of his generation. Despite the isolation, however, Davis persevered in his chosen occupation; he was proud to be an officer of the United States Army.[236]

Benjamin Oliver Davis, the youngest child of Louis and Henrietta Stewart Davis, was born on May 28, 1880 in Washington, D.C., where his father worked as a messenger in the office of the Commissioner of Internal Revenue. Henrietta Davis was a nurse. As a two-income family, they were able to own their own home.

Young Benjamin attended Lucretia Mott Elementary School, one of the few integrated schools in the District of Columbia. Pomeroy Street, where they lived, was in a neighborhood on the outskirts of the city where both whites and blacks lived. He was not aware of any racial distinctions, and he played with the other neighborhood children and went hunting with them for small game.

Benjamin first considered a military career while still in elementary school. The father of one of his classmates organized the boys into a paramilitary group with uniforms and wooden guns. They were taught the manual of arms and close order drill. At the time, young Davis was particularly impressed with the Ninth Cavalry, a black regiment assigned to Ft. Myer across the Potomac River. He saw them participate in the inaugural parade for Grover Cleveland in 1893.

Benjamin attended high school at the segregated M Street High School, where most of the teachers had degrees from highly regarded colleges. He chose the academic program with its Latin requirement because he was "more interested in solving the problems considered hardest by the other boys" and because many English words had Latin roots. He played on the baseball and football teams. In 1896, he was chosen captain of the football team, which held the Howard University football team to a tie that year.

Benjamin joined the Cadet Corps, which used real weapons. Each cadet was given a Springfield rifle, a cartridge belt, and a bayonet scabbard. He received additional instruction in the manual of arms and close order drill. Drill instructor Major Arthur Brooks, commanding officer of the First

Separate Battalion, District of Columbia National Guard, appointed him Second Lieutenant in Company D. Eventually, he was promoted to Captain of Company B.

In his senior year at M Street High School, Benjamin took courses at Howard University and played on their football team. This positive experience was his only exposure to college-level courses.

Benjamin almost became a soldier earlier than he anticipated when the battleship *USS Maine* exploded and sank in Havana harbor, and Congress declared war on Spain. The District of Columbia National Guard was mobilized and marched to a campsite. However, when the impact on the operation of the federal government was realized, since most guardsmen were federal employees, the National Guard was recalled. This terminated Davis's career with the Guard. He looked for other opportunities.

During the Spanish-American war, the War Department created positions for African-American officers. Davis recruited enlisted men for the Eighth U.S. Volunteer Infantry (USVI), and on July 8, 1898, he accepted a commission as First Lieutenant in Company G. The Eighth USVI assembled at Ft. Thomas, Kentucky, where Davis was assigned to train the company in close order drill. He learned about military principles and army customs from Lt. Andrew Smith, a twenty-eight-year veteran of the Regular Army. Lt. John Proctor, who had served in the Ninth Cavalry, taught Davis how to ride; it became a lifelong activity for him.

Davis first encountered racial discrimination at Ft. Thomas, where officers messes were established according to rank as well as race. Captains and above, all of whom were white, ate in one mess; Lieutenants, all of whom were African Americans, ate in another mess; and field and staff officers, who were also white, ate in the third mess. However, two African-American staff officers—an assistant surgeon and the chaplin, who were   Captains—had to use the Lieutenants' mess.

In October 1898, the Eighth USVI was sent to guard supplies at Chickamauga Park, Georgia, where they encountered overt racial prejudice. Their colonel, Col. Huggins, realized that racial hostility posed "a source of constant danger" for his men, and that whites in the region were "ready to distort and magnify every instance of misconduct." In February 1899, the regiment was mustered out. Their General's request that the regiment be assigned further service, possibly in the Philippine Islands, was denied. Col. Huggins suggested that Davis apply for a commission in the Regular Army and wrote a letter of recommendation for him.

Upon Davis's return home to Washington, D.C., his father attempted to obtain an appointment to the U.S. Military Academy for him. A member of President McKinley's staff told him that appointing an African American to West Point "was not politically feasible at that time." Davis applied for a commission in one of the volunteer regiments being formed to occupy the Philippine Islands. Despite being "strongly recommended" by Col. Huggins and receiving letters of support from Senator Shelby Cullom of Illinois and from Mrs. (General) John Logan, he was not appointed.

Davis was determined to pursue an army career. He decided to enlist, serve two years as an enlisted man, and then take the competitive examination for a commission. He and his friend, John Proctor from the Eighth USVI, enlisted at the same time. The recruiter was pleased to get an experienced soldier, Proctor, who had served in the ninth Cavalry, and another, Davis, with proven administrative skills. They were assigned to Troop I at Ft. Duchesne, Utah, which had been established in 1886 to control the Ute Indians. Ft. Duchesne, which was home to troops totaling 150 men, was 170 miles from the nearest municipality, Salt Lake City.

Ft. Duchesne was staffed principally with older, experienced soldiers from whom Davis could learn about customs of the service and the history of the men who fought the Indian Wars. Davis learned much about the officer / enlisted man relationship. Generally, African-American enlisted men viewed the commander of their troop as a father figure. In return, officers tried to help the men with their concerns and problems. The officers and men served long years together and developed a strong sense of loyalty.

In his role as troop clerk, Davis became aware than many of the men could not even write their own name. He helped them; they were proud when they could sign their name to the payroll.

In August 1899, Davis reapplied for a commission. Col. Huggins again recommended him and Mrs. John Logan wrote another letter noting that Davis was "anxious" to earn a commission by "faithful, efficient, and gallant service." Again, his request was denied, although his friend, John Proctor, was accepted. Davis knew that his path was a difficult one; in 1894, Davis's lieutenant, Charles Young, who had come to Ft. Duchesne from Wilberforce University in Ohio, was the only African-American officer in the U.S. Army.

In 1901, Sergeant Major Davis took the competitive examination for a Regular Army commission and was one of two African Americans who received a commission. The other was John E. Green, who had served two years in the infantry. Davis and Green would pursue parallel careers for the next thirty years.

Davis and his troop embarked from San Francisco for the Philippines, where the U.S. Army was attempting to conclude the Spanish-American War. In Manila, Davis was informed that he had passed the examination for a Regular Army commission. He was commissioned a Second Lieutenant and assigned to Troop F of the Tenth Calvary. Most of his assignments in the field were to locate and suppress insurgents in the rebellion. He interacted with the Filipinos daily and learned to speak Spanish and Visayan. His ability to learn languages easily served him well over the course of his career.

In the fall of 1902, Troop F was ordered home and stationed at Ft. Washakie, Wyoming. Davis was the only black officer of the Troop's eight commissioned officers. Established in a career, he decided that it was time to marry. He returned to Washington, D.C. on a thirty-day leave to court Elnora Dickerson, a neighbor whom he had admired during their school days. Elnora was one of nine children in a middle-class family whose father, a teamster, had encouraged education for his children. Benjamin and Elnora were married on October 23, 1902.

At Ft. Washakie, Davis served as adjutant, head of the commissary, and post quartermaster. He was an active participant in the officers' school and wrote several papers on military training. He received excellent efficiency reports and, in May 1904, was promoted to First Lieutenant. Their first child, Olive, was born that year. A year later, he was assigned as Professor of Military Science and Tactics at Wilberforce University in Ohio. The University had been founded in 1856 by the Methodist Episcopal Church, but, by the late 1800s, the African Methodist Episcopal (A.M.E.) Church, a black denomination, supported the school. A military program had been established at Wilberforce in the early 1890s.

Charles Young had preceded Davis at Wilberforce. When Davis had difficulty with the transition from serving with the army in the field to a college setting, Young urged him to complete his tour at the University and to set an example for his students and teach them discipline. Davis bought a horse and kept himself in good physical condition. He and Elnora enjoyed socializing with the black community in Wilberforce and in nearby Xenia.

In Davis's opinion, he did not get sufficient support from the school administration to allow him to be successful with his military program for the students. Nevertheless, when his three-year tour of duty was completed, the administration requested that he stay on because of his achievements with the program. However, Lt. John E. Green was assigned to Wilberforce instead.

In late 1909, Davis was assigned as military attaché in Liberia. His office was in the American Legation in Monrovia. The few U.S. military attachés at the time were assigned to countries that were military powers, such as England, France, and Germany. However, black officers, including Young, Davis, and Green, were assigned to Liberia or Haiti.

Liberia's independence had been threatened by France and Britain, which had colonies that were neighbors of Liberia. The U.S. government appointed a commission which recommended that a private loan assist Liberia in refinancing its debt and that a small number of U.S. Army officers be sent to Liberia to help train its frontier police. Davis was expected to provide the U.S. War Department with detailed reports on Liberia's military capability and on events in the region affecting the military.

Davis decided early in his assignment that the Liberian

Army was ineffective and in need of a complete reorganization. He reviewed his reforms with the Liberian Secretary of State, who not only approved of his recommendations but asked him to accept an appointment in the Liberian Army. U.S. Army Chief of Staff General Leonard Wood ruled that Davis's role was advisor to the Liberian Army, and, as an officer of the U.S. Army, he could not join the Liberian Army.

In 1911, Davis reminded the War Department that he had not had a troop assignment for six years. He was assigned to Troop 1, Ninth Cavalry, at Ft. D. A. Russell near Cheyenne, Wyoming. His friend, Charles Young, replaced him as military attaché in Liberia. On December 18, 1912, Benjamin O. Davis, Jr., the second child of Benjamin and Elnora, was born. He was destined to follow his father in a military career.

In 1913, the Ninth Cavalry was assigned to the border between Arizona and Mexico. A failed revolutionary attempt in Mexico had caused unrest along the border with the United States. During Davis's three years on the border, he was either in command of his troop or second in command. He experienced his first combat at Naco, Arizona, where his troop came under fire from Mexican troops under the command of General Alvaro Obregon and by Yaqui Indians. Several of his men were wounded.

In December 1915, Davis was promoted to Captain and assigned to Wilberforce University, which had been without a Professor of Military Science and Tactics since 1913 when Lt. Green had been reassigned. Davis had many opportunities to indulge in his hobby, horseback riding, and the family was happy at Wilberforce until tragedy struck. Elnora died giving birth to their second daughter, Elnora. Davis was devastated. He was left with three young children: Olive was eleven and Benjamin was three. During this difficult time, Sadie

Overton, an instructor at Wilberforce University, helped Davis care for the children.

During World War I, Davis served with the Ninth Cavalry in Luzon in the Philippines while his children stayed with his parents in Washington, D.C. In August 1917, an occurrence in Houston, Texas influenced Davis's career as well as the career of other African Americans serving in the U.S. military. A battalion of blacks of the Twenty-fourth Infantry encountered racial prejudice, and several soldiers were beaten by white policemen. Out-of-control armed black soldiers swept through Houston, killing sixteen Hispanics and whites and wounding others.

A court martial was convened, and thirteen black soldiers were sentenced to hanging for their actions; however, they were hung before the army announced the verdict. Subsequent courts martial dictated more hangings, although President Wilson commuted some of the death sentences. African Americans expressed outrage over the incident, which reminded them of a 1906 incident in which three black companies of the Twenty-fifth Infantry shot up Brownsville, Texas. President Roosevelt discharged the three companies without honor when they refused to confess their guilt.

The African-American community was convinced that the soldiers in Houston did not receive a fair hearing. The Houston incident affected the War Department's policies during World War I and after the war. It hesitated to use African Americans in combat or to assign large numbers of black troops to posts in the South. These policies had an impact on Davis's career during World War I and between World Wars I and II.

In the Philippines, Davis served as commander of the supply troop and then as post quartermaster prior to being promoted to Major and given command of the Third Squadron of the Ninth Cavalry. In June 1918, Davis was promoted to the temporary rank of Lieutenant Colonel in the National Army. He commanded the First Squadron, served as Provost Marshal, and polished his command of Spanish. In the fall of 1918, he toured China and Japan, where he was impressed by the people.

Davis thought that he had a good working relationship with his commanding officer, Col. John W. Heard, a Mississippian, until he became aware that the Colonel preferred white officers and did not favor an officer corps of mixed races. When Davis's orders to return to the United States were delayed, he said, "I am getting to the point where I am beginning to believe that I have been kept as far in the background as possible."[237] Davis was incensed by an article in the *Army and Navy Journal* that stated that a black officer was not promoted because blacks "were deficient in moral fiber, rendering them unfit as officers and as leaders of men." Davis developed an attitude of tolerating racial insults while working behind the scenes to moderate them.

Davis proposed to Sadie Overton, and they were married in December 1919 in Manila. Shortly after their marriage, conditions within the Ninth Cavalry improved, and officers and their families were permitted to tour the Philippines. Davis and Sadie took advantage of this prior to returning to the United States to rejoin his children.

Davis's next assignment was as Professor of Military Science and Tactics at Tuskegee Institute in Alabama. He was promoted to Lieutenant Colonel as was John E. Green, who had returned as Professor of Military Science and Tactics at Wilberforce University. Davis's role at Tuskegee was to develop discipline in the students and to instruct them in infantry subjects. The structure of military training was representative of the Reserve Officer Training Corps (ROTC). Davis received good fitness reports at Tuskegee, and his work in providing military training was highly regarded.

Davis's next assignment was as instructor, Second Battalion, 372nd Regiment, Ohio National Guard. The family moved to Cleveland, where the two younger children were enrolled in integrated schools. Olive Davis received an undergraduate degree and a master's degree in Social Service Education from Western Reserve University. The Ohio National Guard requested that Davis's four-year assignment be extended to five years. In 1929, Davis was reassigned to Wilberforce University, where Lt. Col. John Green had just completed his tour of duty. Davis's salary was at the top of the range for his rank, and he had invested well. The family toured Europe, where Davis improved his French.

In November 1929, Lt. Col. Green retired from the army after thirty years of service. Davis was now the only African-American officer in the U.S. Army. In March 1931, Davis was promoted to Colonel and became the highest ranking black officer in the U.S. military until that time. Upon completion of this tour of duty at Wilberforce, the President of Tuskegee requested that Davis be reassigned to his Institute. That tour of duty was followed by one last assignment to Wilberforce University.

Benjamin, Jr. attended Western Reserve University before transferring to the University of Chicago. In 1932, at the suggestion of a Congressman from Chicago, he accepted an appointment to the U.S. Military Academy, where he endured the "silent treatment" from the cadet corps because of his race. For four years at West Point:

> No one spoke to me except in the line of duty
> ... they were going to enforce an old West
> Point tradition—"silencing"—with the object
> that they would make my life so unhappy that
> I would resign. Silencing had been applied in
> the past to certain cadets who were considered
> to have violated the honor code and refused to
> resign. In my case there was no question of
> such a violation, which would have been for-
> mally cited by the Honor Committee; I was to
> be silenced solely because cadets did not want
> blacks at West Point. Their only purpose was
> to freeze me out. What they did not realize was
> that I was stubborn enough to put up with their
> treatment to reach the goal I had come to
> attain.[238]

In 1936, Benjamin, Jr. graduated from West Point, the first African American to do so since Charles Young in 1889. Later in his career, many of his classmates denied that they had given him the silent treatment.

In 1938, Davis, Sr. was assigned as instructor and later as Commander of the 369th New York National Guard in New York City. He was highly regarded in this assignment. On October 26, 1940, Benjamin O. Davis was promoted to Brigadier General and became the first African American to attain that rank. He received orders to report to Ft. Riley, Kansas, as Commander of the Fourth Brigade, Second Cavalry Division.

Benjamin and Sadie Davis lived on the post, down the street from the division commander, Maj. Gen. Terry Allen. Officers in the Fourth Brigade were formal with Brig. Gen. and Mrs. Davis. Army etiquette dictated that officers call upon the arrival of a new commanding officer; however, there was no ongoing social activity. Recreational facilities on the post were segregated. The Davis family could not go to the segregated officers' club or movie theater. Benjamin, Jr. was assigned as his father's aide. Social life was virtually restricted to activities, such as playing bridge, for two couples: Benjamin, Sr. and Sadie, and Benjamin, Jr. and his wife, Agatha. Davis rode frequently, as he did throughout his army career.

In June 1941, General George Marshall asked Davis if he would consider an assignment in the Office of Inspector General. Davis accepted the assignment willingly; he was one of two assistant inspector generals. Since the War Department had no separate dining room for blacks, instead of eating in a segregated lunch room in another building, Davis usually skipped lunch.

An ongoing problem as the army added more African-American volunteer soldiers was their treatment by white military police and by white civilian police in towns near army posts. The solution was to confine black soldiers to the base that, unfortunately, had limited recreational facilities, and the few that they had were segregated.

In August 1941, Davis was asked to investigate racial disturbances in Fayetteville, North Carolina, near Ft. Bragg. Black soldiers and white military policemen had fought, with fatalities on both sides. Davis attempted to determine the cause of the incident and to try to prevent it from happening again. Even with the aid of the FBI, results were inconclusive. Some of the African-American soldiers were reacting to bad conditions generally. Davis demanded better living quarters and requested that programs be instituted to improve leadership training of unit commanders. He also began to push for new facilities to be desegregated, not segregated, and for blacks to be assigned to all functional areas of the army.

During the summer of 1941, Davis visited the flying facilities being constructed at Tuskegee, Alabama, where his son was stationed. Benjamin, Jr. underwent flight training and became a fighter pilot. He was promoted to Lieutenant Colonel in 1942. He had a distinguished war record commanding fighter units over Africa and Italy.

In September 1942, Davis was assigned to temporary duty in England to help military personnel there address racial problems. He met with General Eisenhower, who asked him to investigate racial incidents and recommend solutions for them. Lt. Gen. John C. H. Lee, Commander of the Services of Supply, was extremely supportive of his efforts. Davis met many famous people in London. Lady Astor called out to him from her car while he was walking with Admiral Harold Stark, U.S. Navy. She invited him to lunch at Cliveden to meet Lord Astor.

Davis was interviewed by a staff writer for the London *Times,* whom he told that blacks were "profuse in their praise" of the way they were treated in Britain. In Bristol, he met Eleanor Roosevelt who was there on a visit to Red Cross clubs. She was impressed with his work and passed the word on to Washington. The U.S. Embassy in London asked Davis to make an address for the British Broadcasting Corporation. One of his successes in England was in increasing the number of African Americans accepted for Officer Candidate School. He was impressed when he saw black and white Canadian soldiers in integrated units.

In 1943, with larger numbers of African Americans entering the military, racial unrest increased. In dealing with these problems, Davis was viewed as "all soldier"; he had good military bearing and spoke clearly and crisply. One complaint he heard repeatedly was of the perceived slow promotion of blacks in the army. He replied to this complaint by citing his personal experiences. Davis felt that it was "utterly impossible for any white man to appreciate what the colored officers and soldiers experience in trying to develop a high morale under the present conditions."[239]

Davis's superior officer at the Office of Inspector General, General Virgil Peterson, had a high opinion of him: "His dignified and courteous manner and the esteem in which he, as the senior Negro officer in the Army, is held by members of his race, together with his understanding of their problems, have rendered his services to this Department, and to the Army at large, of great value in assisting in the solution of matters involving Negro troops."[240]

Davis continued to address the Army's reluctance to use African-American troops in combat. In his opinion, the troops were ready if the Army chose to use them. Finally, in 1944, the Ninety-second Division was sent to Italy, where they fought Germans in Northern Italy for the next year and a half. Considering their lack of combat experience, they fought well.

Davis finished the war in the European Theater of Operations working for General John C. H. Lee. In August 1944, he was quoted in a press release: "I'm thoroughly pleased with the performance and conditions under which Negro troops are operating here, especially their performance under fire."[241] In February 1945, Davis was awarded the Distinguished Service Medal for his efforts "in the establishment of better understanding of the problems involved in effective employment of the Negro soldier." His experiences during World War II made him realize that segregation could not continue in the armed forces without continual unrest.

Integration in the Army began on a limited basis late in the war.

Prior to the end of the war, General Lee recommended Davis's promotion to Major General. All of the arrangements had been made, but, with the end of the war, all promotions were put on hold. Davis did not attain his dream of a second star. General Lee told him that if the war had lasted longer, he would have been promoted.

Davis stayed on active duty until July 14, 1948, when he completed fifty years of service. His retirement ceremony was held in the oval office at the White House. President Harry Truman presided. On July 20, 1948, President Truman signed an executive order ending segregation in the U.S. armed forces, something that Davis had worked hard for over the years. Davis continued to do public service in his retirement.

Brigadier General Benjamin O. Davis died on November 26, 1970 of acute leukemia. He received full military honors and was buried in Arlington National Cemetery several hundred feet from the grave of President John F. Kennedy. Benjamin Davis, Jr. said that: "his father had been a great man, a good storyteller, and above all, a man who had filled his life with the U.S. Army."

Marvin E. Fletcher, in his book, *America's First Black General: Benjamin O. Davis, Sr.,* noted: "Davis persevered in his chosen occupation; he was proud to be an officer of the United States Army.... In doing his duty, he helped improve the United States Army. Despite his isolation, he achieved a measure of success. The life of Benjamin O. Davis did prove that one could advance and achieve success by doing one's job to the best of one's ability."[242]

During the Eisenhower administration, Benjamin O.

Davis, Jr. was promoted to Brigadier General and in 1965 attained his final rank as Lieutenant General in the U.S. Air Force. He retired five years later. Subsequently, at the end of a week-long visit to the U.S. Military Academy, he noticed his picture on a wall in the Visitors Center with the caption "World War hero, helped integrate Air Force." On the drive home, he admitted to his wife, Agatha, that the week was "the best week I ever spent at West Point."[243]

CHAPTER 7

ENTREPRENEURS / ACHIEVERS

"Oh! Much may be made by defying
    The ghosts of Despair and Dismay;
And much may be gained by relying on
    'Where there's a will, there's a way'"

Eliza Cook, *Where There's a Will There's a Way*

Chapter 7 provides examples of men and women who displayed determination in a wide range of endeavors. They had significant accomplishments during their lifetimes because they were resolved to achieve their objectives.

Lillian Gilbreth's determination allowed her to make significant contributions to the field of motion study and to the people side of the work environment. Initially, she was sufficiently strong-willed not to be dominated by her autocratic husband. Then, as one of the first women in the consulting business, she had to prove herself in male-dominated industry. When her husband died suddenly, she became, at the age of forty-six, the head-of-household for their eleven children, responsible for their well-being and their education. She ran the consulting business until she was offered a position as an Engineering Professor at Purdue University.

Steve Jobs did not invent the personal computer; however, he played a major role in creating the personal computer industry. Jobs visited Xerox's Palo Alto Research Center and was impressed with its innovations to make the personal computer user-friendly through devices such as the mouse, the use of menus (action lists), and icons for pull-down screens. Jobs incorporated these features into the next Apple Computer product, the Macintosh. Making the personal computer easy to use created a new industry. *Time* magazine observed his role as a visionary, "Jobs, more clearly that any of his contemporaries, recognized the computer as a tool not for top-down corporate repression but for bottom-up individual empowerment and creativity."

Sojourner Truth began her life as a slave in the North with few of life's amenities. In young adulthood she received a call to spread the Christian word and became a traveling preacher. She earned her keep by doing chores in the farmhouses that she visited. She became a popular public speaker known for her witty repartee. She spoke on reform topics, including the antislavery movement and the women's rights movement. In later life, she earned living expenses from the sale of her book. Truth could have remained a servant and charwoman for her entire lifetime, but she was determined to take a more active role in life helping others.

Roald Amundsen devoted his life to exploration. He was so focused on exploring that he never married. When Admiral Peary beat him to the North Pole, he shifted his attention to the other Pole. His competition with Robert Falcon Scott to discover the South Pole occupied newspaper headlines for months. Amundsen succeeded because he had prepared himself for a lifetime for his task. He was determined to reach the Pole first. Scott was no less determined; however, Amundsen made better decisions than Scott, who chose to use Manchurian ponies and motorized sledges for transportation.

Knute Rockne was a motivator who was able to get the best from his athletes. He was successful in all of his endeavors: coach, teacher, author, and motivational speaker. He was resolved to win even if he had to tell a white lie to get the best from his players. When his team discovered that he had bent the truth to spur them on, they accepted it, knowing his strong determination to win. His speaking ability was notable; he gave inspirational talks to meetings of sales departments in the automotive industry.

Determination contributed to the success of these individuals in industry and in a wide range of endeavors. They inspire us.

LILLIAN GILBRETH (1878-1972) Motion Study Pioneer and Consultant

"To state that it is in the field of human relationships that Lillian Gilbreth's personal contribution to management will endure is not to detract from her earlier work with her pioneer husband in motion study. That she was one of the pioneers, too, in building management securely into the field of ... engineering adds both strength and scope to her contribution. Engineering needed, for its own professional development, emphasis in the human factors in work."[244]

Edna Yost, *Frank and Lillian Gilbreth*

The story of Lillian Gilbreth cannot be told without also telling the story of her husband, Frank Gilbreth. Lillian and Frank Gilbreth, management consultants and specialists in motion study, were classic examples of two halves that make up the whole, or, more accurately, perfect the whole. He was not college educated; she had a Ph.D. in Psychology. He began his working career as a bricklayer and moved into motion study from the trades.

Before they married, Frank told Lillian of his intention to teach her all facets of his construction business and of his consulting activities. Although her undergraduate and masters degrees were in liberal arts, she did not question his plan. She concentrated on the people side of their contracts and consulting work, thus compensating for one of his shortcomings.

Lillian and Frank Gilbreth, "efficiency experts," were an incredible team in scientific management, which ultimately became part of the field of industrial engineering. Frank's specialty was motion study, which he describes in the foreword of his 1911 book, *Motion Study, A Method for*

Increasing the Efficiency of the Workman:

> The aim of motion study is to find and perpet-
> uate the scheme of perfection. There are three
> stages in this study:
> 1. Discovering and classifying the best
>   practice
> 2. Deducing the laws
> 3. Applying the laws to standardize pract-
>   ice either for the purpose of increasing
>   output or decreasing the hours of labor,
>   or both[245]

Lillian's strength was the application of psychology to scientific management in optimizing the human factors, or the "people" component of their projects. Individually, each was missing part of the total package. Together, because they complemented each other extremely well, they provided the total package to their clients.

In the introduction to Lillian's and Frank's 1917 book, *Applied Motion Study*, George Iles describes the authors:

> Frank B. Gilbreth is a versatile engineer, an
> untiring observer, an ingenious inventor, an
> economist to the tips of his fingers; first and
> chiefly, he is a man.... Every page [of this
> book] has taken form with the aid and counsel
> of Mrs. Gilbreth, whose *Psychology of
> Management* is a golden gift to industrial phi-
> losophy. And thus, by viewing their facts from
> two distinct angles we learn how vital phases
> of industrial economy present themselves to a
> man and to a woman who are among the
> acutest investigators of our time.[246]

In the foreword of Edna Yost's book, *Frank and Lillian Gilbreth, Partners for Life*, A. A. Potter, Dean of Engineering at Purdue University, summarizes the personal characteristics of the Gilbreths:

> The outstanding characteristics of Frank Bunker Gilbreth were: an alert and incisive mind; great ability to observe, analyze, synthesize, and correlate quickly and soundly; an insatiable intellectual curiosity and inquisitiveness; unbounded enthusiasm, zeal, courage, and determination; marked optimism, great vitality, deep foresight, and a most remarkable manner of inspiring others to accept his ideas.

> Lillian Moller Gilbreth, like her husband-partner, has an innate urge for the best and the first-rate, has unusual courage and optimism, loves people and work, has a talent for winning cooperation, and is a person of few antagonisms. Lillian Gilbreth not only won high recognition for her own contributions in motion study and applied psychology, but has preserved, enhanced, and increased the appreciation on the part of industry of the pioneering work of both Gilbreths in the field of management.[247]

Frank Gilbreth was born on July 7, 1868 in Kendall's Mills, Maine to Hiram and Martha Bunker Gilbreth. Young Frank was confident and willing to work hard. He wanted to earn money immediately—not in four years after graduating from college. Also, although his mother could afford to send him to college, he was not comfortable attending school while she worked. She was disappointed when he decided to skip college to learn the construction contracting business from the bottom up.

In July 1885, Frank joined the Thomas J. Whidden Company, contractors and builders, to learn the bricklaying trade. Shipbuilding was the only field that paid higher wages than the building trades. Because of its relatively high wages, construction attracted a higher grade of workmen than most of the other trades. Frank's first contacts were with these workers, and it influenced his attitude favorably toward his fellow workmen.

In his training for a supervisory job, Frank had the opportunity to learn other construction skills, such as carpentry, stone masonry, concrete work, roofing, tinsmithing, cast-iron work, and blacksmithing. However, bricklaying was his specialty. He was promoted to assistant foreman within two and a half years and then to foreman. His goal was to be a partner in the business within ten years. Thomas Whidden had given him the impression that the goal was attainable.

In 1892, Frank patented a scaffold for bricklayers that used platforms resting on adjustable frames at three levels. In a later design, it was suspended from jacks. His scaffold kept the rising wall at the same height for the bricklayer, thus minimizing stooping and stretching to lay bricks. He submitted other patents, including one for the Gilbreth Waterproof Cellar to prevent leaky cellars due to the daily rising of the tide in the Boston area.

At the age of twenty-seven, Frank realized that becoming a partner of the Whidden Company in the short term was unlikely. Applications of his two inventions were not receiving the attention that they required, so he left Whidden to establish his own business. He supported his mother and his

Aunt Kit; however, he had no reservations about starting out on his own. His first employees were J. W. Buzzell, a civil engineering graduate of Worcester Polytechnic Institute who became his second in command, and Anne Bowley, who efficiently ran his office.

Frank's third invention was a portable concrete mixer that relied on gravity to move concrete through a trough. This mixer was effective on small construction jobs, and the invention generated income to use on other projects. It also sold well in England.

Frank traveled widely, but he had time for meeting and dating young women. He was full of energy and had a good sense of humor; he was a popular bachelor. His cousin, Minnie Bunker, arrived in Boston with three young women whom she was chaperoning on a trip to Europe. Lillian Moller was one of Minnie's responsibilities. Frank met his future bride and partner when he gave Minnie and her charges a sightseeing tour of Boston. Lillian Evelyn Moller, the oldest surviving child of William and Annie Delger Moller, was born in Oakland, California on May 24, 1878. Annie was never in strong health after her firstborn child died in infancy. Lillie learned the responsibilities of caring for children and maintaining a home at an early age. Although she was born into a well-to-do family, her personality was shaped by the responsibility that was thrust upon her in her youth.

Lillie's childhood was a happy one in a family steeped in discipline of the children. She earned good grades in school. In high school, she studied music with composer John Metcalfe and wrote poetry. She wanted to attend the University of California at Berkeley, but her father initially disapproved because he believed she would never have to support herself.

Finally, her father was willing to let her matriculate at Berkeley. Lillie majored in modern languages and philosophy and also enrolled in history, mathematics, and science courses. She performed in student-produced plays in college and surprised herself with her confidence on the stage. She earned a Phi Beta Kappa key and was selected as the first woman Commencement Day speaker at the University.

Lillie earned an M.A. at Berkeley and planned to continue with courses leading to a Ph.D. degree. The summer that she received her M.A. degree was the one reserved for the planned trip to Europe with Minnie Bunker. The four women visited New York and Boston before boarding their ship bound for Europe. Frank gave the young women from California a grand tour of Boston in his new Winton-six motorcar. He included many new buildings on his tour, and his conversation was sprinkled with observations such as "ready for occupancy forty-nine days after the contract was signed."

The Winton's engine quit on the trip, and Frank was confronted with a gathering of children taunting him about his shiny, new car that would not run. Lillie was impressed with Frank's smiling, unruffled response to their teasing. Lillie kept the children's attention with stories while Frank obtained help fixing the car. He was impressed with Lillie's ability to keep the children occupied.

Frank suggested that she use her literary background to help him write about his many experiences in the construction business. It was obvious to both of them that they were on the same wavelength. They knew that they would see each other again when Lillie returned from Europe.

1903 was an important year in Frank's personal life and his business life. The fields of management and industrial engineering were not well-defined at the time. Frederick W. Taylor presented his classic paper number 1003, "Shop Management," to the American Society of Mechanical Engineers that year. Taylor's specialty was time study, but the field became known generically as scientific management.

When Lillian returned from Europe, Frank met the ship and was introduced to her parents, who were impressed with him. He spent the Christmas holidays with Lillian and her family in Oakland. When he proposed to her, he made it clear that he expected her to participate in his business activities, and that his mother and his Aunt Kit would live with them after they were married. Although they were engaged for ten months, Frank and Lillian spent only six days together between her return from Europe and their marriage in the Moller home in California on October 19, 1904.

Frank agreed with Lillian's continuing her work on a doctorate, but he suggested that she change her minor in psychology to her major. He recognized the future importance of the application of psychology in industry.

Lillian realized very early in their marriage that she had signed up for both a marital and a business partnership for life. Frank immediately began to educate her about his business. He started by saying: "First I want to teach you about concrete and masonry. 'Bond' is the term we use to express the relationship of joints in masonry."[248] Then he made a sketch so that she could understand the concept clearly.

Lillian had some adjustments to make. She was brought up in a sufficiently wealthy family that women were not expected to have a job. Frank had the reverse experience. His mother supported the family when his father died, and the wife of one of his fellow contractors ran her own contracting firm and even competed for contracts with her husband.

Frank's mother, Martha, was in charge of the household, and he was frequently away on business trips. It was difficult for Lillian not to be mistress in her own home, but she had the personality to deal with it. Both Frank and Lillian wanted a large family, but she was surprised to hear that he wanted twelve children. She was not dismayed by this; Lillian was the oldest of nine children. Her background of playing second fiddle to her attractive, personable younger sister and her fears as a young woman that she was not attractive to men probably helped her adapt to life with her strong-willed husband.

In addition to pursuing demanding careers, Lillian and Frank had twelve children, one of whom died in childhood. In 1948, two of their children, Frank Gilbreth, Jr. and Ernestine Gilbreth Carey, published the story of their family in *Cheaper by the Dozen,* which was made into a movie.

Frank was accused by his friends as having more children than he could keep track of. In one of the family stories, Lillian was out of town giving a lecture and left Frank in charge of their brood. When she returned, she asked him how everything had gone in her absence. He responded, "Did not have any trouble except with that one over there, but a spanking brought him into line." Lillian pointed out, "That is not one of ours, dear; he belongs next door."[249]

No one in the family remembers this actually happening. They attribute it to the fact that the only thing Frank liked more than telling a story about Lillian was telling one about himself. However, the children remembered that two redheaded children lived next door, and all of the Gilbreth children were either redheads or blondes.

Frank applied his motion study concepts at home as well as on his construction projects. He buttoned his vest from the bottom up because it took only three seconds; from the top down took seven seconds. He installed process charts in the bathrooms for the children to initial in the morning after they had brushed their teeth, taken a bath, combed their hair, and made their bed. At night, the children initialed a work sheet after they had weighed themselves, completed their homework, washed their hands and face, and brushed their teeth. It was regimentation, but Frank thought that discipline was important in shepherding twelve offspring through their day.

Lillian was a quick study in learning the construction business. Sometimes her opinions differed from his, particularly on the people side of the business. He thought that workmen always wanted to do what he thought they should do; she realized that this was not always true.

Their work became a joint effort that was not divided into her contribution and his contribution; it was their effort. The contracting and construction aspects of the business did not really appeal to her. The people side of the business interested her, and she was a vital contributor in documenting her husband's thoughts on management—the planning of work and the efficient accomplishment of projects.

Their business grew substantially. They had construction sites around the country, including many on the West Coast. As their family grew, Frank disliked being away from home frequently. He conveyed these thoughts to Lillian in many "Dear Chum" letters.

In December 1907, Frank met Frederick Taylor, the "Father of Scientific Management." Taylor concentrated on time study, and Frank specialized in motion study. Frank thought that if a job were done in its most efficient way, the time that it took would be at a minimum. Later, the two specialties would merge into time and motion study.

Taylor, who was ten years older than Frank, became Chief Engineer for the Midvale Steel Company in the 1880s. He had an imaginative and probing mind. While others worked to improve the technology of producing steel, Taylor concentrated on making the workers who produced the steel more efficient.

Management training at the time was accomplished by apprenticeship programs. Taylor was the first to apply the inductive method to the challenges of managing a factory. His initial emphasis on time study was a means of reducing the pay of nonproducers. Eventually, he applied the inductive method to both the administration and the operation of a factory. He divided work into two distinct functions, planning and execution; also, he set finite, standardized tasks for all workers to allow the application of a bonus or a penalty to each worker's pay.

One of the differences in the outlook of Taylor and Frank was their viewpoint about unions. Taylor had had mainly negative experiences with unions of lower skilled workers; Frank had experienced principally positive experiences with unions of higher skilled workmen. A shortcoming of Taylor's landmark paper, "Shop Management," is that he advocated time study of existing methods. He did not stress the improvement of those methods. Doing tasks more efficiently was the goal of Frank's motion study approach.

Although Lillian had three babies in the first three years of their marriage, she worked actively in the business, including climbing scaffolds when necessary. Frank's influential book, *Bricklaying System*, was published in 1909, one year after he published *Concrete Construction*. In 1911, he published *Motion Study: A Method for Increasing the Efficiency of the Workman*. Lillian's help was vital to Frank in compiling and editing his thoughts in preparing the books for publication.

Lillian observed that Frank had a good relationship with his workers and informally was using the little-understood principles of psychology as they existed at the time. She suggested combining these principles of psychology with the practice of management. Frank considered her "a very remarkable woman," who had moved from being his student / assistant to his junior partner and was moving up to even greater responsibility.

In 1911, Frederick Taylor published his seminal work, *The Principles of Scientific Management*. Although Taylor gave credit to others who contributed to the development of his principles, it was becoming apparent that he was not going to credit Frank as a contributor to the subject of motion study.

In his book and in a paper published in *Engineering* in London that was reprinted in the *American Society of Mechanical Engineering Transactions*, Taylor observed that "motion study has been going on in the United States with increasing volume." Taylor also observed that his colleague in time study, Sanford Thompson, was "perhaps the most experienced man in motion study and time study in the country."

In 1912, a difficult year for Frank and Lillian, the Gilbreth business was operating under financial stress because Frank did not want to apply for additional loans and be controlled by bankers. Also that year, the two oldest daughters, Anne and Mary, contracted diphtheria at school. Six-year-old Anne was able to fight off the disease, but her younger sister succumbed. Mary's death devastated Frank and Lillian. After her death, both parents had difficulty talking about the loss of their daughter.

When she recovered from this blow, Lillian completed her

doctoral dissertation, "The Psychology of Management," at the University of California at Berkeley. The University approved her dissertation, but required her to complete an additional year of resident study before awarding her Ph.D.

Lillian and Frank had the dissertation published serially in the periodical, *Industrial Engineering*. In 1914, Sturgis and Walton published it in book form — by L. M. Gilbreth as cited in *Industrial Engineering*. If the fact that the author was a woman was known, it was not publicized. When Frank was asked if L. M. Gilbreth was related to him, he responded, "Only by marriage."

Frank's next construction project was in Providence, Rhode Island, home of Brown University. Brown offered a Ph.D. program in Applied Management that fit Lillian's needs precisely. She was now a full partner with Frank in developing scientific motion study methods. The move to Providence had the additional benefit of getting the children away from their home in Montclair, New Jersey, where their sister Mary had died.

With six children at home, the Gilbreths had to establish a regimen that permitted Lillian to complete her studies while Frank spent long hours on his construction projects. They hired a housekeeper, a handyman, and a Pembroke College student who served as an au pair girl for the children. Frank's mother was in her late seventies but was in excellent health and helped with the household duties.

At Brown University, Lillian continued to develop the concept of micro-motion techniques and also studied the elimination of fatigue. Fatigue in the workplace was mental as well as physical, and she sought ways of combining the psychological aspects with the concept of motion study. Both Lillian and Frank participated in a series of summer programs at Brown. Frank undertook assignments with companies in Europe, and he was returning from one of those jobs when Lillian received her Ph.D. from Brown University. The Gilbreths moved back to Montclair, New Jersey after Lillian finished her studies.

In the United States, Frank and Lillian applied their motion study techniques at companies such as Cluett Peabody, Pierce Arrow, U.S. Rubber, and Eastman Kodak. Lillian usually accompanied Frank on the first plant visit for their projects when they were sizing up the task ahead. Gilbreth Associates had managers capable of directing projects, including their first employee, J. W. Buzzell; however, Lillian was Frank's only partner. In his letters to her at this time, his salutation had evolved from "Dear Chum" to "Dear Boss."

The Gilbreths believed that a maximum of seventeen elements were required to complete a motion cycle:

- Search
- Find
- Select
- Grasp
- Position
- Assemble
- Use

- Dissemble
- Inspect
- Transport, loaded
- Pre-position for next operation
- Release load
- Transport, empty

- Wait, unavoidably
- Wait, avoidably
- Rest, necessary for overcoming fatigue
- Plan

In the spring of 1921, an honorary membership in the Society of Industrial Engineers was awarded to Lillian in Milwaukee. For the first time in his life, words failed Frank. He was so happy for her that no words came out when he was called upon to speak. The resulting applause rescued him. She claimed that the honorary membership was due to Frank's overstressing her contributions, but her own book,

Psychology of Management, was highly regarded and frequently quoted.

In 1924, the Gilbreths planned to attend the World Power Conference in London and the International Management Congress in Prague. Early one morning, Frank prepared to go to Manhattan to have their passports renewed. He called from the railroad station in Montclair to tell Lillian that he had forgotten to bring the passports with him. She left the telephone to look for them and when she returned, there was no one on the line. The police asked a neighbor to come to her house and tell her that Frank had dropped dead in the telephone booth.

Lillian and the family were heartbroken. They were a close-knit family, and all of the children revered their father. According to his wishes, he had a simple funeral service with no music or flowers. Several days later, Lillian sailed for Europe as Frank would have advised her to do. She attended the World Power Conference in London and then traveled to Prague for the International Management Congress. She read the paper that they had prepared for Frank to read in Prague, chaired the session at which he was scheduled to preside, and was made an honorary member of the Masaryk Academy in his place. She controlled her emotions with difficulty as members of the Congress paid many tributes to her husband.

When she returned home, she consulted with the eleven Gilbreth children about their future. Frank and Lillian had placed a priority on a college education for all of the children, and she intended to honor that plan. Lillian's mother invited her and the children to move in with her and to take advantage of the California educational system. However, consulting opportunities for Lillian were greater on the East Coast, where she was better known.

Lillian listed her goals for the future:

- Provide a home, a living, and love for the family.
- Maintain Frank's work. Teach his ideals and techniques to younger people who would keep them alive and progressing.
- Push forward cooperative research projects in the areas of his interests, especially the motion study aspects of problems affecting the health and efficiency of human beings in industry.

Her first project was a request from Johnson & Johnson to establish a facility to train employees in motion study techniques. This task meshed with an activity that she and Frank had already planned. She continued Frank's ongoing projects and began work on a new assignment for R. H. Macy and Company. When she had spent the insurance money and the money received from selling their car, she had to borrow from her mother to help pay for living and school expenses. All of these loans were eventually repaid in full.

Lillian faced significant challenges. At the age of forty-six, she had to venture out on her own without the backing and advice of her strong-willed husband. However, Lillian had inner strengths that she drew upon. She needed these strengths at a time when women were not universally accepted in industry.

Initially, she was faced with providing the necessary discipline for her teenage children, particularly her sons. Then she had to cope with providing for forty-four years of college education, four years for each of her eleven children. In time their eleven bachelor degrees included three from the University of Michigan and two from Smith College.

In October 1930, with the country struggling with the Great Depression, Lillian was asked to head the women's unit of the President's Emergency Committee for Employment.

She devised a plan to use women's clubs and other national organizations to conduct job surveys and to determine how to use the unemployed.

The Chairman of the Committee for Employment credited Lillian with "conceiving a new method to apply to an old evil ... a brilliant conception and carried through with speed and skill."[250] Following her success with this program, she was asked to serve with the President's Organization on Unemployment Relief.

In 1935, Lillian was invited by President Elliott of Purdue University and Dean Potter of its Engineering School to join the Purdue faculty. They offered her an appointment as Professor of Management that allowed her time for outside consulting. This appointment provided her with the opportunity of passing on the principles of motion study to younger people and gave her more employment stability than consulting provided during the Depression.

Initially, she was required to be away from Montclair, where her younger children were still in school, for three weeks out of every four. Her Purdue experience was very rewarding for her; she retained her appointment there until her retirement in 1948. Lillian remained in good health as she grew older. She followed the physical exercise program that Frank had devised for her to use after the births of their children.

In 1931, Lillian was awarded the first Gilbreth Medal by the Society of Industrial Engineering "for distinguished contribution to management." She received many honors, including an honorary Master of Engineering degree from the University of Michigan and an appointment as the only woman delegate to the World Engineering Congress in Tokyo.

One of her greatest honors was awarded at an annual joint meeting of the American Society of Mechanical Engineers and the American Management Association: "To Dr. Lillian Moller Gilbreth, and to Dr. Frank B. Gilbreth posthumously ... the 1944 Gantt Medal, in recognition of their pioneer work in management and their development of the principles and techniques of motion study."[251] Lillian was considered the First Lady of Engineering in her later years.

STEVE JOBS (1955-   ) Founder of Apple Computer Corporation

"His tenacity is what makes him great. Several years after leaving Steve's employ, Susan Barnes conducted a study about family run businesses. She found that the key to success was 'pure staying power, persistence, continually believing in something, doggedness to get things done, and continual optimism.' That was a good description of Steve Jobs. Steve was beaten down many times but 'he kept getting off the mat,' she says."[252]

> Alan Deutschman, *The Second Coming of Steve Jobs*

Steve Jobs was the first to envision that people would buy a computer for their home because they wanted to do some business tasks or to run educational applications for themselves or their children. Furthermore, he foresaw the need to link the home with a "nationwide communications network," now called the Internet. Jobs's role in the formation of the personal computer industry is described by Nathan Aaseng in *Business Builders in Computers:*

> Steve Jobs was the first person who saw the personal computer as a mass consumer product. He triggered the transformation of personal computers from hobby toys into useful products for the home and business. Jobs then went on to introduce a second revolution in personal computers—the user-friendly, point and click operating systems that are now standard. While Jobs did not originate the ideas that went into the Macintosh ... his drive and energy helped bring the revolutionary computer into existence.[253]

Steve Jobs was born on February 24, 1955 in San Francisco. Shortly after his birth, he was adopted by Paul and Clara Jobs. Paul Jobs worked for a finance company in Palo Alto; the family lived in nearby Mountain View. Young Steve was smart but was known as a loner. He was not subjected to much discipline as a child, and he was used to getting his way. He was not interested in team sports so he became a swimmer, where emphasis was on individual achievement.

Paul Jobs's hobby was buying and fixing up old cars. He took his son with him when he negotiated for cars and parts. This early experience helped Steve to develop his strengths as a negotiator.

Steve became interested in electronics at the age of ten. Many Hewlett-Packard engineers lived in his neighborhood, and he was intrigued with many electronics projects assembled in neighborhood garages. One neighbor instructed Jobs in electronics and enrolled him in the Hewlett-Packard Explorer Club, where he learned about calculators, diodes, holograms, and lasers.

Because Steve did not like the high school in Mountain View, his father secured a position as a machinist in Los Carlos and moved the family. Through a mutual friend, Jobs met Steve Wozniak. Jerry Wozniak, an electrical engineer at Lockheed, had instructed his son in electronics. Steve Wozniak was only eighteen when he met Jobs, but his knowledge of electronics was advanced for his age. He had won prizes in local electronics fairs against tough competition. He had already expanded his design for a one-bit adder-subtractor into a ten-bit parallel adder-subtractor, a precursor to a computer.

One of Jobs's first projects for the Explorer Club was building a frequency counter. He needed parts and obtained them with the boldness for which he later became known. He looked up Bill Hewlett in the Palo Alto phone book. Hewlett answered the phone and talked with Jobs for twenty minutes. He not only gave him the parts he needed but also gave him a summer job at Hewlett-Packard assembling frequency counters. Later, when Jobs needed another part, he called the Burroughs Corporation in Detroit collect, and asked them to donate it to him.

During high school, Jobs worked at a surplus electronics warehouse store in Sunnyvale, where he learned electronic part pricing. He purchased capacitors, resistors, and microchips at flea markets and resold them at a profit.

Wozniak enrolled at the University of Colorado but returned to San Francisco after one year. He took programming courses at the local community college and later enrolled at the University of California at Berkeley.

Despite his parents' objections, Jobs enrolled at Reed College in Portland, Oregon. Reed was a liberal school, and its students considered themselves anti-establishment. Jobs and a fellow student, Daniel Kottke, studied Zen Buddism and Yoga. They became vegetarians and visited the Hare Krishna temple frequently. Jobs dropped out of school but stayed on the periphery of Reed. He lived in an unheated room and supported himself by maintaining electrical equipment. He usually went barefoot and only wore his sandals when it snowed.

In 1974, Jobs returned home and interviewed for a job at Atari as a technician. He insisted that they hire him, so they did. Nolan Bushnell had founded Atari in 1972 to develop video games. His first big success was the game "Pong." Jobs wanted to travel to India, as one of his Reed friends had done the previous summer. Jobs asked Atari's Chief Engineer to pay his way to India "to see his guru." The Chief Engineer laughed at him but thought of a way to give him time off. He asked Jobs to stop in Germany on his way to India.

Atari had a grounding problem with circuit boards in the games they sold in Germany partly due to the difference between sixty-cycle and fifty-cycle power. The Chief Engineer gave Jobs a short course in ground loops. In Germany, Jobs solved the problem in two hours by ensuring that the chassis in which the board was inserted was properly grounded.

Jobs's friend Kottke joined him in India. They were moved by the poverty, which was greater than they had expected. Jobs's summer in India caused him to question many of his Eastern beliefs. His friends thought that his disillusionment with India made him seem detached. In the fall of 1974, Jobs returned home and contacted Wozniak.

Wozniak had dropped out of Berkeley during his junior year, married, and accepted a position as an engineer in Hewlett-Packard's calculator division. He became a regular attendee at meetings of the Homebrew Computer Club, a gathering place for computer hobbyists, engineers, programmers, and suppliers.

Attendance at Club meetings increased exponentially after the January 1975 issue of *Popular Electronics* was circulated. It included an article about the Altair 8800 computer kit produced by MITS in Albuquerque, New Mexico. The Altair central processing unit used an Intel 8080 microprocessor. The Altair was a collection of parts with meager documentation and little input / output capability. It required substantial knowledge of electronics to assemble, was usually missing parts, and cost $495. Orders from hobbyists for this first mail-order computer overwhelmed MITS. The Altair operating system was developed by Bill Gates and Paul Allen, who later founded Microsoft Corporation.

Wozniak designed his own computer. Initially, he based his design on the Motorola 6800 microprocessor, but later replaced it with the MOS Technology 6502. He drew on his previous experience in building a computer with limited capability in a neighbor's garage and in designing a "Computer Converser" for Call Computer. Wozniak was adept at designing efficient circuit boards with a minimum of components; the circuit board for this computer was no exception.

Wozniak took his computer to meetings of the Homebrew Computer Club, but they were not interested in it because it was not based on the Intel 8080 used in the Altair. He offered to give away circuit diagrams of his computer to club members, but Jobs suggested that they sell them. Better yet, Jobs suggested that they make the circuit-board computers and sell them. On April 1, 1976, Jobs and Wozniak formed a partnership called Apple Computer to make and sell computers. Jobs chose the name because it came before Atari in the phone book and because he liked the Beatles—Apple was the name of their record label.

Jobs invited Ron Wayne, Atari's Chief Field Service Engineer, to join the partnership to do artwork, advertising layout, and documentation. Wayne was given ten percent of Apple Computer, and Jobs and Wozniak each took forty-five percent. Wayne, a conservative engineer in his forties, favored low risk investments such as precious metals and stamps. He became nervous when Apple Computer committed substantial amounts of money for circuit-board parts. He withdrew from the partnership, a move that he regretted later.

Jobs found a source for economical circuit boards. He had gained experience in dealing with circuit-board houses when he negotiated circuit-board work for Wozniak's Computer Converser. Jobs developed a reputation as a tough negotiator. He was called "the rejector," because he usually turned down early designs and estimates.

Jobs met an electronics retailer at a Homebrew Club meeting who offered to buy fifty circuit-board computers, now called Apple I, for $500 each. Apple Computer needed start-up capital, but no one was willing to lend it to them. Jobs had $1,000 from the sale of his van plus a small nest egg from selling Atari the video game "Breakout" that Wozniak had designed. Jobs's loan requests were turned down by banks and by his previous employer at the electronics warehouse store.

Finally, Jobs found a supplier of electronics parts in Palo Alto who would sell them $20,000 worth of parts on credit with no interest if they paid within thirty days. Jobs's sister had married and moved out of their parents' home, so they used her bedroom to assemble the circuit boards. The Jobs' garage is usually noted as the first location of Apple Computer. The garage was used when the work volume over-flowed Jobs's sister's bedroom. Their customer was unhappy with the first delivery of the Apple I because it lacked a display, a keyboard, a power supply, and software. Nevertheless, he paid in cash.

Jobs hired his sister and his old friend Kottke to insert components into circuit boards. A classmate of Jobs at Reed kept the company's books. Wozniak obtained a $5,000 loan from friends to keep the enterprise going. In the fall of 1976, Jobs and Wozniak took Apple I to a computer fair in New York City. Commodore Business Machines offered to buy Apple Computer, but they thought that $100,000 and annual salaries of $36,000 a year for Jobs and Wozniak was too much to pay for a garage-based operation.

Jobs offered to sell Apple Computer to Nolan Bushnell of Atari and was turned down; Bushnell saw no future in microprocessors. Wozniak approached Hewlett-Packard about buying Apple, but they did not want to get into that "dubious" market. Finding no buyers for the company, Jobs and Wozniak addressed the shortcomings of the Apple I.

Wozniak had already started to design the next generation computer, so Jobs farmed out the design of the power supply. Jobs insisted upon a power supply that required no cooling fan. After another designer failed with a cassette interface, Wozniak designed a straightforward interface for use in loading BASIC programming language into the computer. Jobs devised a wooden case for the Apple I made by a local cabinet maker. It was heavy and did not dissipate heat well; unfortunately, it cost almost as much as the circuit board.

When Apple Computer outgrew their bedroom / garage operation, Jobs contracted out the insertion of components into circuit boards. The company he chose did not want the work, but Jobs succeeded with his "I'm not going to leave here until you agree" approach. Wozniak's next-generation computer incorporated a case, a keyboard, and a power supply. It was designed to be used a with a standard television set as the display, both to hold down the cost and because it was less intimidating to the user.

Wozniak added expansion slots to the Apple II to be used by suppliers of add-on circuit boards. This important feature started a new industry when other vendors realized how easy it was to design and build products for the Apple II. Wozniak also designed a read-only memory chip to hold the BASIC programming language, thus eliminating the cassette interface. Jobs found a designer for Apple II's plastic case through contacts at Hewlett-Packard.

Jobs had been an individual in search of a cause. In promoting the personal computer, he had found his cause. He had a knack for convincing talented people to undertake projects for Apple.

One of Jobs's important early decisions was his choice of an advertising / public relations firm. He asked Intel who had handled their recent advertising campaign and was told it was the Regis McKenna Agency. McKenna turned him down. Jobs persisted; he called McKenna three or four times a day until he agreed to take on Apple as a client. McKenna's first action was to change the logo. Wayne had designed the original black and white logo with Isaac Newton sitting under a tree with one apple on a limb. McKenna redesigned the logo using an apple with multicolored bands and a bite, or byte, taken out. Apple used that logo until it was replaced in 1998.

The fledgling enterprise needed capital to expand. Jobs asked Nolan Bushnell of Atari to recommend a venture capitalist. Bushnell suggested Don Valentine of Sequoia Ventures, but Valentine was not interested. Valentine told Jobs and Wozniak they were not thinking big enough; he suggested that they talk with Mike Markkula, who had made his first million when Intel went public. Markkula, who had retired at the age of thirty-three, offered to devote four years to Apple and provide $250,000 to develop and manufacture the Apple II in return for a one-third ownership in the company.

Markkula's offer was dependent upon Wozniak leaving Hewlett-Packard and working for Apple full time. Wozniak refused even though his division of Hewlett-Packard was moving to Oregon, and he did not want to move. He changed his mind when a friend told him that he did not have to become a manager; he could continue as an engineer.

Markkula helped Jobs and Wozniak prepare a business plan. On January 3, 1977, Apple Computer Company was incorporated and, within three months, bought out the partnership for $5,308.96. Jobs, Wozniak, and Markkula each owned thirty percent and Rod Holt, designer of the power supply and finisher of Wozniak's projects, owned ten percent.

Markkula's strengths were business planning and marketing strategy. He had no desire to be President of Apple; he recommended his friend, Michael Scott, who was responsible for producing $30 million worth of components a year at National Semiconductor. Scott was an aggressive manager who could make tough decisions, in contrast to the diplomatic, mild-mannered Markkula.

As he had on Apple I, Jobs worked closely with the circuit-board contractor. The board, due to Wozniak's original design of sixty-two chips and integrated circuits and to Jobs's efforts as "rejector," was a work of art. It was easy to produce and it looked good when the cover was raised. Jobs persisted in negotiating bargain-basement prices for Apple's components.

Neither Markkula nor Scott could get along with Jobs; daily confrontations occurred between Scott and Jobs, partly because Markkula pushed off all of his dealings with Jobs onto Scott. Jobs was openly critical of the work of the young employees. As the business increased and company operations became more formal, Jobs went in several directions at once.

Wozniak fitted in less well with the expanding organization and was not consulted as often as he had been. The close working relationship between him and Jobs began to change. Wozniak spent so much time at Apple that his marriage broke up. He gave his wife fifteen percent of his Apple stock in the divorce settlement.

In early 1977, Apple II was demonstrated in an attention-gathering booth at a computer fair in San Francisco. Jobs bought the first suit he ever owned to wear at the fair. 13,000 attendees were captivated by Apple II, and 300 orders were placed.

During 1977, Markkula worked hard to obtain additional capital to fuel Apple's growth. He was amazingly successful. In January 1978, financing arrangements were completed, and Apple was valued at $3 million. Venrock, a venture firm that invested Rockefeller money, invested $288,000; Don Valentine, who earlier had declined investing in Apple, invested $150,000; Arthur Rock, who had made millions on Intel and Scientific Data Systems stock, invested $57,600. Rock also became an important advisor to the fledgling enterprise. Henry Singleton of Teledyne invested $108,000 and agreed to serve on the Board.

In early 1978, Wozniak completed his design for a floppy disk drive, and it went into production. Wozniak considered it his best design; it added important functionality to the Apple II by allowing programmers to produce software that could be transferred from computer to computer reliably.

Later in 1978, Markkula suggested that Apple enter the education market. His daughter was learning grade school math, and he could see the enormous potential of the market. His efforts ultimately led to the establishment of the Apple Education Foundation. The education market became a lucrative one for Apple.

The next product was an enhanced Apple II, Apple Plus, that had an improved startup routine and an updated version of BASIC. Memory was doubled to 48 kilobytes. However, enhancement was not enough; the company provided additional improvements that customers and dealers had requested by:

- Increasing the width of the display from forty to eighty characters
- Providing lower-case as well as upper-case letters
- Providing additional memory to accommodate more sophisticated programs
- Ensuring compatibility between the Apple II and new machines
- Bundling the software and providing it with the purchase of the hardware

Wozniak was not directly involved with the new machine, the Apple III, as he had been on earlier products. Jobs designed the case first and then made the designers fit within it as best they could. The designers did not have enough space, but Jobs would not enlarge the case. As a result, they designed a circuit board to piggyback onto the motherboard. To save money, they did not use gold contacts (that do not corrode) to connect the boards. The connectors corroded, and Apple III was not reliable. Fortunately, sales of Apple II, which had little competition in 1979, were strong.

Apple sold an additional $7,273,801 worth of stock that year. Also in 1979, the spreadsheet application entered the marketplace. Dan Fylstra, a Boston software entrepreneur, developed VisiCalc on an Apple II and offered it to Apple for $1 million. Apple declined; nevertheless, when VisiCalc was shipped in the fall of 1979, it only ran on the Apple II. The availability of a spreadsheet application and of Wozniak's floppy disk drive spurred Apple II sales.

Following Apple III's limited success, Jobs needed a new goal. He hired two Hewlett-Packard managers, one to manage software development and the other to manage engineering.

Jobs's goal was a machine based on 16-bit architecture, rather than the Apple II 8-bit architecture, to sell for $2,000. The new machine, Lisa, was large, awkward-looking, and based on the 68000, the new microprocessor from Motorola.

Lisa was slow in both processing and in screen refreshment speed, but the software group had been innovative in using bit-mapping that provided a one-to-one correspondence between the bits in the computer memory and the picture elements (pixels) on the screen. Screen resolution was considerably higher than that of the Apple II and III. Jobs did not think that Lisa was "sexy" enough, and he did not think it was the right product for the office environment. He sought a partner; he considered IBM and Xerox despite the fact that Apple considered IBM the enemy.

Xerox had invested in Apple's second private investment placement. Jobs contacted the Xerox Development Corporation, the company's venture capital unit, and offered to let them invest $1 million in Apple if they would give him a tour of their Palo Alto Research Center (PARC). PARC had a talented staff of computer scientists who had made many breakthroughs that Xerox had failed to exploit. Xerox purchased 100,000 shares of Apple at $10.00 and opened their doors to Jobs. The twenty-five-year-old entrepreneur had gotten his way again.

Larry Tesler of PARC demonstrated their Alto personal computer to Jobs and seven Apple developers, who were enthusiastic when they saw Alto's potential. User interaction with the Alto was revolutionary through the use of icons, menus (action lists), partitions of the screen (windows), and a "mouse." Jobs was moved by what he saw. He shouted: "Why aren't you doing anything with this? This is the greatest thing! This is revolutionary!" After the demonstration, Jobs hired

Tesler to work for Apple. Later, Alan Kay, one of PARC's principal computer science visionaries, joined Apple and eventually became an Apple Fellow.

In August 1980, Markkula reorganized Apple into three divisions:

- Personal Computer Systems (Apple II and III)
- Professional Office Systems (Lisa)
- Accessories (add-on circuit boards, disk drives, printers, etc.)

Jobs had hoped to be given line authority of a division; instead, he was named Chairman of the Board.

On December 12, 1980, Apple Computer Corporation went public. Apple's 4,600,000 shares sold out within the first hour in the most oversubscribed initial public offering since Ford Motor Company had gone public in 1956. Apple was worth $1.778 billion on the stock market. The company had reached the Fortune 500 faster than any company in history. Forty new millionaires were made that day, including:

- Jobs, whose fifteen percent of the outstanding shares was worth $256 million.
- Markkula, who owned $239 million of Apple stock.
- Wozniak, who was worth $135.6 million.
- Scott, the President, who owned Apple stock worth $95.5 million.
- Holt, a key designer, who was worth $67 million.
- Wozniak's ex-wife, whose divorce settlement stock was worth $42 million.

Without line responsibility, Jobs was again without a project. He needed a subject for his evangelism. The Macintosh personal computer was the next project to provide an outlet for his zeal. Macintosh was in the R & D phase and had already survived one attempt by Jobs to kill it. Scott had rescued the project. Jef Raskin and his team of two developers planned a "luggable" machine that would be easy to use and would sell for about $1,000. Hardware and software designers would work together from the beginning, and software would be offered as part of the purchase price of the machine.

Jobs promoted the Macintosh within Apple, and three developers were immediately added to the team. Jef Raskin had based the design on the Motorola 6809 microprocessor. Jobs insisted that the 6809 processor be replaced with the faster Motorola 68000; Raskin was overruled.

Jobs challenged Burrell Smith to redesign the Macintosh based on the 68000 by the end of 1980. Smith was a Wozniak-type designer who liked simple designs and worked on a project night and day until it was done. He also had Wozniak's ability to evaluate the elements of a complex design in his head. The Macintosh design had one circuit board that used off-the-shelf parts, compared to Lisa's five circuit boards with some custom components. Furthermore, it was twice as fast as Lisa and could be produced at one-third the price. Jobs took over the project and brought in developers from the successful Apple II, including Wozniak and Holt. Jobs managed the Macintosh Division when it was formed.

As the Macintosh development effort expanded, Jobs pulled talent from the rest of the company. In fact, he frequently and loudly announced that the future of the company was with the Macintosh "pirates." Ultimately, however, this split between Macintosh developers and other Apple developers divided the company. The development deadlines for the Macintosh were so tight that it forced them to contract writing some of the programs outside of Apple.

The first software developer Jobs sought out was Bill Gates of Microsoft, who wrote the first BASIC programs for personal computers. Gates and his partner, Paul Allen, provided the operating system software (eventually called MS / DOS) for IBM's personal computers. Gates negotiated a non-exclusive agreement with IBM that allowed Microsoft to license IBM's operating environment to other customers.

Jobs and Scott, Apple's President, had a tempestuous working relationship. Scott was one of the few people that Jobs could not intimidate. Unfortunately, Scott's abrasive personality intimidated younger employees. Scott fired the Vice President of Engineering and was attempting to do that job in addition to his own. Finally, he was edged out by Markkula, who had brought him into the company.

Markkula was in a difficult position because his four-year arrangement with Apple was almost over. He looked outside Apple for a new president. He wanted John Sculley, President of Pepsi-Cola USA, who had taken market share from Coca-Cola. Initially, Sculley was not interested in joining Apple. Jobs flew to New York City and courted Sculley. After many long conversations about the future of Apple, Jobs asked Sculley if he intended to sell sugar water to children for the rest of his life when he could be doing something important with personal computers. The financial package Apple offered to Sculley was difficult to turn down.

Sculley spent many hours learning the technology. Within his first year on the job, he realized that cuts would have to be made. Apple II was carrying the company, and Lisa was a distinct disappointment. He streamlined the organizational structure and eliminated 1,200 jobs to keep the company profitable. Jobs retained his position as manager of the Macintosh Division in addition to serving as Chairman of the Board. Sculley redirected the company from producing most of its own software to increased reliance on outside software developers, an approach similar to IBM's.

The first disagreements between Jobs and Sculley occurred in 1983. By 1984, when Macintosh sales were considerably below Jobs's estimates, the rift was obvious to everyone. Apple lowered the price of Macintosh from $2,495 to $1,995, but sales continued to be disappointing. The initial demand for Apple IIc had declined; eventually 200,000 had to be sold through a liquidator. An attempt to market Lisa as Macintosh XL wasn't successful. In 1985, Wozniak left the company. He was unhappy with Apple's direction, particularly the lack of recognition of Apple II's contribution to the company's bottom line and the dearth of Apple II development funds.

At the Board meeting on April 11, 1985, Sculley removed Jobs as manager of the Macintosh Division and replaced him with Jean-Louis Gassee, the successful head of Apple France. Jobs then attempted to have Sculley removed as President and CEO. However, he misjudged Sculley's support from the Board of Directors. Finally, their disagreements became so disruptive that the Board suggested that Sculley force Jobs out of the company.

When Jobs left Apple, he formed a new computer company called NeXT. He attracted many key Apple developers to his start-up. Apple was alarmed by the loss of critical personnel and was concerned about a potential loss of technology. Jobs sought start-up capital for NeXT; Ross Perot invested $20 million for sixteen percent of the company. Jobs was only moderately successful with NeXT, which generated some income by selling software to Apple. In 1997, Apple's sales and earnings plummeted, and Jobs returned to Apple Computer as interim CEO and led Apple's rebound. He became CEO in 2000.

Steve Jobs and Steve Wozniak made significant contributions to the computer industry. Working out of a garage, they succeeded where large corporations had failed; they pioneered the personal computer revolution. In 1985, President Reagan awarded National Technology Medals to Jobs and Wozniak at the White House. Together, they provided the expertise, determination, and vision to found an industry within an industry. In doing so, they changed the home and workplace environment forever.

SOJOURNER TRUTH (1797-1883) Antislavery and Women's Rights Activist.

"When we follow her from one field of labor to another, her time being divided between teaching, preaching, nursing, watching, and praying, ever ready to comfort and assist, we feel that, for one who is nobody but a woman, a black woman, and an old woman, born and bred a slave, nothing short of the Divine incarnated in the human form could have wrought out such grand results."[255]

Frances Titus, Sojourner Truth's friend and companion

Sojourner Truth's accomplishments are not widely known. Her book, *The Narrative of Sojourner Truth,* a combination of scrapbook and memoir with a chapter on her death, is only partially helpful in documenting her life. In the introduction to Truth's book, Nell Irvin Painter provides a summary of Sojourner's significance:

> Tall, black Sojourner Truth—ex-slave, abolitionist, women's rights activist—stands today for strong African-American women, for the strength of all women. She embodied "the slave" as female and "the woman" as black, having achieved that status in her own times.... An indefatigable lecturer, Truth rounded out the two most important reform movements of the early nineteenth century.... Truth's fame rests on her speech: her preaching, her singing, and her mastery of lightning repartee.[256]

An example of Truth's quick repartee was her response to the comments of a minister at a women's rights convention in

1853 in Akron, Ohio. The minister told the convention that women were inferior to men because they were weaker and had to be helped into a carriage, carried over mud puddles, and provided with the best seat. Truth responded by telling the minister that no man had ever helped her into a carriage, carried her over a puddle, or given her the best seat. She then asked the question for which she is known, "And aren't I a woman?" She rolled up her sleeve and said, "Look at me. Look at my arm! I have plowed, and planted, and gathered into barns, and no man could head me, and aren't I a woman?"[257]

Sojourner Truth was born in Hurley, New York in the Hudson River Valley about 1797. Her parents were slaves owned by farmer Johannes Hardenbergh; the date of her birth was not recorded. She was born Isabella Hardenbergh, the ninth child of Betsey and James Hardenbergh; she changed her name to Sojourner Truth when she was forty-six.

Slaves, who constituted fifteen percent of the population of New York State by 1723, were an important part of the State's economy although the North had only a fraction of the number of slaves in the South. Dutch settlers in New Amsterdam had imported slaves beginning in 1626. British settlers continued to bring in slaves after New Amsterdam became New York in 1664.

Isabella grew up speaking Dutch, not English. Johannes Hardenbergh died in 1800, leaving Isabella's family and ten other slaves to his son, Charles. The slaves all lived in the cellar of Hardenbergh's limestone farmhouse. Water entered the basement through cracks in the walls when it rained; the only light came from a small casement window. During winter, they lit a fire in the middle of the mud floor and wrapped themselves in old blankets. Hardenbergh forced them to live in harsh conditions; however, he gave them a small plot of land to grow crops to trade for food and clothes. Isabella's mother was a very religious woman who taught them that they were under God's protection. She advised them that if they sought God's aid when they were in need, he would help them.

In 1808, Charles Hardenbergh died, and Isabella's family was split up. Earlier, Isabella's older brother and sister had been taken from their parents and auctioned off at a slave market. Betsey and James were freed from slavery and continued to live in the cellar, but Isabella was sold to John Nealy of Kingston, New York. She was beaten regularly because she spoke only Dutch and the Nealys spoke only English. She was unable to understand many of Mrs. Nealy's orders. Mr. Nealy beat Isabella because she was slow in learning English.

When Isabella's father heard about her beatings, he persuaded Martin Schryver, a farmer, fisherman, and tavern owner, to buy his daughter. She was a hard worker who helped the fishermen, hoed corn, chopped wood, and gathered hops in the fields for making homemade beer served at the tavern. Later, she became known for smoking a pipe, a habit that began while she lived with the Schryvers.

In 1810, Isabella was sold to John Dumont, a farmer in New Paltz, New York. Dumont was kind to his new slave, but Mrs. Dumont was cruel to her. Isabella quietly tolerated the abuse and became a more religious person. In her late teens, she married Thomas, one of the Nealy's slaves, and moved back with the Nealys. Their daughter, Diana, was born in 1815. Four more children were born over the next twelve years.

On July 4, 1827, the New York State Legislature passed an emancipation law, and Isabella and Thomas were freed.

Nealy had told her that he would free her one year early, but he broke his promise. She decided to run away. Unfortunately, the only child she could take with her was Sophie, the youngest. A nearby farmer, whom she asked where she should go, directed her to the home of Quakers Isaac and Maria Van Wagener. Nealy came to their home to claim Isabella and Sophia; Isabella refused to return with him. Van Wagener offered to pay for Isabella and her daughter. Nealy, who knew that Isabella would not return to work for him willingly, gave in.

Van Wagener told her that she was a free woman. She was happy with the Quaker family but was saddened to hear that her son, Peter, had been sold to an Alabama plantation owner. When she heard that New York's emancipation law forbid shipping slaves out of state, she filed a lawsuit against the owner who sold Peter south. Isabella was determined to have Peter returned to the North. After some delays, she won her lawsuit and her son was returned to her. She was one of the first African-American women in the United States to win a case in court.

Isabella became more devout and was active in the local Methodist church. Although she was happy with the Van Wageners, she felt that she was living an overly sheltered life. Also, her wages were low, and she knew that she could earn significantly more in New York City. In the summer of 1828, she and Peter moved to New York, where she found employment as a servant in the homes of New York's merchants. Peter planned to go to sea after studying in a navigation vocational school. Isabella joined the Zion African Church, where she became an active member. She vigorously professed her faith by reciting from the Bible and by giving moving sermons.

Isabella was determined to help reduce the suffering of the poor. She devoted considerable time and effort to the Magdalene Asylum, where she taught homeless women skills to help them find employment. Elijah Pierson, the director of the Magdalene Asylum, and his wife, Sarah, were intensely religious. They "purified" themselves by fasting without food or water for four or more days at a time. After the death of Sarah Pierson by excessive fasting, Isabella moved into the meetinghouse and became a servant for and avid follower of Elijah Pierson.

In May 1832, Isabella responded to a knock on the door of the meetinghouse and was confronted by a robed man calling himself Matthias, who asked to see Elijah. The man, who had started life as Robert Matthews of Albany, New York, told her that he was Matthias, God the Father, and that he had the power to do all things. Matthews and Pierson, self-proclaimed ministers, established a religious community called Zion Hill (later called Kingdom) on a farm owned by Benjamin and Ann Folger along the Hudson River.

Harmony reigned in the community until Matthews, the only one who had not contributed financially, demanded control over the others. Isabella became disillusioned with the community when the principals argued and conducted unusual rituals. Pierson died, and his family accused Matthews of poisoning him and taking his money. Matthews was arrested for murder but was acquitted in April 1835. Several books were published that documented many rumors about the community.

Isabella, who returned to New York City, was drawn into the scandal and was accused of contributing to the disharmony at Kingdom. She provided the press with letters of reference she had received from previous employers. Those references and the account of newspaper journalist Gilbert Vale, "The Narrative of Isabella, or Fanaticism: Its Source and Influence," cleared her name. She sued Folger and the newspaper that had published the libelous article about her. Again, she won her lawsuit. She went back to work for the Whitings, a family whom she knew from her earlier stay in New York City.

Isabella attempted to reunite with her daughters, who had stayed on the Dumont farm until they had fulfilled their obligations. However, when they left the farm, they did not want to move to New York City. Also, she was concerned about her son, Peter, who had become a delinquent before signing on as seaman on a merchant ship. She received letters from him until communications between them ended in 1841.

During the summer of 1843, Isabella left New York and went on the road as a traveling preacher. She was excited and somewhat apprehensive about her new challenge; however, she knew that the Lord would provide. She began in Brooklyn and walked toward Long Island. She decided that the name given to her as a slave was not suitable to her new role as a pilgrim. She called herself "Sojourner," which she felt was appropriate for someone who planned to "travel up and down the land, showing the people their sins, and being a sign to them." Initially, she did not have a last name in mind to go with Sojourner. She chose Truth because she thought it would be a good last name for one of the Lord's pilgrims.

On her travels, Truth quoted the Bible widely from memory and inspired the farmers with whom she stayed. She asked them, "How can you expect to do good to God unless you first learn to do good to each other." In return for food, shelter, and hospitality, she did housework and washed their clothes. From Long Island, she crossed Long Island Sound to preach in Connecticut and Massachusetts. In late 1843, she traveled to Northampton, Massachusetts, where she joined the Northampton Association of Education and Industry, a cooperative community led by Samuel Hill. She did not agree with all of their tenets, and she let them know how she felt; nevertheless, they respected her. While at Northampton, she met abolitionists George Benson and David Ruggles and anti-slavery activists and speakers Frederick Douglass and William Lloyd Garrison.

In 1846, the Association of Education and Industry closed and Truth became a housekeeper for George Benson and other abolitionists. She was actively involved in the antislavery movement. The following year, Olive Gilbert, a Northampton friend of Truth, suggested that she dictate her life story. *The Narrative of Sojourner Truth* was published in 1850. Sales of the book at abolitionist meetings helped to support her.

Truth also became active in the Women's Rights Movement while living in Northampton. In October 1850, she attended the national Women's Rights Convention in Worcester, Massachusetts, where she met women's rights leaders Lucretia Mott, Elizabeth Cady Stanton, and Lucy Stone. Douglass and Garrison also attended the convention. Garrison and his friend, Wendell Phillips, persuaded Truth to go on the lecture circuit and give speeches for the abolitionist cause. Phillips, among others, was impressed by the spell with which Truth held audiences. He observed: "Rachel [the actress] had the power to move and bear down a whole audience by a few simple words. I never knew but one other human being who had that power, and that was Sojourner Truth."[258]

In 1850, the year that the Fugitive Slave Law and the

Compromise of 1850 Act were passed, Truth's audiences were occasionally hostile. She stood her ground despite threats of violence. She joined the antislavery campaign led by George Thompson, the English abolitionist, and spoke in Rochester, New York before traveling to the Midwest.

In May 1853, she attracted national publicity when she spoke at a women's rights convention in Akron, Ohio. A minister told the convention that domination of women by men was justified by the fact that Jesus Christ was a man. He said, "If God had desired the equality of women, He would have given some token of His will through the birth, life, and death of the Savior." Truth asked the minister, "Where did your Christ come from?" When the minister did not answer, Truth provided the answer: "From God and a woman. Man had nothing to do with Him."[259]

Truth told the attendees of the convention, "But we'll have our rights; see if we don't; and you can't stop us from them; see if you can. You may hiss as much as you like, but it is coming. Women don't get half as much rights as they ought to; we want more, and we will have it."[260] She continued her tour through Ohio and Michigan. Eventually, she traveled through all of the New England and Middle Atlantic states as well as nine Midwestern states and Virginia.

When Truth was heckled, she relied on her wit to respond to the hecklers. An Ohio heckler asked her, "Old woman, do you think that your talk about slavery does any good? Do you suppose that people care what you say? Why, I don't care any more for your talk that I do for the bite of a flea." She replied, "Perhaps not, but, the Lord willing, I'll keep you scratching."[261]

In 1857, Truth moved to Battle Creek, Michigan, where strong abolitionist residents had welcomed her on previous visits. Following the U.S. Supreme Court's Dred Scott decision that Congress did not have the right to pass laws restricting slavery, Truth returned to the lecture circuit. She believed that the slaves could be freed without civil war. She encountered particularly angry crowds in Indiana and was arrested on many occasions. When released, she went back on the road.

In 1853, Truth had a memorable meeting with Harriet Beecher Stowe, author of *Uncle Tom's Cabin,* at Stowe's home in Andover, Massachusetts. Stowe wrote an article for the April 1863 *Atlantic* magazine in which she referred to Truth as the "African sibyl," comparing her with an ancient prophetess. Stowe praised Truth's intellect and speculated about her potential achievements if she had had the benefit of an education.

On October 29, 1864, Truth visited President Abraham Lincoln at the White House to "advise" him. She thanked Lincoln for all that he had done for African Americans and told him not to worry about his critics. She predicted that he would win the election in November. Truth brought with her a copy of her "Book of Life," a compilation of journal notes that had been edited for her. President Lincoln inscribed it, "For Aunty Sojourner Truth, A. Lincoln, Oct. 29, 1864." Truth commented that: "I felt that I was in the presence of a friend, and I now thank God ... that I always have advocated his cause and have done it openly and boldly."[262]

Truth remained in Washington, D.C. to help with the freedmen's villages, in which living conditions were horrible. Ex-slaves lived in shacks in refugee camps with inadequate food and clothing. She was saddened by Lincoln's assassination on April 14, 1865, but was jubilant with the passage of the Thirteenth Amendment to the U.S. Constitution, which declared that "neither slavery nor involuntary servitude ... shall exist within the United States or any place subject to their jurisdiction." She stayed in the nation's capital to fight in the struggle against racial prejudice.

While in Washington, Truth attempted to board a streetcar with a white friend. The conductor pushed Truth and told her to "get out of the way and let this lady in." Truth told him, "I am a lady too." A white passenger asked the conductor if blacks were allowed on the streetcar. The conductor grabbed Truth by the shoulder and told her to get off. When she refused, he shoved her, dislocating her shoulder. Truth sued for assault and battery and won her case. The conductor was fired. This incident occurred ninety years before Rosa Parks refused to give up her seat on a bus to a white man in Montgomery, Alabama.

On March 31, 1870, Truth met with President Ulysses S. Grant at the White House. Initially, President Grant and Truth were formal with each other but became less formal after they had talked for a while. Truth thanked the President for working toward justice for blacks. He replied that he would work for equal rights for everyone. The meeting ended with Grant signing Truth's "Book of Life."

In early 1882, Truth became seriously ill. Ulcers covered her legs and arms, and she was in considerable pain. She lapsed into a coma and died on November 26, 1883. A thousand mourners visited her house and formed a procession behind the hearse that conveyed her body to a nearby church for her funeral.

Sojourner Truth displayed determination during her entire lifetime in defending her own rights and attempting to obtain rights for others. Olive Gilbert, to whom Truth dictated *The Narrative of Sojourner Truth,* observed:

She has ever listened to the still, small voice in her soul, and followed where it led. She has clothed the naked, and fed the hungry; been bound with those in bondage, and remembered her less fortunate brothers when released from chains herself. She has upheld the right and true, denouncing wrong in high places as well as low.[263]

ROALD AMUNDSEN (1872-1928) Discoverer of the South Pole

"Resolution ... is omnipotent. He that resolves upon any great, and at the same time, good [objective], by that very resolution, has scaled the chief barrier to it. He will find it removing difficulties, searching out or making means, giving courage for despondency, and strength for weakness; and like the star in the East, to the wise men of old, ever guiding him nearer and nearer to the sum of all perfection."

T. Edwards

The life of Roald Amundsen is a notable example not only of determination in achieving personal goals but also of courage. From his youth, Amundsen planned a career as an explorer. To please his mother, he enrolled in medical school but dropped out when she died.

Amundsen was driven to explore the world to the exclusion of everything else, including marriage. He set his long-term goals at the age of fifteen after reading of the exploits of Sir John Franklin, the British explorer who attempted to find the Northwest Passage. Amundsen never wavered from his goals and eventually discovered the South Pole and the Northwest Passage that Franklin lost his life trying to discover. Amundsen was the first person to visit both the North Pole and the South Pole.

Roald Amundsen, the youngest of four sons, was born on July 16, 1872 on a farm near Borge, Norway. During his first year, his parents moved to Oslo, then known as Christiania. He became familiar with skating, skiing, and snowshoeing at an early age as did all young Norwegians. Amundsen was fourteen when his father died.

As a teenager, Amundsen built himself up physically to prepare for demands that would be placed upon him later. He hiked and skied and was physically very active. He played soccer in secondary school, not because he liked the sport but as part of his conditioning program. He slept with his bedroom window wide open during the winter to condition himself to the cold, something rarely done in Olso winters. He spent most of his free time in outdoor activities.

When he graduated from secondary school, Amundsen enrolled at the University of Olso to prepare for his medical studies. When his mother passed away during his third year, he dropped out of college. In later years, he looked back with relief that he left the university to pursue enthusiastically his life's goals.

Soon after dropping out of college, Amundsen was called up for compulsory military service. He welcomed it because he considered it his duty to serve and it afforded him an opportunity for additional physical training. Army medical doctors were amazed by his muscle development and his physique. They were so impressed with his physical development that they neglected to examine his eyes thoroughly. If they had, his farsightedness would have caused him to fail the examination.

Amundsen trained hard, enjoyed his army service, and was encouraged to make the army his career. Compulsory military training in Norway included several weeks of intensive training each year after completion of the initial obligation. At the age of twenty-two, he decided that he needed a challenge of his physical endurance. He convinced a friend, Leif Bjornsen, to undertake a winter trek that had not been accomplished before.

A forbidding plateau called the Hardangervidda lies west

of Oslo. The plateau is 6,000 feet above sea level and extends over seventy-five miles toward the west coast of Norway in the direction of Bergen. Lapps pastured herds of reindeer on the central plateau during the warmer months of the year, but they left during the winter. They had built a few crude huts to use in the cold, rainy periods of autumn.

Mogen farm was located near the eastern edge of the Hardangervidda, and Garen farm was near the western edge of the plateau. No one had ever crossed the plateau from one farm to the other. This presented Amundsen with precisely the challenge that he was seeking.

Amundsen and Bjornsen skied to Mogen on the first leg of their journey and stayed a week with an older couple while waiting for a storm to end. The family tried to persuade Roald and Leif to turn back because of the danger that they faced. As soon as the storm subsided, however, the friends began their journey across the plateau, traveling light because Amundsen estimated that they could reach Garen in two days. In addition to their skis and snowshoes, they carried only chocolate bars, crackers, an alcohol lamp, sleeping bags made from reindeer hide, a map, and a compass.

At the end of the first day they found one of the herders' huts. It had been boarded up, and the chimney was covered to keep out the snow. Leif injured his hand while removing boards to gain access to the hut. They made porridge from a sack of flour that they found there. They had to wait two days for the weather to clear enough to resume their trek. They found no hut at the end of the second day and had to sleep in the open. They stopped when it became too dark to see the crevasses.

Amundsen attempted to protect himself from the weather by digging a hole in the snow. When he awoke, he could not move and was having difficulty breathing. He was entombed by the wet snow that had fallen during the night and had turned to ice. He could hear Leif attempting to dig him out with a ski pole. It took several hours of hard work.

Amundsen discovered that the bags containing their food had disappeared, either sunken into slush and covered with ice or taken by a wild animal. They trudged onward until Amundsen realized that he was alone. Leif had fallen into a snow-covered crevasse about thirty-feet deep. He was unhurt but could not climb out unaided. With difficulty, Amundsen pulled him out. They traveled four more days without food; area streams provided drinking water. Finally they reached a haystack from the previous growing season.

Leif was too tired to move the next morning, but Amundsen reconnoitered the area and found a set of ski tracks. He followed them until he caught up with the skier. They went back and woke up Leif and then went to the near-by farm, Mogen, the farm from which they had started. Later, the story unfolded. The farmer at Garen, at the western edge of the plateau went looking for sheep that had strayed and found two pairs of ski tracks coming from the East and bending back around toward the East. He was astounded to see tracks at all, let alone tracks bending back upon themselves.

Amundsen and Leif had traversed twice a plateau that had not been traversed once previously. Amundsen learned three things from this outing:

• Ensure that the planning for the expedition is sound.
• Be well versed in the techniques of navigation.
• Do not take any unnecessary chances.

In 1894, Amundsen signed on as a deckhand on a sailing ship to learn seamanship and navigation. He sailed for three years and felt that he was ready to take the examination for

Captain, but he did not have the necessary experience. In 1897, in Antwerp, Belgium, he signed on as first mate on the ship, *Belgica,* scheduled to sail to Antarctica as the Belgian Antarctic Expedition. The Captain was Adrien DeGerlache, a Belgian. Dr. Frederick Cook of Brooklyn, New York, the ship's doctor, was the only member of the ship's company with polar experience. He had sailed five years previously with Robert Peary on an expedition to Greenland.

On August 23, 1897, the *Belgica* sailed southward. The ship made numerous landings in Antarctica, and the crew did some of the early mapping of the continent. Captain DeGerlache was determined to sail as far south as he could. They found themselves 100 miles within the ice pack, encircled by ice, with no channels to the open sea. Since they had not planned on wintering over in the Antarctic, they did not have sufficient food or supplies. The only winter clothing they had on board was enough for a small shore party, not enough for the entire crew.

The crew suffered from scurvy, and eventually the Captain and the expedition commander were prostrated by it. Dr. Cook and Amundsen provided leadership for the crew, who initially refused to eat seal and penguin meat. Dr. Cook and Amundsen convinced them that their survival depended upon it. They were trapped in the ice for thirteen months until they broke through with the help of explosive charges.

Recording meteorological readings for an entire year was one of the achievements of the expedition. The readings served as a basis for the early climatology of the region. Another achievement was the advancement of the training and experience in polar exploration of Roald Amundsen.

Amundsen's next goal was to lead an expedition of his own. He passed his examination for a master's license and visited the well-known explorer, Dr. Fridjof Nansen, who warned him of a life of hardship and that the life of an explorer and marriage were not compatible. Amundsen told him that his goals were set and asked for a letter of reference to use in obtaining backers for an expedition. The letter helped in raising funds, obtaining supplies, and gaining technical support. Amundsen worked at two jobs to raise money.

In 1900, Amundsen made a down payment on a forty-seven-ton fishing boat that was twenty-seven-years old, the same age as he was. The sloop *Gjoa* was sixty-nine-feet long with a beam of twenty-one and a half feet, carried 300 yards of canvas, and had an auxiliary gasoline engine. His critics thought that he needed a larger vessel for expeditions; however, he intended to push his small ship between the ice floes instead of breaking the ice with a larger ship.

Obtaining sufficient financial support was difficult, even with Dr. Nansen's letter. On June 15, 1903, Amundsen received a letter from the Bailiff that warned him of a potential lawsuit and seizure of his ship and supplies unless he paid his bills. He decided not to wait to see if the Bailiff was serious. During the night of June 15, 1903, Amundsen and his crew of six sailed from Oslo to find the Northwest Passage through over a hundred miles of land masses in the Canadian Arctic to Alaska. He was about to accomplish what Sir John Franklin failed to do in four attempts. Franklin perished on his last expedition of two ships, the *Erebus* and the *Terror,* along with 105 members of the crews, between 1845 and 1847. They were not found until 1854. Exploration was a hazardous occupation.

Guided by the writing of Sir Leopold McClintoch, Amundsen chose a route south of the most obvious one due west from Boothia Peninsula. A shipboard fire broke out but was put out quickly. West of the peninsula, the *Gjoa* ran aground on a shoal, and many supplies had to be jettisoned to lighten the ship to refloat her. Coming off the shoal, the rudder was moved upward off its hinges, and Amundsen could not steer the ship. Fortunately, the rudder pins later fell back into place of their own accord.

The *Gjoa* and her crew collected meteorological information in the Canadian Arctic for two winters. They verified Ross's placement of the magnetic North Pole years previously and encountered two Eskimo villages that were friendly to them. On August 26, 1905, they sighted the American whaler, *Charles Hansen,* of San Francisco. Captain James McKenna of the *Charles Hansen* congratulated Amundsen on finding the Northwest Passage and told him that he and his crew planned to winter over near Hershel Island. The *Gjoa* wintered over there also, but Amundsen did not want to wait until spring to tell the world of his accomplishment. He went by dogsled to Eagle City, Alaska, site of the nearest telegraph station.

On October 19, the *Gjoa* arrived in San Francisco, where Amundsen and his crew were feted with a parade, a banquet, and receptions. The Norwegian Colony of San Francisco raised funds to buy the *Gjoa* and to donate her for exhibition in Golden Gate Park. Amundsen went on the lecture circuit describing his expedition and his visits with the Eskimo communities. He was invited to meet with President Theodore Roosevelt.

Amundsen earned enough money on the lecture tour to pay his debts in Norway. However, many of his creditors refused to accept payment; they were happy to have participated in a successful venture.

Amundsen prepared for his next expedition, to the North

Pole. Dr. Nansen offered him a ship that he had designed for polar exploration; smooth, rounded sides reduced the possibility of being crushed by ice. The *Fram* was 119-foot long and had a beam of thirty-six foot. She was a much larger and more comfortable ship than the *Gjoa*. Amundsen planned to sail the *Fram* around to Alaska and then, using the drift theory espoused by Dr. Nansen, become frozen in the Arctic ice pack and drift to, or over, the North Pole.

However, while Amundsen was preparing for this expedition, word was received that Admiral Robert E. Peary had reached the North Pole by sledge on April 6, 1909. Amundsen was extremely disappointed, and many of his backers dropped out. He changed his plans but told no one of his new plans. Some of his backers wondered why he was proceeding to the North Pole after it had already been discovered. Others wondered why he was loading a thirteen-foot by twenty-six-foot prefabricated hut on the *Fram* if he planned to drift over the North Pole. Also, he loaded ninety-seven sled dogs and coal, which he could easily obtain in Alaska.

Amundsen realized that he could not hide his new plans for long. On September 10, 1910, after taking on supplies at Funchal, Madeira Islands, he announced to the crew that their destination was the Bay of Whales, Antarctica. He sent a telegram to Captain Robert Falcon Scott in Melbourne, Australia, who was also preparing an expedition to Antarctica: "Am going south—Amundsen."

Amundsen's expedition party landed at the Bay of Whales and set up the hut two miles from where the *Fram* was anchored. From this base camp, Amundsen's men established several supply depots along their route that crossed the Axel Heiberg Glacier and the Devil's Glacier. Three tons of food were stored for later consumption.

Scott's base camp was established at Cape Evans, 400 miles away. Unlike Amundsen, who was relying on Husky sled dogs for transportation, Scott was using Manchurian ponies and motorized sledges; he had developed a distrust for sled dogs on earlier expeditions. Scott's ship, *Terra Nova,* without Scott, who was establishing a string of supply depots along his route at the same time that Amundsen was establishing his, put in at the Bay of Whales while en route to King Edward VII Land. The two parties cautiously exchanged information; both were very much aware that they were in a race for the South Pole.

The *Fram* left for Buenos Aires from which she started a transoceanic survey eastward to the west coast of Africa. She would return to the Bay of Whales the following summer to pick up the nine-member expedition. They had to wait until the Antarctic spring—autumn in the Northern Hemisphere—to arrive before they could begin their quest for the Pole. After a start aborted by consistent cold weather, Amundsen and four of his men set out for the Pole on October 19, 1911. Their food caches along their path were marked by flags mounted on twenty-foot-long bamboo poles.

Scott had to carry considerable food for his Manchurian ponies and fuel for his motorized sledges. Amundsen had more options than Scott; his dogs could be killed for food for other dogs and for members of the expedition, if necessary. In fact, the first option was used. Amundsen and his men had several accidents en route to the Pole, mainly when dogsleds broke through a thin crust or fell into a crevasse in poor visibility.

Amundsen's party planted a Norwegian flag when it reached the South Pole on December 14, 1911 and placed additional flags at the four compass points ten miles from the central flag. They began their return to their base camp on December 17 and arrived there on January 25.

The Scott expedition was less fortunate. It reached the flag and the tent left by Amundsen on January 18, 1912. All five men in the Scott party perished on the return trip to their base as determined by records found later. They died eleven miles from one of their food caches. At the end, they were on foot; the ponies and motorized sledges had failed them. One member of the Scott party, Petty Officer Evans, died of a head injury, and another member, Captain Lawrence Oates, walked away from the camp with no intent of returning when he began to slow the others down.

In November 1912, a search party found the corpses of the three remaining men in the party, Scott, Bowers, and Wilson, along with Scott's diary and some photographs. In his diary, Scott left the message "Had we lived, I should have had a tale to tell of the hardihood of my companions which would have stirred the heart of every Englishman. These rough notes and our bodies must tell the tale."[264]

At Hobart, Tasmania, Amundsen went ashore to send a message to Norway that he had discovered the South Pole. However, the Royal Society of England responded, "We will wait to hear from Scott. His expedition was well equipped, while this adventurer who was supposed to have gone to the North Pole and claims to have wound up at the South Pole could not possibly have done it." Textbooks were printed in England that gave Scott credit for the discovery of the South Pole. When Scott's diary was found, he gave credit to Amundsen for his discovery. Amundsen was awarded honors by many governments and scientific societies, including the National Geographic Society in the United States.

Amundsen returned to Norway, where he invested in the

shipbuilding business, made profitable by World War I. He had another ship built, the *Maud,* named for Norway's Queen. On July 15, 1918, he sailed along the Arctic coast of Russia to Alaska. This five-year voyage was only moderately successful. Toward the end of this trip, his business manager defrauded him, causing Amundsen to declare bankruptcy.

Amundsen returned to the United States to raise funds by lecturing to finance another expedition. He met American financier Lincoln Ellsworth, who offered to finance an expedition by seaplane to the North Pole and to share leadership with Amundsen. This unsuccessful expedition was followed by an expedition over the North Pole by dirigible. They dropped flags over the North Pole. Amundsen became the first person to visit both the North Pole and the South Pole, one by air and one by surface transportation.

Following this dirigible flight, Amundsen retired from exploring. However, another team crashed while attempting to fly over the North Pole in a dirigible. Amundsen was asked to help the rescue party. His aircraft developed engine trouble shortly after taking off from Spitzbergen and crashed into the sea, killing all on board.

Amundsen's wish was, "When death comes to me, may it do so while I'm busy at my life's work, while I'm doing something good and useful."[265] On the maps of the world, Amundsen Glacier, Amundsen Gulf near the Beaufort Sea in the Arctic, and Amundsen Sea off the Walgreen Coast in the Antarctic mark the explorer's accomplishments.

KNUTE ROCKNE (1888-1931) Inspirational Football Coach

"Anyone who can fire the manhood of others as he did is in every way admirable ... We all have latent powers that need to be stirred and wakened; Rockne did this, not merely for the men of the Notre Dame squad but for all the healthy young men of the country. Just as we learn history best through the biographies of great men, so in the chronicle of our own time, the life of Knute Rockne, exerting an extraordinary influence for the good, will be remembered."[266]

Staff Writer, Youngstown *Vindicator*

Knute Rockne's won-lost percentage established him as one of the winningest of college football coaches. During a thirteen-year period that included five undefeated seasons, his teams won 105, lost twelve, and tied five games. He did not invent the forward pass, but he did as much as any coach to make it an integral part of the game of football.

Rockne expanded upon many of the techniques instituted by Jesse Harper, his predecessor as football coach at Notre Dame. He implemented the backfield shift with such precision that the rulebook was changed to lessen its impact. Also, he optimized the play of a small lineman in misdirecting a larger opposing lineman and perfected the style that became known as the Notre Dame system.

Above all, Rockne was a motivator. He could inspire a subpar team to get the most out of their talents. On many occasions, his teams beat opposing teams who clearly were more talented. In addition to his coaching duties, he was a highly regarded chemistry instructor at Notre Dame and the author of two books. At the time of his death in 1931, he was traveling to Hollywood to sign a movie contract and to investigate other opportunities with the movie industry.

Knute Rockne was born in Voss, Norway on March 4, 1888 to Lars and Martha Gjermo Rokne (the c was added after they immigrated to the United States). Knute was the second oldest of five children and the only son. Knute's father, like his grandfather and great-grandfather, was a blacksmith and mechanical repairman. He manufactured high-quality two-wheeled carriages that were marketed in England and Germany; he sold several carriages to Kaiser Wilhelm for his personal use.

Lars won a prize at a fair in Liverpool and traveled to the United States to display his carriage at the 1893 World's Fair in Chicago. He was successful at the World's Fair and decided to settle in Chicago. He sent for his family, who arrived in the spring of 1893. Young Knute was known for two attributes, awkwardness and adventuresomeness. Before leaving Bergen, he climbed up into the ship's crow's nest and had to be removed by the crew.

The Rockne family moved to the Logan Square district of Chicago where Knute entered Brentano grade school. He immediately distinguished himself academically and was recognized by his teacher for his learning potential and his memory. The Logan Square district was a heterogeneous melting-pot of many nationalities; it had many corner lots for football and baseball games. Most of the football games were between the Irish and the "Swedes," with anyone of Scandinavian extraction being called a "Swede."

Knute's parents thought that football was too rough for him, but he was allowed to play baseball. During a fight at a sandlot baseball game, Knute was hit with a baseball bat on the bridge of his nose, changing its shape forever. After that incident, playing baseball was forbidden, and football was allowed. He played on the scrub football team in high school, but he excelled on the track team.

In 1907, Rockne worked for the U.S. Post Office in Chicago with the goal of saving $1,000 for college expenses. He ran in track meets for the Illinois Track Club to keep in good physical condition. Two of his track friends were going to Notre Dame; they told Rockne that his chances of finding part-time work were better at Notre Dame than at the University of Illinois where he had been planning to go.

In September 1910, Rockne enrolled as a freshman at Notre Dame and worked as a janitor in the chemistry lab. Initially, he played inter-hall football for his dormitory and then became the starting fullback for the freshman football team. When Rockne arrived in South Bend, the Notre Dame varsity football team record was ninety-five wins, thirty losses, and ten ties for a .760 winning percentage. They had beaten Michigan and were definitely a team on the rise.

Rockne was the starting left end on the Notre Dame team from 1911 through 1913 and was team captain in his senior year. During his four years at Notre Dame, the varsity football team won twenty-four games, lost three, and tied one; none of the losses occurred in the three years that Rockne played for the varsity.

During the summer before his senior year, Rockne and Gus Dorais, the starting quarterback, practiced the forward pass in their off hours from their summer jobs. Although the forward pass became legal in 1906, it was little used. When a pass was thrown, the receiver would stop, turn, catch the ball in his chest, and then turn to go downfield. Rockne practiced catching the ball in his hands on the dead run. Later, as a coach, Rockne developed a reputation with pass plays, but he always gave credit to other coaches, including Pop Warner and Amos Alonzo Stagg, for evolving the forward pass.

In the fall of 1913, Notre Dame played Army for the first time. The game was played at West Point; the Army team had superior size and was a strong favorite. Army took an early lead with their running game. Rockne, at left end, faked a limp, causing the defensive back covering him to back off. Gus Dorais hit Rockne with a pass for a touchdown. When Army defended against the pass, Irish fullback Ray Eichenlaub ran through the line. Notre Dame won 35-13, surprising everyone except the victors.

Rockne also ran on the track team, played flute in the college orchestra, boxed in area smokers to earn spending money, and acted in theatrical productions. He majored in pharmacology and chemistry and graduated magna cum laude. Father Julius Nieuwland, Professor of Chemistry and the inventor of synthetic rubber, considered Rockne the most remarkable student in his experience.

When he graduated, Rockne worked as a high school football coach in St. Louis but returned to Notre Dame when offered the positions of instructor in chemistry, assistant football coach, and track coach. Now that he was gainfully employed, he proposed to Bonnie Skiles whom he had met the previous year on his summer job. They were married on July 15, 1914; Gus Dorais was the best man.

Rockne was an assistant coach to Jesse Harper for four years at Notre Dame, which continued to add major schools to its schedule. In the game with Wabash in 1916, Harper was ill, and Rockne was acting head coach. The team experienced for the first time Rockne's pre-game and half-time motivational talks. He concluded by saying, "Now go out there and crucify them." Notre Dame won 60-0. An earlier Notre Dame coach, Shorty Longman, had challenged the team with: "Go out and conquer. It's the crisis of your lives."[267] Unfortunately, Shorty gave the same speech at every game.

Rockne's innovations in four years as assistant coach were polishing the backfield shift and "flexing" the ends wider or closer in to the tackles in conjunction with the backfield shift, giving the runner more blockers. Also, he evolved the "boxing tackle" with head feints and diversion of the bulk of the tackle, thus allowing a lighter lineman to handle a heavier tackle. Use of these techniques was called the "Rockne" system or the "Notre Dame" system.

After four years as assistant coach, Rockne felt that he was ready to be a head coach; he seriously considered an offer to coach at Michigan State. However, a relative of Jess Harper passed away, and Harper had to leave to manage the family ranch. He suggested that Rockne replace him as head coach, and the administration agreed.

In the fall of 1916, George Gipp arrived on the Notre Dame campus. After graduating from high school, he had worked in the construction industry and driven a taxi for two years. He had played neither football nor baseball in high school but had established a reputation in amateur baseball. He thought that he might play that sport at Notre Dame. He tried out for the inter-hall football team for his dormitory but quit after one practice. He was a loner who had difficulty adjusting to college life.

Rockne first encountered Gipp on a practice field drop-kicking the football fifty yards, consistently, without much effort. Rockne suggested that he try out for the freshman football team; thus began the legend. In his first game, against Western State Normal, Gipp received the call to punt from the quarterback but instead drop-kicked a sixty-two-yard field goal to win the game.

In 1920, late in a game against Indiana, Gipp, with a dislocated shoulder, added to the legend with a slashing touchdown through the line to win the game. In addition to playing in the offensive backfield, Gipp also played defensive back and was the place-kicker / punter. Rockne claimed that no one ever completed a pass in a zone defended by Gipp.

Gipp caught a bad cold and did not start the Northwestern game. After the crowd had called for him for three quarters, he went in and completed his first two passes for touchdowns. However, he was exhausted and had chills. He had to leave the game and was taken to St. Joseph's Hospital. His condition worsened, and he decided to convert to Catholicism.

When Gipp lay near death, he told Rockne: "Sometime, Rock, when the team is up against it, when things are wrong, and the breaks are beating the boys—tell them to go in there with all they've got and win just one for the Gipper. I don't know where I'll be then, Rock, but I'll know about it, and I'll be happy."[268] George Gipp died on December 14, 1920 at St. Joseph's Hospital; he was twenty-five-years old. His cold and chronic tonsillitis had led to pneumonia. He died of a streptococcal infection.

Rockne expanded the football schedule. In 1922, Notre Dame played Georgia Tech for the first time. Tech had an excellent team, and the fans in Atlanta intimidated their opponents with rebel yells. In his pre-game pep talk, Rockne read telegrams to the team, including one from the Mayor of South Bend and one from the President of the Alumni Association. Finally, Rockne told the team that his four-year-old son was ill and had been taken to the hospital. All of the players knew and loved Billy; they were touched. Hesitantly, Rockne removed one last telegram from his pocket and read it to the team: "PLEASE WIN THIS GAME FOR MY DADDY. IT IS VERY

IMPORTANT TO HIM."[269] Notre Dame won 13-3.

When they returned to South Bend, the usual large crowd at Union Station welcomed the team home. One of the first to greet them was a happy and healthy Billy Rockne, who had not been near a hospital since his birth. Rockne would use any technique to motivate his players. Star running back Jim Crowley explained:

> But the guys on the team never considered they'd been taken in by Rock. There wasn't anything to forgive. We were used to Rock's drama—the real and the theatrical—and we'd find out over the next couple of years that Rock would use any ploy he could think of to get the most out of us, whether it was at practice or at a game.[270]

In the fall of 1921, the players who became known as the "four horsemen" entered Notre Dame. Initially, Rockne was not impressed by them. The four backs (Jim Crowley, Elmer Layden, Don Miller, and Harry Stuhldreher) were thrown together by an injury to the starting fullback, Paul Castner, who broke his pelvis in the game against Butler. Crowley and Layden had been sharing the left halfback position. Layden was moved to fullback to replace the injured Castner.

The four horsemen were light compared with today's teams, but they had speed and precision. The principal factors in the "Notre Dame shift" were coordination and synchronization. Supposedly, Rockne devised the shift after watching the precision of a line of chorus girls. Plays were rehearsed over and over in slow motion until the backs achieved the necessary precision.

The four horsemen received their name on October 18,

1924 at the Army-Notre Dame game at the Polo Grounds in New York. George Strickler, the student reporter from Notre Dame, was seated three feet away from Grantland Rice in the press box. The previous week, Strickler had seen the movie starring Rudolph Valentino based on *The Four Horsemen of the Apocalypse* by Blasco Ibáñez. A member of the press observed that the Notre Dame backfield was going to maul Army. Strickler said, "Just like the four horsemen." Grantland Rice glanced at Strickler and then looked out at the field.

The next day, Grantland Rice reported in the New York *Tribune:* "Outlined against a blue-gray October sky, the Four Horseman rode again. In dramatic lore they were known as Famine, Pestilence, Destruction, and Death. These are only aliases. Their real names are Stuhldreher, Miller, Crowley, and Layden."[271] When the team returned to South Bend, Strickler told Rockne that he wanted to take a picture of the backs in full uniform mounted on four horses. Rockne thought that none of them had probably ever been on a horse before, but he agreed to do it. The photograph was widely distributed.

Rockne took Catholic instruction from Father Vincent Mooney and was baptized on November 20, 1925. Not many people knew about it; in fact, his sons were not told. The next morning, the Rockne's second son, Knute, Jr. received first communion. When his father walked down the aisle with him, Knute, Jr. reminded his father that only Catholics could receive communion. At the communion rail, Father Mooney told Knute, Jr. that his father had been baptized the previous day. This was the first that his sons had heard of his conversion to Catholicism.

Rockne was in demand nationally as a football coach. Other universities, including Columbia and Ohio State, made lucrative offers to entice him to leave Notre Dame. However, he wanted to stay. He became a syndicated writer and a radio personality and was in demand as an inspirational speaker, particularly for sales meetings for the automotive industry. For the Studebaker Corporation, Rockne developed sales programs based on concepts learned in football but applied to business, such as:

- "Selection—ability to select superior human material
- Training—ability to teach his men
- Supervision—salesmen would respond to Rockne's 'perfect' type of discipline
- Inspiration—his understanding contact with individuals as well as the group"[272]

Rockne had lobbied for a new football stadium for years, but at Notre Dame academic needs always took precedence over athletic programs. Finally, funding for the new stadium was approved, and Rockne worked closely with the designers. He was personally involved even in laying out the parking lots and choosing material for the seats.

On the morning of March 31, 1931, Rockne boarded a Fokker trimotor NC-999 operated by Transcontinental Airlines for its Kansas City to Los Angeles flight. He was going to Hollywood to sign a film contract. He had been asked to play a coach in the movie that RKO was making from the stage musical, *Good News*.

Over Bazaar, Kansas, en route to Wichita, the Fokker encountered icing conditions and was buffeted by a bad storm. Blown off course, the plane crashed. None of the six passengers or crew survived. One theory advanced for the crash was damage to the propeller on the engine on the right wing. A farmer saw the right wing detach from the fuselage, causing the aircraft to dive straight down from about 650 feet.

Rockne was forty-three-years old when he died. Over 100,000 people lined the streets of South Bend when Rockne's casket was transported from Union station to Sacred Heart Church on the Notre Dame campus for the funeral Mass. It was attended by 1,400 mourners. The nation was stunned. Mrs. Rockne received many condolences, including messages from President Hoover, ex-President Coolidge, and King Haakon of Norway. Will Rogers said:

> We thought it would take a President or a great public man's death to make the whole nation, regardless of age, race, or creed, shake their heads in real sorrow ... Well, that's what this country did today, Knute, for you. You died one of our national heroes. Notre Dame was your address but every gridiron in America was your home.[273]

EPILOGUE

"Don't bother about genius. Don't worry about being clever. Trust to hard work, perseverance and determination. And the best motto for the long march is: 'Don't grumble. Plug on!'"

Sir Frederick Treves

The thirty-five individuals whose lives are described in this book displayed a high level of determination in striving to attain their goals and to achieve their purpose in life. Although determination is one of the principal factors in achieving one's goals, receiving support from relatives, teachers, mentors, and colleagues can also be a major factor.

Florence Nightingale's achievements are impressive, and many of these accomplishments were due to her high level of motivation and her relentless determination. Her friend, Sidney Herbert, Secretary of War during the Crimean War and later Chairman of the Royal Sanitary Commission, supported her requests for supplies and additional nursing staff. His significant support continued even when his health began to fail; he realized the value of Nightingale's pioneering work in medical services.

Henry Schliemann's young Greek wife, Sophia, provided him with contacts within the society of Athens and worked with him in the field, even wielding a shovel. They were a compatible couple; her interest in archaeology was equal to, or at least approached, his own. Schliemann was a driven man whose personal characteristics helped him to achieve success; however, Sophia was a major factor in his accomplishments.

Elizabeth Barrett was a widely acclaimed poet when she met Robert Browning. Initially, her literary reputation exceeded his. After they were married, they helped each other improve their poetry. She knew that he was destined to be one of England's most-respected literary figures. Elizabeth and Robert were better poets than they would have been had they not received each other's advice and support.

Horatio Nelson was the Royal Navy's most successful admiral while still a young man. His organizational and motivational abilities contributed heavily to his success. His personal characteristics of aggressiveness and determination to win every engagement made him a formidable opponent. Nelson never entered battle thinking that he might lose, even when he was significantly outnumbered. He knew that his captains were extremely capable and would not let him down. They had the vision and the discipline to take the correct actions even if they could not see the signals from the flagship.

Lillian Gilbreth was very capable and had many strong personal characteristics; however her working relationship with her husband, Frank, allowed them to achieve more working as a team than either could have achieved as individuals. Frank knew the construction and technical side of the business, but he was weak on the people side of their work. She did not let his ego get in the way of their working together; they had a loving marriage and an extremely successful business partnership.

Steve Jobs is an innovator with many strong qualities that contributed to his success, including his aggressiveness and his vision. His contributions to the founding of the personal computer industry were significant. However, since he did not have a technical education, he needed to collaborate with a technical person. Steve Wozniak was that person. Together they enabled Apple Computer to get off to a good start. Each needed the capabilities of the other to attain the success that they ultimately achieved.

Examples of determined individuals who have benefitted from the support of others are all around us. We have role models among our relatives, friends, and acquaintances. Occasionally, we read in newspapers and magazines about people who inspire us. Brooke Ellison and her mother are examples of this.

Brooke Ellison was hit by a car on her first day of class in the seventh grade. Doctors did not think that she would survive. After thirty-six hours in a coma, she awoke as a quadriplegic with no feeling below her neck. Among her first words was the question, "When can I get back to school?" She returned to school with her mother, Jean Marie, sitting next to her in every class.

A ventilator pumps air through Brooke's trachea into her lungs thirteen times a minute. She steers her wheelchair by touching her tongue to a retainer in the roof of her mouth. Brooke says: "This is just the way my life is. I've always felt that whatever circumstances I confront, it's just a question of continuing to live and not letting what I can't do define what I am."[274]

When Brooke was accepted to Harvard University, her mother lived with her in her dormitory suite in Harvard Yard. Although Brooke did her own research on the Internet and dictated term papers into a voice-actuated personal computer, her mother turned book pages for her and raised her hand in class when Brooke wanted to respond to a question or contribute to classroom discussion. Harvard accommodated her needs by customizing her dormitory room and by moving a class on history of the opera for which she had enrolled because the original building was not wheelchair accessible.

In June 2000, Brooke, who maintained an A- average,

graduated from Harvard University with a bachelor's degree in psychology and biology. She was honored by her classmates who asked her to address them on senior class day. Her goals are to write her autobiography and to travel around the country as a motivational speaker. She said, "Anywhere people feel they need encouragement, that's where I hope to be."[275]

* * *

PRESS ON

"Nothing in the world can take the place of persistence.

Talent will not; nothing is more common than unsuccessful men with talent.

Genius will not; unrewarded genius is almost a proverb.

Education alone will not; the world is full of educated derelicts.

Persistence and determination alone are omnipotent."

Anonymous

(Appeared on the cover of a program for a memorial service for Calvin Coolidge in 1933.)

NOTES

Prologue

1 Dumont, Theron Q. *The Power of Concentration*.
(Chicago: Advanced Thought Publishing, 1918) 52-53.

2 Deci, Edward L. *The Psychology of Self-Determination*.
(Lexington, MA: Lexington Books, 1980) 19.

3 James, William. *The Principles of Psychology, Volume II*.
(Cambridge: Harvard UP, 1981) 1098.

Introduction

4 Dumont 53.

5 Clancy, Frank. "If You Ever Get A Second Chance In Life,
You've Got To Go All The Way."*USA Weekend*. 10-12 Dec. 1999:
9.

6 Clancy 9.

7 Clancy 10.

Chapter 1

8 Hare, Lloyd C. M. *The Greatest American Woman: Lucretia Mott*.
(New York: American Historical Society, 1937) Preface.

9 Bryant, Jennifer Fisher. *Lucretia Mott: Guiding Light*.
(Grand Rapids, MI: Eerdmans, 1996) 133.

10 Graham, Maureen. "Lucretia Mott."*Women of Power and Presence:
The Spiritual Formation of Four Quaker Women Ministers*.
(Wallingford, PA: Pendle Hill, 1990) 29.

11 Bryant 144.

12 Bryant 145.

13 Bryant 146.

14 Bryant 129.

15 Mott, Lucretia. "Discourse on Women." Philadelphia: n. p., 1849.

16 Bryant 138.

17 Bryant 167.

18 Foster, Warren Dunham, ed. *Heroines of Modern Religion*.
(Freeport, NY: Books for Libraries, 1970) 114.

19 Kerr, Andrea Moore. *Lucy Stone: Speaking Out for Equality*.
(New Brunswick: Rutgers UP, 1992) 42.

20 Kerr 46.

21 Hays, Elinor Rice. *Morning Star: A Biography of Lucy Stone 1818-1893*. (New York: Harcourt, Brace & World, 1961) 312.

22 Strachey, Lytton. "Florence Nightingale." *Eminent Victorians*. (New York: Harcourt Brace Jovanovich, 1918) 156.

23 Woodham-Smith, Cecil. *Florence Nightingale: 1820-1910*. (New York: McGraw-Hill, 1951) 33.

24 Woodham-Smith 34.

25 Woodham-Smith 38.

26 Woodham-Smith 51.

27 Strachey 138-139.

28 Woodham-Smith 61.

29 Woodham-Smith 85.

30 Boyd, Nancy. "Florence Nightingale." *Three Victorian Woman Who Changed the World*. (New York: Oxford UP, 1982) 183.

31 Boyd 183.

32 Strachey 149.

33 Woodham-Smith 199.

34 Strachey 163.

35 Woodham-Smith 185.

36 Woodham-Smith 225.

37 Woodham-Smith 81.

38 Ross, Ishbel. *Child of Destiny: The Life Story of the First Woman Doctor*. (New York: Harper & Brothers, 1949) 83.

39 Ross 87.

40 Ross 97.

41 Chambers, Peggy. *A Doctor Alone, A Biography of Elizabeth Blackwell: The First Woman Doctor 1821-1910*. (London: Abelard-Schuman, 1958) 42-43.

42 Ross 108.

43 Ross 111.

44 Ross 118.

45 Chambers 58.

46 Ross 121.

47 Ross 121.

48 Chambers 87.

49 Ross 204.

50 Ross 287.

51 Ross 291.

52 Cazden, Elizabeth. *Antoinette Brown Blackwell: A Biography.* (Old Westbury, NY: Feminist Press, 1983) 31.

53 Cazden 31.

54 Kerr, Laura. *Lady in the Pulpit.* (New York: Woman's Press, 1951) 53.

55 Cazden 51.

56 Cazden 52.

57 Cazden 75.

58 Cazden 77.

59 Cazden 83.

60 Cazden 87.

61 Cazden 98.

62 Cazden 252.

Chapter 2

63 Winston, Richard. *Thomas Becket.* (New York: Alfred A. Knopf, 1967) 7.

64 Winston 12.

65 Knowles, David. *Thomas Becket.* (Palo Alto: Stanford UP, 1970) 13.

66 Vann, Joseph, ed. "Saint Thomas Becket." *Lives of the Saints with Excerpts from Their Writings.* (New York: John J. Crawley, 1954) 211.

67 Vann "Saint Thomas Becket" 212-213.

68 Vann "Saint Thomas Becket" 214.

69 Vann "Saint Thomas Becket" 215.

70 Winston 346.

71 Vann "Saint Thomas Becket" 218.

72 Marius, Richard. *Thomas More: A Biography.* (New York: Alfred A. Knopf, 1984) 191.

73 Fremantle, Anne. "Thomas More." *Saints Alive: The Lives of Thirteen Saints.* (Garden City: Doubleday, 1978) 191.

74 Reynolds, E. E. *Saint Thomas More.* (New York: P. J. Kenedy & Sons, 1953) 55.

75 Reynolds *Saint Thomas More* 192-193.

76 Fremantle 106.

77 Fremantle 111.

78 Reynolds, E. E. *Saint John Fisher*. (New York: P. J. Kenedy & Sons, 1965) 295.

79 Wilby, Noel MacDonald. *Saint John of Rochester*. (New York: Paulist Press, n.d.) 6-7.

80 Reynolds *Saint John Fisher* 30.

81 Reynolds *Saint John Fisher* 59-60.

82 Wilby 23.

83 Wilby 28.

84 Reynolds *Saint John Fisher* 276-277.

85 Reynolds *Saint John Fisher* 284-285.

86 Cowie, Leonard W. *Martin Luther: Leader of the Reformation*. (New York: Praeger, 1969) 6.

87 Cowie 29.

88 Cowie 30-31.

89 Cowie 32.

90 Cowie 32.

91 Cowie 33.

92 Cowie 36.

93 Stepanek, Sally. *Martin Luther*. (New York: Chelsea House, 1986) 35.

94 Cowie 38.

95 Cowie 44.

96 Cowie 45.

97 Cowie 45-46.

98 Cowie 49-50.

99 Cowie 50.

100 Cowie 57-58.

101 Cowie 58.

102 Cowie 59.

103 Cowie 106.

104 Cowie 88.

105 Cowie 112.

106 Maynard, Theodore. *Saint Ignatius and the Jesuits*. (New York: P. J. Kenedy & Sons, 1956) 199.

107 Caraman, Philip. *Ignatius Loyola: A Biography of the Founder of the Jesuits*. (New York: Harper & Row, 1990) 30.

108 Vann "Saint Ignatius of Loyola" 347.

109 Vann "Saint Ignatius of Loyola" 348.

110 Vann "Saint Ignatius of Loyola" 350.

111 Yust, Walter, ed. "Society of Jesus." *Encyclopedia Britannica*. Vol 13. (Chicago: William Benton, 1957) 10.

Chapter 3

112 Brackman, Arnold C. *The Dream of Troy*. (New York: Mason & Lipscomb, 1974) 235.

113 Honour, Alan. *The Unlikely Hero: Heinrich Schliemann's Quest for Troy*. (New York: McGraw-Hill, 1960) 90.

114 Honour 142.

115 Honour 154.

116 Honour 169.

117 Brachman 225.

118 Braymer, Marjorie. *The Walls of Windy Troy: A Biography of Heinrich Schliemann*. (New York: Harcourt, Brace & World, 1960) 176.

119 Dubos, René. *Pasteur and Modern Science*. (Madison, WI: Science Tech, 1960) 24-25.

120 Untermeyer, Louis. *Makers of the Modern World*. (New York: Simon & Schuster, 1955) 104-105.

121 Dubos 95-96.

122 Untermeyer 108.

123 Untermeyer 110-111.

124 Untermeyer 111-112.

125 Reynolds, Moira Davison. *How Pasteur Changed History: The Story of Louis Pasteur and the Pasteur Institute*. (Bradenton, FL: McGuinn & McGuire, 1974) 10.

126 Dibner, Bern. *Wilhelm Conrad Röntgen and the Discovery of X-Rays*. (New York: Franklin Watts, 1968) 39.

127 Egan, Louise. *Thomas Edison: The Great American Inventor*. (New York: Barron's Educational Series, 1987) 144-145.

128 Untermeyer, Louis. *Makers of the Modern World*. (New York:

Simon & Schuster, 1955) 360.

129 Jakab, Peter L. *Visions of a Flying Machine: The Wright Brothers and the Process of Invention*. (Washington: Smithsonian Institution, 1990) 10.

130 Untermeyer 365.

Chapter 4

131 Still, William. *The Underground Rail Road*. (Philadelphia: Porter & Coates, 1872) 655.

132 McGowan, James A. *Station Master on the Underground Railroad, The Life and Letters of Thomas Garrett*. (Moylan, PA: Whimsie Press, 1977) 38.

133 McGowan 72.

134 McGowan 77.

135 McGowan 57.

136 Smedley, R. C. *History of the Underground Railroad*. (Lancaster, PA: Office of the *Journal,* 1883) 240.

137 Haskins, James. *Get on Board: The Story of the Underground Railroad*. (New York: Scholastic, 1993) 31-33.

138 Coffin, Levi. *Reminiscences of Levi Coffin, The Reputed President of the Underground Railroad*. (Cincinnati: Robert Clarke, 1898) 13.

139 Coffin 727.

140 Coffin 729.

141 Altschuler, Glenn C. *Andrew D. White—Educator, Historian, Diplomat*. (Ithaca: Cornell UP, 1979) 15.

142 White, Andrew Dickson. *Autobiography of Andrew Dickson White*. Vol. I. (New York: Century, 1907) 298.

143 White 298.

144 Wechsberg, Joseph, ed. *The Murderers Among Us: The Simon Wiesenthal Memoirs*. (New York: McGraw-Hill, 1967) 8.

145 Noble, Iris. *Nazi Hunter: Simon Wiesenthal*. (New York: Julian Messner, 1979) 131.

146 Noble 130.

147 Wechsberg 35.

148 Wechsberg 39.

149 Wechsberg 40.

150 Wechsberg 48.

151 Wechsberg 55.

152 Wechsberg 58.

153 Wechsberg 123.

154 Wechsberg 171.

155 Wechsberg 172.

156 Wechsberg 176.

Chapter 5

157 Stack, V. E. ed. *How Do I Love Thee? The Love-Letters of Robert Browning and Elizabeth Barrett.* (New York: G. P. Putnam's Sons, 1969) xx.

158 Stack xx-xxi.

159 Stack xxi.

160 Stack xxii.

161 Stack xxv.

162 Markus, Julia. *Dared and Done: The Marriage of Elizabeth Barrett Browning and Robert Browning.* (New York: Alfred A. Knopf) 165.

163 Markus 211.

164 Forster, Margaret. *Elizabeth Barrett Browning: A Biography.* (New York: Doubleday, 1988) 279.

165 Forster 359.

166 Forster 366.

167 Forster 366.

168 Yust, Walter, ed. "Elizabeth Bartlett Browning." *Encyclopedia Britannica. Vol. 4.* (Chicago: William Benton, 1957) 275.

169 Cogniat, Raymond. *Gauguin.* (New York: Harry N. Abrams, 1963) 5-6.

170 Gauguin, Pola. *My Father Paul Gauguin.* (New York: Alfred A. Knopf, 1937) 66.

171 Estienne, Charles. *Gauguin: Biographical and Critical Studies.* (Cleveland, World, 1953) 28.

172 Estienne 29.

173 Estienne 29.

174 Cogniat 25.

175 Cogniat 39.

176 Steinberg, Barbara Hope. *Gauguin*. (New York: A & W Visual Library, 1976) 20.

177 Cogniat 47.

178 Cogniat 50.

179 Cogniat 51.

180 Gauguin 214.

181 Estienne 89.

182 Estienne 91.

183 Estienne 90.

184 Estienne 99.

185 Estienne 96.

186 Steinberg 10.

187 Hughes, Robert. "Seeing Gauguin Whole at Last." (*Time Magazine*. 9 May 1988) 76.

188 Gauguin x.

189 Mizener, Arthur. *The Far Side of Paradise: A Biography of F. Scott Fitzgerald*. (Boston: Houghton Mifflin, 1965) xviii-xix.

190 Mizener 337-338.

191 Miller, Douglas T. *Frederick Douglass and the Fight for Freedom*. (New York: Facts on File, 1988) 19.

192 Douglass, Frederick. *Narrative of the Life and Times of Frederick Douglass*. (New York: Thomas Y. Crowell, 1966) 406-407.

193 Huggins, Nathan Irvin. *Slave and Citizen: The Life of Frederick Douglass*. (Boston: Little, Brown, 1980) vii.

194 Douglass 103.

195 Miller 69, 75.

196 Miller 131.

197 McClard, Megan. *Harriet Tubman: Slavery and the Underground Railroad*. (Englewood Cliffs, NJ: Silver Burdett, 1991) 62.

198 Cosner, Shaaron. *The Underground Railroad*. (New York: Franklin Watts, 1991) 47.

199 Taylor, M. W. *Harriet Tubman*. (New York: Chelsea House, 1991) 22.

200 Taylor 23.

201 McClard 43.

202 McClard 48.

203 McClard 75.

204 Taylor 43.

Chapter 6

205 Wilkinson, Clennell. *Nelson.* (London: George G. Harrap, 1931)
    291.

206 Wilkinson 153.

207 Warner, Oliver. *Victory: The Life of Lord Nelson.* (Boston:
    Little, Brown, 1958) 152.

208 Wilkinson 167.

209 Warner 354.

210 Warner 354.

211 Wilkinson 296.

212 Southey, Robert. *Life of Nelson.* (London: J. M. Dent & Sons, 1813)
    260.

213 Southey 262.

214 Bringhurst, Newell G. *Brigham Young and the Expanding American
    Frontier.* (Boston: Little, Brown, 1986) vii-viii.

215 Palmer, Richard F. and Karl D. Butler. *Brigham Young:
    The New York Years.* (Provo, UT: Charles Redd Center for Western
    Studies at Brigham Young University, 1982) 4.

216 Bringhurst 13.

217 Bringhurst 20.

218 Bringhurst 21.

219 Palmer and Butler 75.

220 Catton, Bruce. *U. S. Grant and the American Military Tradition.*
    (Boston: Little, Brown, 1954) 11.

221 Green, Horace. *General Grant's Last Stand.* (New York:
    Charles Scribner's Sons, 1936) 227.

222 Green 281.

223 Green 287.

224 Green 290-291.

225 Green 297.

226 Green 299.

227 Green 306.

228 Green 312.

229 Green 314-315.

230 Green 320-321.

231 Tachau, Frank. *Kemal Atatürk*. (New York: Chelsea House, 1987) 91.

232 Tachau 15.

233 Kinross, Lord. *Atatürk: A Biography of Mustafa Kemal, Father of Modern Turkey*. (New York: William Morrow, 1965) 93.

234 Kinross 111.

235 Fletcher, Marvin E. *America's First Black General: Benjamin O. Davis, Sr*. (Lawrence, Kansas: UP of Kansas, 1989) viii.

236 Fletcher 176.

237 Fletcher 54.

238 Davis, Benjamin O., Jr., *Benjamin O. Davis, Jr., American*. (Washington: Smithsonian Institution Press, 1991) 27.

239 Fletcher 120.

240 Fletcher 117.

241 Fletcher 132.

242 Fletcher 176-177.

243 Davis 426.

Chapter 7

244 Yost, Edna. *Frank and Lillian Gilbreth: Partners for Life*. (New Brunswick: Rutgers UP, 1949) 353-354.

245 Gilbreth, Frank B. *Motion Study*. (New York: Van Nostrand, 1911) v.

246 Gilbreth, Frank B. and L. M. Gilbreth. *Applied Motion Study*. (New York: Sturgis & Walton, 1917) xi.

247 Yost vii-viii.

248 Yost 114.

249 Gilbreth, Frank B., Jr. and Ernestine Gilbreth Carey. *Cheaper by the Dozen*. (New York: Thomas T. Crowell, 1948) 3.

250 Yost 333.

251 Yost 359.

252 Deutschman, Alan. *The Second Coming of Steve Jobs*. (New York: Broadway Books, 2000) 298.

253 Aaseng, Nathan. "Steve Jobs." *Business Builders in Computers*.

(Minneapolis: Oliver, 2000) 124.

254 Smith, Douglas K. and Robert C. Alexander. *Fumbling the Future*. (New York: William Morrow, 1988) 241.

255 Taylor-Boyd, Susan. *Sojourner Truth: The Courageous Former Slave Whose Eloquence Helped Promote Human Equality*. (Milwaukee: Gareth Stevens, 1990) 58.

256 Painter, Nell Irvin, ed. *Narrative of Sojourner Truth*. (New York: Penguin, 1998) vii.

257 Taylor-Boyd 30.

258 Taylor-Boyd 25.

258 Krass, Peter. *Sojourner Truth*. (New York: Chelsea House, 1988) 19.

260 Taylor-Boyd 49.

261 Truth, Sojourner. *Narrative of Sojourner Truth: A Bondswoman of Olden Time*. (Battle Creek, MI: Review and Herald, 1884) 215.

262 Taylor-Boyd 38.

263 Taylor-Boyd 42.

264 Vaeth, J. Gordon. *To the Ends of the Earth: The Explorations of Roald Amundsen*. (New York: Harper & Row, 1962) 109.

265 Vaeth 208.

266 Wallace, Francis. *Knute Rockne*. (Garden City: Doubleday, 1960)

267 Wallace 47.

268 Steele, Michael R. *Knute Rockne: A Bio-Bibliography*. Westport, CT: Greenwood Press, 1983.

269 Brondfield, Jerry. *Rockne: The Coach, The Man, The Legend*. (New York: Random House, 1976) 5.

270 Brondfield 5.

271 Steele 29.

272 Wallace 252.

273 Wallace 265.

Epilogue
274 Rochester *Democrat and Chronicle*. "Harvard Student Is Profile in Courage." 17 May 2000: 15A.

275 Rochester *Democrat and Chronicle* 15A.

BIBLIOGRAPHY

Aaseng, Nathan. "Steve Jobs." *Business Builders in Computers*. Minneapolis: Oliver, 2000.

Allen, John, ed. *One Hundred Great Lives*. New York: Journal of Living Publishing, 1944.

Altman, Linda Jacobs. *The Importance of Simon Wiesenthal*. San Diego: Lucent Books, 2000.

Altschuler, Glenn C. *Andrew D. White—Educator, Historian, Diplomat*. Ithaca: Cornell UP, 1979.

Andrist, Ralph K. *The Erie Canal*. New York: American Heritage, 1964.

Arrington, Leonard J. *Brigham Young: American Moses*. New York: Alfred A. Knopf, 1985.

Bacon, Margaret Hope. *Valiant Friend: The Life of Lucretia Mott*. New York: Walker, 1980.

Bainton, Roland H. *Here I Stand: A Life of Martin Luther*. New York: Meridian, 1995.

Bartlett, John *Familiar Quotations*. Boston: Little, Brown, 1955.

Beard, Annie E. S. *Our Foreign-Born Citizens*. New York: Thomas Y. Crowell, 1955.

Bentley, Judith. *Harriet Tubman*. New York: Franklin Watts, 1990.

Bernard, Jacqueline. *Journey Toward Freedom: The Story of Sojourner Truth*. New York: W. W. Norton, 1967.

Bilstein, Roger E. *Flight in America 1900-1983: From the Wrights to the Astronauts*. Baltimore: Johns Hopkins UP, 1984.

Bishop, Morris. *A History of Cornell*. Ithaca: Cornell UP, 1962.

Blackwell, Alice Stone. *Lucy Stone: Pioneer of Woman's Rights*. Boston: Little, Brown, 1930.

Bobbé, Dorothie. *DeWitt Clinton*. New York: Putnam, 1968.

Boyd, Nancy. *Three Victorian Woman Who Changed the World*. New York: Oxford UP, 1982.

Brackman, Arnold C. *The Dream of Troy*. New York: Mason & Lipscomb, 1974.

Braymer, Marjorie. *The Walls of Windy Troy: A Biography of Heinrich Schliemann*. New York: Harcourt, Brace & World, 1960.

Bringhurst, Newell G. *Brigham Young and the Expanding American Frontier*. Boston: Little, Brown, 1986.

Brock, Ray. *Ghost on Horseback: The Incredible Atatürk*. Boston:

Little, Brown, 1954.

Broderick, James. *Saint Ignatius Loyola: The Pilgrim Years 1491-1538*. New York: Farrar, Straus and Cudahy, 1956.

Brondfield, Jerry. *Rockne: The Coach, the Man, the Legend*. New York: Random House, 1976.

Brown, Jordan. *Elizabeth Blackwell*. New York: Chelsea House, 1989.

Bryant, Jennifer Fisher. *Lucretia Mott: Guiding Light*. Grand Rapids, MI: Eerdmans, 1996.

Butcher, Lee. *Accidental Millionaire: The Rise and Fall of Steve Jobs at Apple Computer*. New York: Paragon House, 1988.

Caraman, Philip. *Ignatius Loyola: A Biography of the Founder of the Jesuits*. New York: Harper & Row, 1990.

Catton, Bruce. *U. S. Grant and the American Military Tradition*. Boston: Little, Brown, 1954.

Cazden, Elizabeth. *Antoinette Brown Blackwell: A Biography*. Old Westbury, NY: Feminist Press, 1983.

Chalmers, Harvey II. *The Birth of the Erie Canal*. New York: Bookman, 1960.

Chambers, Peggy. *A Doctor Alone, A Biography of Elizabeth Blackwell: The First Woman Doctor 1821-1910*. London: Abelard-Schuman, 1958.

Clancy, Frank. "If You Ever Get A Second Chance In Life, You've Got To Go All The Way." *USA Weekend*. 10-12 Dec. 1999: 9.

Coffin, Levi. *Reminiscences of Levi Coffin, The Reputed President of the Underground Railroad*. Cincinnati: Robert Clarke, 1898.

Cogniat, Raymond. *Gauguin*. New York: Harry N. Abrams, 1963.

Cosner, Shaaron. *The Underground Railroad*. New York: Franklin Watts, 1991.

Cousins, Margaret. *The Story of Thomas Alva Edison*. New York: Random House, 1965.

Cowie, Leonard W. *Martin Luther: Leader of the Reformation*. New York: Praeger, 1969.

Cromwell, Otelia. *Lucretia Mott*. Cambridge: Harvard UP, 1958.

Crouch, Tom D. *The Bishop's Boys: A Life of Wilbur and Orville Wright*. New York, Norton, 1989.

Daintith, John and Anne Stibbs, eds. *Bloomsbury Treasury of*

Quotations. London: Bloomsbury Publishing, 1994.

Davies, Michael. *Saint John Fisher: The Martyrdom of John Fisher, Bishop, During the Reign of King Henry VIII*. Long Prairie, MN: Neuman Press, 1998.

Davis, Benjamin O., Jr., *Benjamin O. Davis, Jr., American*. Washington: Smithsonian Institution Press, 1991.

De Angelis, Gina. *Lucretia Mott*. Philadelphia: Chelsea House, 2001.

Debré, Patrice. *Louis Pasteur*. Baltimore: Johns Hopkins UP, 1998.

Deci, Edward L. *The Psychology of Self-Determination*. Lexington, MA: Lexington Books, 1980.

Deutschman, Alan. *The Second Coming of Steve Jobs*. New York: Broadway Books, 2000.

Dibner, Bern. *Wilhelm Conrad Röntgen and the Discovery of X-Rays*. New York: Franklin Watts, 1968.

Douglass, Frederick. *The Life and Times of Frederick Douglass*. New York: Thomas Y. Crowell, 1966.

Dowling, Maria. *Fisher of Men: A Life of John Fisher, 1469-1535*. New York: St. Martin's, 1999.

Dubos, René. *Pasteur and Modern Science*. Madison, WI: Science Tech, 1960.

Dumont, Theron Q. *The Power of Concentration*. Chicago: Advanced Thought Publishing, 1918.

Edwards, Mark, and George Tavard. *Luther: A Reformer for the Churches*. Philadelphia: Fortress Press, 1983.

Egan, Louise. *Thomas Edison: The Great American Inventor*. New York: Barron's Educational Series, 1987.

Erikson, Erik H. *Young Man Luther: A Study in Psychoanalysis and History*. New York: W. W. Norton, 1958.

Esterer, Arnulf, K. *Discoverer of X-Rays: Wilhelm Conrad Röntgen*. New York: Julian Messner, 1968.

Estienne, Charles. *Gauguin: Biographical and Critical Studies*. Cleveland: World, 1953.

Fitch, Suzanne Pullon, and Roseann M. Mandziuk. *Sojourner Truth as Orator: Wit, Story, and Song*. Westport, CT: Greenwood Press, 1997.

Fletcher, Marvin E. *America's First Black General: Benjamin O. Davis, Sr.* Lawrence, KS: UP of Kansas, 1989.

The Forbes Scrapbook of Thoughts on the Business of Life. New York: Forbes, Inc., 1968.

Forster, Margaret. *Elizabeth Barrett Browning: A Biography*. New York: Doubleday, 1988.

Foster, Warren Dunham, ed. *Heroines of Modern Religion*. Freeport, NY: Books for Libraries, 1970.

Fremantle, Anne. *Saints Alive: The Lives of Thirteen Saints*. Garden City: Doubleday, 1978.

Gauguin, Pola. *My Father Paul Gauguin*. New York: Alfred A. Knopf, 1937.

Geddes, George. *Origin and History of the Measures that Led to the Construction of the Erie Canal*. Syracuse: Summers, 1866.

Geison, Gerald L. *The Private Science of Louis Pasteur*. Princeton: Princeton UP, 1995.

Gibbs-Smith, Charles H. *The Aeroplane: An Historical Survey of its Origins and Development*. London: Her Majesty's Stationery Office, 1960.

Gilbreth, Frank B. *Motion Study*. New York: Van Nostrand, 1911.

Gilbreth, Frank B. and L. M. Gilbreth. *Applied Motion Study*. New York: Sturgis & Walton, 1917.

Gilbreth, Frank B., Jr. and Ernestine Gilbreth Carey. *Cheaper by the Dozen*. New York: Thomas T. Crowell, 1948.

Graham, Maureen. *Women of Power and Presence: The Spiritual Formation of Four Quaker Women Ministers*. Wallingford, PA: Pendle Hill, 1990.

Grant, Madeleine P. *Louis Pasteur, Fighting Hero of Science*. New York: McGraw-Hill, 1959.

Grant, Ulysses S. *The Personal Memoirs of U. S. Grant*. Cleveland: Long, 1952.

Green, Horace. *General Grant's Last Stand*. New York: Charles Scribner's Sons, 1936.

Green, V. H. H. *Luther and the Reformation*. New York: G. P. Putnam's Sons, 1964.

Greenfield, Howard. *F. Scott Fitzgerald*. New York: Crown, 1974.

Gritsch, Eric W. *Martin—God's Court Jester: Luther in Retrospect*. Philadelphia: Fortress Press, 1983.

Hall, Josef Washington. *Eminent Asians: Six Personalities of the New East*. New York: D. Appleton, 1929.

Hallowell, Anna Davis. *James and Lucretia Mott: Life and Letters*. Boston: Houghton, Mifflin, 1884.

Hare, Lloyd C. M. *The Greatest American Woman: Lucretia Mott*. New York: American Historical Society, 1937.

Harris, Sherwood. *The First to Fly: Aviation's Pioneer Days*. Blue Ridge Summit, PA: Tab / Aero, 1970.

Hart, Michael H. *The 100: A Ranking of the Most Influential Persons in History*. Secaucus, NJ: Citadel Press, 1987.

Haskins, James. *Get on Board: The Story of the Underground Railroad*. New York: Scholastic Press, 1993.

Hays, Elinor Rice. *Morning Star: A Biography of Lucy Stone 1818-1893*. New York: Harcourt, Brace & World, 1961.

Holland, Frederic. *Frederick Douglass: The Colored Orator*. New York: Funk & Wagnalls, 1895.

Honour, Alan. *The Unlikely Hero: Heinrich Schliemann's Quest for Troy*. New York: McGraw-Hill, 1960.

Howard, Fred. *Wilbur and Orville: A Biography of the Wright Brothers*. Mineola, NY: Dover, 1998.

Hubbard, Elbert. *Elbert Hubbard's Scrapbook*. East Aurora, NY: The Roycrofters, 1923.

Huggins, Nathan Irvin. *Slave and Citizen: The Life of Frederick Douglass*. Boston: Little, Brown, 1980.

Hughes, Robert. "Seeing Gauguin Whole at Last." *Time Magazine*. 9 May 1988 77.

Jakab, Peter L. *Visions of a Flying Machine: The Wright Brothers and the Process of Invention*. Washington: Smithsonian Institution, 1990.

James, William. *The Principles of Psychology, Volume II*. Cambridge: Harvard UP, 1981.

Kelly, Fred C. *The Wright Brothers*. New York: Harcourt Brace, 1943.

Kenny, Anthony. *Thomas More*. New York: Oxford UP, 1983.

Kerr, Andrea Moore. *Lucy Stone: Speaking Out for Equality*. New Brunswick: Rutgers UP, 1992.

Kerr, Laura. *Lady in the Pulpit*. New York: Woman's Press, 1951.

Kinross, Lord. *Atatürk: A Biography of Mustafa Kemal,*

Father of Modern Turkey. New York, William Morrow, 1965.

Knowles, David. *Thomas Becket*. Palo Alto: Stanford UP, 1970.

Krass, Peter. *Sojourner Truth*. New York: Chelsea House, 1988.

Kugelmass, J. Alvin. *Roald Amundsen: A Saga of the Polar Seas*.
New York: Julian Messner, 1955.

Leturia, Pedro. *Inigo De Loyola*. Syracuse: LeMoyne College Press,
1949.

Levy, Alan. *The Wiesenthal File*. Grand Rapids, MI: Eerdmans, 1993.

Macklem, Michael. *The Life of John Fisher of Rochester*.
Ottawa, Ontario: Oberon Press, 1967.

Marius, Richard. *Thomas More: A Biography*. New York:
Alfred A. Knopf, 1984.

Markus, Julia. *Dared and Done: The Marriage of Elizabeth Barrett
Browning and Robert Browning*. New York: Alfred A. Knopf, 1995.

Mason, Theodore K. *Two Against the Ice: Amundsen and Ellsworth*.
New York: Dodd, Mead, 1982.

Maynard, Theodore. *Saint Ignatius and the Jesuits*. New York:
P. J. Kenedy & Sons, 1956.

McClard, Megan. *Harriet Tubman: Slavery and the Underground
Railroad*. Englewood Cliffs, NJ: Silver Burdett, 1991.

McGowan, James A. *Station Master on the Underground Railroad.:
The Life and Letters of Thomas Garrett*. Moylan, PA:
Whimsie Press, 1977.

McKissack, Patricia C. and Frederick. *Sojourner Truth: Ain't I a Woman*.
New York: Scholastic Press, 1992.

Miller, Douglas T. *Frederick Douglass and the Fight for Freedom*.
New York: Facts on File, 1988.

Mizener, Arthur. *The Far Side of Paradise: A Biography of F. Scott
Fitzgerald*. Boston: Houghton Mifflin, 1965.

Mott, Lucretia. "Discourse on Women." Philadelphia: n. p., 1849.

Noble, Iris. *Nazi Hunter: Simon Wiesenthal*. New York: Julian Messner,
1979.

Painter, Nell Irvin, ed. *Narrative of Sojourner Truth*. New York:
Penguin, 1998.

Palmer, Richard F. and Karl D. Butler. *Brigham Young: The New York
Years;* Provo, UT: Charles Redd Center for Western Studies at

Brigham Young University, 1982.

Pauli, Hertha. *Her Name Was Sojourner Truth*. New York: Avon, 1962.

Payne, Robert. *The Gold of Troy: The Story of Heinrich Schliemann and the Buried Cities of Ancient Greece*. New York: Funk & Wagnalls, 1959.

Pick, Hella. *Simon Wiesenthal: A Life in Search of Justice*. Boston: Northeastern UP, 1996.

Poole, Lynn and Gray. *One Passion, Two Loves: The Story of Heinrich and Sophia Schliemann, Discoverers of Troy*. New York: Thomas Y. Crowell, 1966.

Reynolds, E. E. *The Field Is Won: The Life and Death of Saint Thomas More*. Milwaukee: Bruce, 1968.

—. *Saint John Fisher*. New York: P. J. Kenedy & Sons, 1965.

—. *Saint Thomas More*. New York: P. J. Kenedy & Sons, 1953.

Reynolds, Moira Davison. *How Pasteur Changed History: The Story of Louis Pasteur and the Pasteur Institute*. Bradenton, FL: McGuinn & McGuire, 1974.

Ridley, Jasper. *Statesman and Saint: Cardinal Wolsey, Sir Thomas More, and the Politics of Henry VIII*. New York: Viking, 1982.

Ring, Frances Kroll. *Against the Current: As I Remember F. Scott Fitzgerald*. Berkeley: Creative Arts, 1985.

Rochester *Democrat and Chronicle*. "Harvard Student Is Profile in Courage." 17 May 2000: 15A.

Rogers, Walter P. *Andrew D. White and the Modern University*. Ithaca: Cornell UP, 1942.

Roper, William. *The Life of Sir Thomas Moore, Knight*. New York: William Morrow, 1950.

Ross, Ishbel. *Child of Destiny: The Life Story of the First Woman Doctor*. New York: Harper & Brothers, 1949.

Smedley, R. C. *History of the Underground Railroad*. Lancaster: Office of the *Journal,* 1883.

Smith, Douglas K. and Robert C. Alexander. *Fumbling the Future*. New York: William Morrow, 1988.

Snyder, Louis L. *Great Turning Points in History*. New York: Van Nostrand Reinhold, 1971.

Southey, Robert. *Life of Nelson*. London: J. M. Dent & Sons, 1813.

Stack, V. E. ed. *How Do I Love Thee? The Love-Letters of Robert Browning and Elizabeth Barrett*. New York: G. P. Putnam's Sons, 1969.

Steele, Michael R. *Knute Rockne: A Bio-Bibliography*. Westport, CT: Greenwood Press, 1983.

Steinberg, Barbara Hope. *Gauguin*. New York: A & W Visual Library, 1976.

Stepanek, Sally. *Martin Luther*. New York: Chelsea House, 1986.

Sterling, Dorothy. *Lucretia Mott: Gentle Warrior*. Garden City: Doubleday, 1964.

Still, William. *The Underground Rail Road*. Philadelphia: Porter & Coates, 1872.

Stone, Lucy. *Loving Warriors: Selected Letters of Lucy Stone and Henry B. Blackwell, 1853-93*. New York: Dial, 1981.

Stoneburner, Carol and John, ed. *The Influence of Quaker Women on American History: Biographical Studies*. Lewiston / Queenston, Ontario: Edwin Mellen, 1986.

Strachey, Lytton. *Eminent Victorians*. New York: Harcourt Brace Jovanovich, 1918.

Surtz, Edward. *The Works and Days of John Fisher*. Cambridge: Harvard UP, 1967.

Tachau, Frank. *Kemal Atatürk*. New York: Chelsea House, 1987.

Taves, Ernest H. *This Is the Place: Brigham Young and the New Zion*. Buffalo: Prometheus Books, 1991.

Taylor, M. W. *Harriet Tubman*. New York: Chelsea House, 1991.

Taylor-Boyd, Susan. *Sojourner Truth: The Courageous Former Slave Whose Eloquence Helped Promote Human Equality*. Milwaukee: Gareth Stevens, 1990.

Toynbee, Arnold. "Mustafa Kemal." *Men of Turmoil*. New York: Minton, Balch, 1929.

Tripp, Rhoda Thomas, ed. *The International Thesaurus of Quotations*. New York: Harper & Row, 1970.

Truth, Sojourner. *Narrative of Sojourner Truth: A Bondswoman of Olden Time*. Battle Creek, MI: Review and Herald, 1884.

Turnbull, Andrew. *Scott Fitzgerald*. New York: Charles Scribner's Sons, 1962.

Untermeyer, Louis. *Makers of the Modern World*. New York: Simon & Schuster, 1955.

Vaeth, J. Gordon. *To the Ends of the Earth: The Explorations of Roald Amundsen*. New York: Harper & Row, 1962.

Vallery-Radot, René. *The Life of Louis Pasteur.* Garden City, NY: Sun Dial Press, 1937.

Vann, Joseph, ed. *Lives of the Saints with Excerpts from Their Writings*. New York: John J. Crawley, 1954.

Wallace, Francis. *Knute Rockne*. Garden City: Doubleday, 1960.

Warner, Oliver. *Victory: The Life of Lord Nelson*. Boston: Little, Brown, 1958.

Wechsberg, Joseph, ed. *The Murders Among Us: The Simon Wiesenthal Memoirs*. New York: McGraw-Hill, 1967.

Wheeler, Leslie, ed. *Loving Warriors: A Revealing Portrait of an Unprecedented Marriage*. New York: Dial, 1981.

White, Andrew Dickson. *Autobiography of Andrew Dickson White*. Vol. I. New York: Century, 1907.

Wiesenthal, Simon. *Justice Not Vengence*. New York: Grove Weidenfeld, 1989.

Wilby, Noel MacDonald. *Saint John of Rochester*. New York: Paulist Press, n.d.

Wilkinson, Clennell. *Nelson*. London: George G. Harrap, 1931.

Wilson, Susan. *Steve Jobs: Wizard of Apple Computer.* Berkeley Heights, NJ: Enslow, 2001.

Winston, Richard. *Thomas Becket*. New York: Alfred A. Knopf, 1967.

Woodham-Smith, Cecil. *Florence Nightingale: 1820-1910*. New York: McGraw-Hill, 1951.

Woodward, W. E. *Meet General Grant*. New York: Liveright, 1928.

Young, Jeffrey S. *Steve Jobs: The Journey Is the Reward*. Glenview, IL: Scott, Foresman, 1988.

Yost, Edna. *Frank and Lillian Gilbreth: Partners for Life*. New Brunswick: Rutgers UP, 1949.

Yust, Walter, ed. *Encyclopedia Britannica. Vols. 4, 13*. Chicago: William Benton, 1957.

INDEX